A Young Scholar's Guide to
Composers

A full year's curriculum in 32 weekly lessons

Melissa E. Craig and Maggie S. Hogan

Bright Ideas PRESS

A Young Scholar's Guide to Composers
by Melissa E. Craig and Maggie S. Hogan

Copyright © 2009 Bright Ideas Press

ISBN: 978-1-892427-46-5
First Edition

Published by Bright Ideas Press
Dover, Delaware

contact@BrightIdeasPress.com
www.BrightIdeasPress.com
877.492.8081

Unless otherwise indicated, Scripture is taken from the New King James Version. Copyright © 1982 by Thomas Nelson, Inc. Used by permission. All rights reserved.

Scripture quotations marked (NIV) are taken from the HOLY BIBLE, NEW INTERNATIONAL VERSION®. NIV®. Copyright © 1973, 1978, 1984 by the International Bible Society. Used by permission of Zondervan. All rights reserved.

Trademarks:
Jeopardy!® is a registered trademark of Jeopardy Productions, Inc.
Lap Book™ is a trademark of Tobin's Lab, Inc.
Google™ is a trademark of Google, Inc.
Play-Doh® is a registered trademark of Hasbro, Inc.

Design and Production by:
David Borrink, Arts & Letters, Inc., www.artsandletters.biz

Other Production Credits:
Copyediting—Elizabeth Torjussen
Proofreading—Emily Andres, Sallie Borrink
Illustrations—Nicole Petersen

To our Lord Jesus Christ, the Creator and Lover of music,
Who throughout the Psalms, commands us to praise Him
with singing and instruments.

Soli Deo Gloria
"To God Alone the Glory"
–J.S. Bach

Acknowledgments

From Maggie

This book would never have been written without the constant prodding (I mean "encouragement") of my dear sister-in-Christ, Melissa Craig. Why you thought I could help write a book on MUSIC still makes me smile!

Without the constant support (and prodding) of my husband, Bob, ("get it written, already"), I would still be researching. Thanks for everything—you are my biggest supporter!

From Melissa

To my dear father, whose tremendous love of music and exceptional musical background and expertise filled our home with magnificent sound and filled my heart with a desire to know and understand it. Without you and Mom, this book would never have been born.

Maggie—if it weren't for your constant support, prodding, patience with your godchildren (who happen to call me Mom), and your vision of a finished product, I would still be collecting resources. And I might get around to writing Schubert...soon.

Bob—you truly kept us going and patiently let Maggie come to visit so we could keep writing. Now that this is finished, we have to come up with a new excuse—I mean reason—for those visits!

My precious husband, Jim, and children, Rebecca, Joshua, Jeremy, and Bethany—you have supported this effort, listened to more classical music than you knew existed, and put up with the constant quizzes—"Do you know who wrote this?" Thank you!

We both also want to thank the following people:

This book would not be what it is without the wonderful insights from two important groups of people: the children in Maggie's local homeschool composer class and Gwynne Hoffecker, her assistant, as well as the 200+ families in our online beta group. Thank you each and every one for your encouragement, attention to detail, keen insights, suggestions, and observations. You all have greatly enhanced the usefulness of this curriculum.

Richard Pinkerton, music editor. Your musical expertise and willingness to carefully go over in minute detail everything we wrote about each composer has elevated the content of this book tremendously. We simply cannot thank you enough!

Nicole Petersen, artist. Your artwork is such a lovely addition to this work; we couldn't imagine not having it. Thanks for the untold hours you spent researching and drawing all those portraits and coloring pages!

Betsy Torjussen, our copyeditor. Your many years of professional experience improved our work tremendously.

Beth Barr, administrative assistant. You compiled the majority of the books in our resource list, created most of the suggested games, and helped with the student review pages. Thank you for your perseverance.

Laura Reisinger, research assistant. Thank you so much, Laura, for taking time out from your own studies to do some preliminary research and writing for us. You did a great job!

David Borrink, our new friend and master of the quick, professional, graphic layout. How do you manage to read our minds?

Table of Contents

Dear Teachers

Because the rules for naming musical pieces are not often taught or explained, we thought it wise to advise our readers as to our choices regarding typographic conventions for the citation of musical works in this book. We followed the styling recommended in *The Chicago Manual of Style*, 15th Edition. Quoted below are the two applicable sections, including several of the examples provided in those sections.

Sect. 8.202 *Operas, songs, and the like.* Titles of operas, oratorios, tone poems, and other long musical compositions are italicized. Titles of songs are set in roman and enclosed in quotation marks, capitalized in the same way as poems (see 8.191–92).

- Handel's *Messiah*
- *Rhapsody in Blue*
- "The Star-Spangled Banner"
- the "Anvil Chorus" from Verdi's *Il Trovatore*

Sect. 8.203 *Instrumental works.* Many instrumental works are known by their generic names—*symphony, quartet, nocturne*, and so on—and often a number or key or both. Such names are capitalized but not italicized. A descriptive title, however, is usually italicized if referring to a full work, set in roman and in quotation marks if referring to a section of a work. The abbreviation *no.* (number; plural *nos.*) is set in roman and usually lowercased.

- B-flat Nocturne; Chopin's nocturnes
- Bach's Mass in B Minor
- Charles Ives's *Concord* Sonata
- the Sixth Symphony; the *Pastoral* Symphony

The exception we made in following these guidelines was that we chose to also italicize the word *symphony, sonata,* etc., when a part of the descriptive name, i.e., the *Pastoral Symphony*, the *Concord Sonata*. Because this is not a scholarly work and because we felt the combination of italicized and non-italicized words in one title looked confusing, we chose to simplify.

We hope that explaining the conventions we used in choosing when to use what typeface for musical names will allow the reader to see that our choices were based on a system, not just arbitrarily assigned. If, in reading this work, you find errors in our attempt to be consistent, please drop us an e-mail. We welcome the opportunity to improve!

Thank you,

Melissa Craig and Maggie Hogan

Introduction

Why Teach the Classical Composers?

There are a number of good reasons for exposing children to classical music and the rich heritage of classical composers. First, music is from the Lord. He created it, and He created us with the ability both to make music and to appreciate music.

Second, although there are many different types of music in other cultures, what is called "classical" music is uniquely part of the heritage of our Western civilization. Becoming familiar with it opens a door into ideas and expressions that are inaccessible to those who have not been introduced to the musical classics. This familiarity allows one to participate in conversations and musical experiences that would otherwise remain a mystery.

Third, research suggests that both listening to and playing classical music is of great value to the development of the brain even in many other aspects of learning, including math, memory, and literacy itself.

Finally, there is the rich satisfaction that comes with the knowledge of having been exposed to great minds and talents and having brought away from it a deeper understanding of music, of self, and of life. It is not always easy to "crack" the code of classical music, but even rudimentary exposure, over time, will increase one's level of enjoyment and understanding.

Although this is just a one-year course, we are not suggesting that teaching classical composers should be a one-time activity. Ideally, you will continue to incorporate classical music into your curriculum, perhaps following the format we have developed or perhaps using other resources.

How to Use This Book

Any music appreciation course taught primarily through a book is lacking one important ingredient: actual music! This is where you play an integral role. It is imperative to play the music of the composers as you study them in order to truly gain any understanding of the classical composers and their music. Fortunately, it is easy to find recordings of music from every composer we will be covering by looking online, at your library, or in catalogs.

Music and the Brain

Although there had been much hype about the now mostly discredited "Mozart Effect," it does not change the fact that there is a growing body of research that points to a strong link between music and positive brain development. From www.sciencedaily.com, accessed May 16, 2008, we read this headline and the beginning of an article about music and brain development:

> ### "First Evidence That Musical Training Affects Brain Development in Young Children"
>
> Science Daily—"*Researchers have found the first evidence that young children who take music lessons show different brain development and improved memory over the course of a year compared to children who do not receive musical training.*
>
> "*The findings, published 20 September 2006 in the online edition of the journal Brain [Oxford University Press], show that not only do the brains of musically trained children respond to music in a different way to those of the untrained children, but also that the training improves their memory as well. After one year the musically trained children performed better in a memory test that is correlated with general intelligence skills such as literacy, verbal memory, visiospatial processing, mathematics and IQ.*[1]"

A Word About Music Lessons . . .

Does this mean that your child is being sadly neglected if you don't provide music lessons? Does this mean that his or her brain will shrivel up and become the size of a lima bean without the experience of piano practice? Of course not! This is just a further bit of motivation to encourage you, in whatever way works best, to provide basic lessons for a year or two. The piano is the typical instrument of choice, although some people prefer the violin, and others find that a recorder is all they can handle space-wise and money-wise.

If your child is provided with a caring and competent teacher, an instrument to use, as well as scheduled and monitored practice time, the lessons are sure to be a success. Despite your best intentions, though, not all children will appreciate music lessons. Encourage your child to try it for one school year. If after that time they are still disinterested, at least you know you have given them the great advantage of exposure to the world of playing music. Many, many adults say how much they now appreciate the gift of music lessons in their childhood, even if at the time they vigorously opposed them. We can't think of anyone who has told us the opposite!

A Kind and Simple Approach to This Curriculum

This course is intended to be as stress-free as possible. The plan is to listen to the recommended music a minimum of three times per week. The read-aloud lesson and the note-taking pages or student review questions should be done on Day One. The hands-on work of timeline, map, and Composer Info-Card can be done on Day Two. In the interest of time, it is certainly feasible to do all the academic work on one day instead of two, but the music listening itself should be spread throughout the week.

Your Schedule

Day One

- Listen to the recommended selections.
- Read the lesson.
- Fill in the note-taking pages or answer the Student Review Questions

Day Two

- Listen to the recommended selections again.
- Fill in the Composer Info-Card.
- Color in the timeline. (See Timeline Directions.)
- Match the composer to his place of birth. (See Map Directions.)

Day Three

- Listen to the recommended selections again.

Listening Directions

- Say the name of the composer.
- Say the name of the selection.
- Play the piece.

We concur with the opinion expressed by Jessie Wise and Susan Wise Bauer in *The Well-Trained Mind*. They write:

> "The first time the child listens to the piece, have her listen to it two or three times in a row. Then make sure she plays it again at the beginning of her next listening period. [Day Two] Familiarity breeds enjoyment. She can do handwork such as Play-Doh™ or coloring books about the composer . . . but nothing that involves words; her attention should be focused on what she hears, not on what she sees."

We would add that some children need to move to the music, some like to draw, and others do best just sitting and staring out the window!

Lessons

Each lesson runs about 1,200 words. Each will take approximately fifteen minutes to read aloud. There will often be unfamiliar vocabulary words within the lessons. These usually are defined for you within the lesson, allowing you to quickly explain them to the student before moving on. (There is also a handy glossary in the Appendix.) A composer who especially captures a child's interest would be worth further research. Fortunately, there are many biographies of composers available now, and there is a plethora of online information available as well. (Please see the caution regarding research below.)

Content Considerations

There are two issues we would like to address here:

1. Historical reliability
2. Spiritual lives

First, as with any research of historical events/people, there is much conflicting information. One source emphatically states "such and such is true," and the other equally reliable source shouts out "absolutely not such and such!" This puts the researcher in a quandary. Whom to believe? If we were writing scholarly papers on the composers, we would spend large blocks of time chasing down original source documents and then having them translated. We would travel to Europe where many of these documents are stored. We would hole up in the Library of Congress, falling asleep over mounds of dusty books. But as exciting as this sounds to us—and it really does—it just isn't feasible to spend that kind of time and money conducting in-depth academic research for a one-year middle-grade curriculum.

However, accuracy is very important to us. What we have chosen to do is to limit ourselves to about a dozen resource books that are generally well regarded and Websites sponsored primarily by universities or other reliable sources. We have tended to use the information that was most often agreed upon by these sources. But you will occasionally run into conflicting information if you do any research yourself. We have been careful, we have read until our eyes have popped, we have taken mountains of notes, and we have submitted our work to our music editor, Richard Pinkerton, for the opinion of someone who is considered an expert in his field of music. However, the truth may still remain elusive. Instead, realize that it is the bigger picture that we are pursuing, and enjoy and appreciate the music!

The second issue, and this is important for you to know as well, is that there is much material available about these composers that is *not* information we feel is appropriate for the age level of the students for whom this book is intended. Composers, even the classical composers, were sinners like the rest of us! It takes no real digging to come across sins of every nature. This leads us to those we included and those we decided to leave out and why.

Obviously, we couldn't include every well-known composer. (In fact, there is plenty of material left for another entire volume!) We had to limit the number of people studied to fit within the time frame of a typical school year. We chose well-known composers who had a great impact on the music world. We included composers known to be Christian, composers known not to be Christian, and composers of whom we have no real way of knowing if they were Christian!

For example, we included Frédéric Chopin—a master of piano compositions and absolutely on just about everyone's list of important classical composers. However, the evidence regarding his conversion to Christianity, possibly on his deathbed, is conflicting and controversial. The difficulty lies within the discussion of his lifestyle, including his having lived for many years with his female companion, George Sand (her pen name), a woman of highly questionable morals. This is an example of the types of issues we had to consider when deciding whom and what to leave in, whom and what to exclude, and how to word certain information.

An example of one we chose to leave out is Richard Wagner. Yes, he is considered one of the finest minds in classical composing, an opera writer in a class of his own. However, we could not write about him in any way without bumping into his blatant and boldly immoral lifestyle. We couldn't gloss over the facts, skip over the stories, or recommend doing "further research" on him! From all the evidence, the man was simply evil (and, interestingly, Hitler's favorite composer).

Note-taking Pages and Student Review Questions

Several note-taking pages follow each of the lessons on the musical eras, and ten student review questions follow each composer's biography. If your student is a competent reader/ writer, it is best for him or her to answer the review questions on paper. Much of this course already involves listening, so doing a little writing at this point is worthwhile. The questions are in a mixed format and cover the vocabulary and main points in each biography lesson. All answers are in the "Lesson Answer Keys" section of the Appendix.

Composer Info-Cards

These cards provide the student with an opportunity for:
- analyzing data.
- reinforcing the main points.
- remembering the points using visual reminders.
- reviewing the information presented.

Directions:
- Copy the Info-Card onto sturdy paper or front and back on card stock. (If paper, then cut it out and paste the front and back onto a 5" x 7" index card.)
- Cut the illustration of the composer out of Appendix section of the book and place it in the appropriate place on the front of the card. (Artistic students may prefer to color this in or draw their own picture.)
- Fill in the name and the musical period on the front as well.
- The back of the card is fairly straightforward. Answer the questions, fill in the birth and death dates, and color in the country of origin on the map. Choose the Composer Info-Card with the correct map on the back for each composer. (For example, almost all of the composers we study were born in Europe, so you will predominantly use the Europe back. But Tchaikovsky was born in Russia and a number of the Contemporary period composers were born in the USA.)
- The trickiest part for some of the cards will be the question regarding the composer's faith. You may need to discuss this with the student or help him or her to decide if there are any clues available in the lesson.

Composer Info-Card Game and Review

- A simple but effective manner of reinforcing the chronology of composers is to mix up the cards on the table, picture side up. Ask the student to stack them in the order of the composers' birth dates. Students can then easily self-check by turning the cards over to check the dates to see if they were right.
- A quick review game is for the parent or one student to hold up the card, picture side facing outward to a student. The student states the name and then lists either the names of the composer's works or three facts.
- Cards should be brought out and reviewed often and can be
  ~ stored in a 5" x 7" index box.
  ~ wrapped in a rubber band.
  ~ placed in envelopes.
  ~ inserted into a Folderbook. (See Folderbook Directions.)

Folderbook Directions

Folderbooks are a simple and interesting way to show what one has learned. Think of them as a place to store tidbits of information, pictures, drawings, maps, etc. By helping your students to learn to organize and display what they have studied, you are training them to sift through ideas, choose what is important, and present it in a logical manner. This kind of learning will be useful for the rest of their lives!

If you are familiar with Lap Books, think of Folderbooks as the simple, quicker version. Instead of multiple layers, a Folderbook consists of just one file folder. Instead of elaborate, clever folds and time-consuming layouts, a Folderbook can be assembled rapidly. Although Lap Books are a wonderful learning tool, sometimes all we have time for is simple!

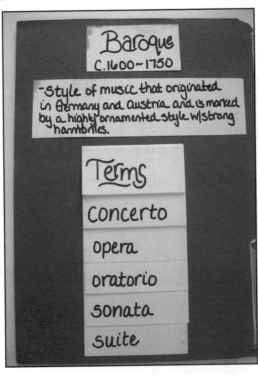
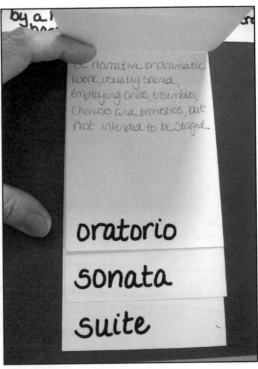

Ideas for your composer Folderbook:

- Paste envelopes inside and put cards with information or smaller books inside the envelopes.
- Include pictures, maps, or timelines as appropriate.
- Make small books or flip books and paste them inside.
- Decorate lists and glue them on.
- Let imagination and creativity be your guide.
- Decorate the cover in an appropriate fashion. Coloring pages make easy covers.

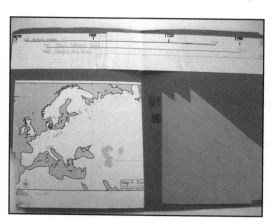  

Timeline Directions

There is a Comparative Timeline page for every fifty-year period, beginning with Vivaldi, the first composer in our study who has been given his own lesson. Use a different color for each musical period: Baroque – red, Classical – blue, Romantic – green, Contemporary – orange. We have provided the birth and death rates for each composer and a shaded line connecting these two dates. The student's aassignment is to use the appropriate color to highlight or draw over this shaded line for each composer. This is a simple method that enables students to see at a glance which composers composed in which period, visually reinforcing what they are learning in the lessons.

We also want students to recognize the relationships between the composers. In this study students will learn that some composers influenced other composers, and some composers were friends. We have assigned a different color for each of those relationships. Friendship will be marked with gold; influence will be marked with purple. If one composer influenced another, draw a vertical line, in purple, from the "influencer" to the one who was influenced. Put an arrow at the end of the line, so the direction of the influence is clear. If the composers were friends, draw a vertical line in gold from one friend to the other.

At the bottom of each timeline page, there is a "Significant Events" line. On it, you'll see that one or two significant events have already been labeled. This is a quick and painless technique useful for seeing where each composer fits into world events. You might like your older students to find a few additional events to add to this line. The significance of these timeline pages is that these composers did not live in isolation but were, indeed, influenced by the people and events around them. This is an effortless visual way to present this information.

There is an Exhaustive Timeline Reference Key on our Website, www.BrightIdeasPress.com, that is a thorough answer key for these timeline activities. The charts in this Reference Key are provided in full color and can be downloaded and printed out.

Map Directions

The mapping exercise in *A Young Scholar's Guide to Composers* is easy and visually powerful. This geography component consists of three maps—a map of Europe (two views, one with an inset of Russia for Tchaikovsky) and a map of the United States. Students should have their own copy of each map. When the student discovers where the composer was born, he simply draws a line from the composer's portrait (found in the border of the map) to the country or state in which the composer was born. Students will use the same color-coding system for musical periods on the map that they use on the timeline.

This map exercise will reinforce several things:

- geography awareness
- visual identification of composers
- recognition of composers within their musical periods

There are two composers whose sphere of influence is as important as their place of birth. In these cases, the student should draw a second line so that both places are represented. These composers are:

- George Frideric Handel (who was born in Germany but did much of his work in England)
- Antonín Dvořák (who was born in Europe, yet was significantly influenced by his time spent in the United States)

We've tried to make this clear in our biographies, but adding it to the map will help to cement the information.

Two Comments:

1. We use the modern-day equivalent of the country's name. There were many small kingdoms in earlier times, especially in the area that is modern-day Germany. Older students may wish to look in a historical atlas and locate the original name.
2. Spellings of composer names can vary widely, depending on which source you consult. We picked a common spelling and tried to remain consistent with it throughout the book.

Endnote

[1]Fujioka, Takako, et al. "One year of musical training affects development of auditory cortical-evoked fields in young children." Brain 129.2593 (2006). <http://brain.oxfordjournals.org/cgi/content/full/129/10/2593>.

Student Introduction

Stop and think for a moment about what really is music. Is music something that sounds good to your ears? Does it have to have a melody? Are drumbeats music? How about raindrops or bird tweets? Humans have been challenged with this question for years. It's interesting to think about what music is or isn't. You may even develop your own definition of music as you study this course. For our purposes, however, we will go with a traditional definition of music. Webster's dictionary says that music is "the science or art of ordering tones or sounds in succession, in combination and in temporal relationships to produce a composition having unity and continuity." What a mouthful! What this means is that music is sounds that have been put together in a purposeful way to produce sounds that go together in meaningful ways.

When did music begin? Music probably began on day six of Creation. We believe that Adam and Eve sang in the Garden of Eden. We read in Genesis that Jubal was a maker of musical instruments. So we can see that God gave people the gift of music, and people have loved music from the start—enough to not only produce music with the voice, but to create instruments that make unique sounds.

Music is found in all different cultures, but in each culture, it sounds different. Have you ever been to a Chinese restaurant where they have played traditional Chinese music? Could you tell that it was Chinese? How about an Indian restaurant? What made it sound Indian? One difference was that the instruments they use are different from the instruments that we are used to hearing. Did you like the way it sounded? Would you like to listen to that kind of music on the radio? Probably not, and here's why:

In our Western culture, we are used to hearing sounds played from a certain kind of scale. If possible, on a piano or keyboard find middle C, and then play all of the white keys up to and including the next C. That is called a scale. All the black keys are half steps, so if the keys were numbered, you would have 1, 1½, 2, 2½, 3—but wait, is there a 3½? No. However, there's a 4½, 5½, and a 6½. But there's no 7 ½. That's because in the scale that we use for Western music, the "natural" half steps are between 3 and 4 and between 7 and 8. When we hear music, that's what we are used to hearing. In other cultures, their scales have natural half steps in different places. People who have grown up there are used to hearing it that way, but we are not. Music based on scales with different half steps sounds strange to us. Some cultures even use quarter steps—or quarter tones—notes whose sounds are squeezed between the notes we see on our piano. We can't even hear quarter steps, because our culture doesn't use them. However, people who have grown up listening to that type of music can.

When music is so foreign to us, it can be difficult to understand because our ears aren't trained that way. Because studying Western music will keep us very busy, we are going to focus only on Western music in this course. As you study other cultures in your history, however, it's a good idea to go to the library or the Internet and listen to some samples of music from those cultures to help you understand them even better.

Frequently, when people study music history, they start in 1678 with Vivaldi in the Baroque period. When you read a book about composers, he is often the first one discussed. But music didn't suddenly start in the Baroque period, with harpsichords and violins and musical notation that everyone knew how to read. All of that had to develop. You will see that although music has progressed a great deal, human nature has not changed much at all, and it is human nature that has spurred on many of these changes. Music that we consider "classical" today (and maybe even boring) was once very controversial. People argued and fought about it! Sometimes it was even banned. People's ears had to become accustomed to the "new" types of music. People within the church even disagreed about what music would be appropriate in a church. Just as they do today!

In this course, we hope to show you why classical music isn't boring. You will listen to different kinds of music and learn about the composers who created the music. Did you know that music can be funny? Haydn wrote a symphony, called the *Farewell Symphony*, in which the people playing the different instruments were to get up one by one and walk off the stage while the rest of the orchestra was playing, until only two violinists were left. (Haydn wrote this piece to make a point to his benefactor—you'll hear this great story in the lesson on him.) Did you know that some music you hear on television today, often during commercials, was written two hundred years ago?

We're going to learn about different time periods in music history and what it was like for the composers growing up then. We'll study composers and see how God influenced their lives—and we'll see that some composers didn't know God at all. We think you'll have fun learning how to listen to music so that you can understand it better. You'll create a "Folderbook" that will help you remember all the things you've learned. Most importantly, you'll begin (or continue) to appreciate one of God's many wonderful gifts to us: the gift of music.

Ancient Music to Music in the Middle Ages

Do you sing in the shower? Have you heard babies make little noises that sound as if they are trying to "sing" to their parents? People have been singing since Adam and Eve in the Garden of Eden. People have been making music since Creation because God created us to love music. We know from reading Genesis that Jubal was the "father of all who play the harp and flute" (Gen. 4:21), so we know that music existed very early in the history of the world. In the Psalms, David speaks of several different musical instruments and says that we should use them to praise the Lord! Examples include:

Psalms 33:2   *Praise the Lord with the harp; make music to Him on the ten-stringed lyre.*

Psalms 43:4   *Then will I go to the altar of God, to God, my joy and my delight. I will praise you with the harp, O God, my God.*

Psalms 57:8   *Awake, my soul! Awake, harp and lyre! I will awaken the dawn.*

Psalms 71:22   *I will praise you with the harp for your faithfulness, O my God; I will sing praise to you with the lyre, O Holy One of Israel.*

Psalms 81:2   *Begin the music, strike the tambourine, play the melodious harp and lyre.*

(NIV)

From paintings and writings found in ancient Mesopotamia, China, and Egypt we know that there were instruments in those civilizations and that they were probably used in religious and official ceremonies. Music from that time was not written down, however, so we really have no idea how it sounded.

The ancient Greeks enjoyed music. The word *music* comes from the Greek word *mousike*. In the Greek culture, music was not played just at ceremonies. It was also used as entertainment in the theater and accompanied the dance. The Greeks were some of the greatest thinkers of the ancient world, and over the years they developed theories about music and its relation to math. The Greeks thought that numbers were the key to the universe, and they found many relationships between numbers and the notes on the musical scale. They even thought that some notes corresponded to certain planets! Because the Greeks frequently wrote about their music, we know what they thought about music, even if we don't know how the music actually sounded.

Music was important to the ancient Romans, too, but as a sin-loving culture, they often used instrumental music to accompany their bad habits and wrongdoing. They were enjoying themselves so much, they didn't write much about it. We know, though, that because of the importance of music and instruments in the pagan Roman lifestyle, early Christians didn't want instruments in their churches at all! Music with instruments was associated with all the wrong things that the Romans did, and they didn't want any part of that in their churches.

In the early **Middle Ages**, there is evidence of some folk music—music played at fairs and in homes by common people. But the first written music didn't appear until about A.D. 1000. For a long time, only church music was written down. Folk music was handed down from one musician to another, just by copying and sometimes adapting and improving the words and music as it was passed down through the generations. Because of this, our study of Western classical music will begin here, with the church music of the Middle Ages.

The early church developed three guidelines for the use of music in Christian worship to differentiate its use from pagan and Jewish music:

1. Music must remind the listener of divine and perfect beauty.
2. Music is a servant to religion. Because nonvocal music cannot teach Christian thoughts, instrumental music is not appropriate in worship.
3. Pagan influences (large choruses, "happy" melodies, and dancing) are not appropriate in worship.

Because worship was the primary focus, the church needed to begin with just the basics. As time went on, other influences began to work their way into worship so that now we have a wide diversity of styles that are considered appropriate.

Early written music didn't look much like our music today. It had a few lines with some spots on them for notes, and it was only one musical line—just the melody. This type of music was called *plainchant*, or **chant**. Some people think that these melodies were passed down through the ages and were originally Jewish or Greek songs. At first, the chants that were sung during **Mass** (which we'll explain later) were different throughout Europe. Pope Gregory, the pope from A.D. 590–604, gets the credit for standardizing the chants, so this type of music is also known as **Gregorian chant**.

Gregorian chants were the only church music during the Middle Ages. Their primary purpose was to help convey the text. The words were far more important than the music. Chants had certain things in common. They were all:

- Sung in **unison**, which means that they were always sung together—everybody sang the same notes and nobody sang any other notes that might distract from the beauty of the melody. (Harmonies were not known yet; they developed over the next several centuries.)
- Sung without instruments.
- Non-metrical rhythm. (This means you can't tap your foot to it.)
- Sung with a smooth progression—the notes usually move by step to the next note up or down—no jumps from high notes to low notes or low notes to high notes.

- Sung in Latin, not English (except for the Kyrie, which is in Greek).
- Additionally, they were all **modal**. This means that they do not follow the major or minor scales that we use in our music today, so sometimes they sound very different from the music we are used to hearing.

Part of the resurgence of chant in the twentieth century was a yearning for its simplicity and beauty without the extravagant harmonies that had been layered onto these simple melodies. Stripped of all that, the chants were, and still are, quite beautiful on their own.

During the Christian church service, Christians fulfill Christ's command to commemorate the Last Supper by taking the bread and the wine. Christians call this ritual Communion. Over time, a standard developed. Certain prayers were said in a certain order when God's people celebrated Communion. This service became known as the **Mass**.

To this day, a form of this Mass is still said in the Catholic Church, in some Anglican churches, and in some Lutheran churches. The Mass is composed of about twenty different prayers, which can be divided into two parts: the Ordinary and the Proper. The **Mass Ordinary** is the standard prayers of the Mass that don't change from day to day. The words that are said in these prayers are always the same. In the **Mass Proper,** other prayers are recited that change according to the day or the part of the church calendar that is being celebrated. Until the middle of the twentieth century, the prayers were always said in Latin, so the names of the prayers might not be familiar to you. Around the year A.D. 1000, the order of the Mass looked like this:

ORDINARY	PROPER
	Introit
Kyrie	
Gloria	
	Collect
	Epistle
	Gradual
	Alleluia or Tract
	Gospel
Credo	
	Offertory
Prayers	
	Secret
	Preface
Sanctus	
Canon	
	Pater Noster
Agnus Dei	
	Communion
Prayers	
	Post-Communion
Benedicamus	

Ancient Music to Music in the Middle Ages

The parts that are in boldface are the parts that were traditionally sung, or chanted. The other parts were traditionally spoken. It is important to be familiar with the Ordinary parts of the Mass, because composers have written music for these parts of the Mass through modern times, and you will come across them throughout our study.

- The **Kyrie** is a plea for mercy: "Lord, have mercy; Christ have mercy. . ." It is sung in Greek instead of Latin.
- The **Gloria** proclaims God's glory: "Glory to God on high. . ."
- The **Credo** is a statement of the Nicene Creed: "I believe. . ."
- The **Sanctus** proclaims the holiness of God: "Holy, holy, holy. . ."
- The **Agnus Dei** proclaims the power of Christ's redemption: "Lamb of God, who takes away the sin of the world."
- The **Benedicamus** is a closing benediction: "Let us bless the Lord."

Music in churches was sung in this traditional way, with these traditional prayers, for hundreds of years. You can still hear chants sung in this beautiful, worshipful form in many churches throughout the world today!

Ancient Music to Music in the Middle Ages

Note-taking Pages

Years: _____ to _____

People have been making music since _____

_____

_____

Genesis 4:21 tells us that Jubal was _____.

_____ found in ancient Mesopotamia,

China, and Egypt, we know that there were musical instruments in those civilizations.

We don't know what ancient music sounded like because _____

_____.

The beginning of the growth of Western classical music started with _____

_____.

The first written music didn't appear until _____ .

This music was called _____ or _____.

Characteristics of chants:

1. _____

2. _____

3. _____ — you can't _____ your foot

4. _____ — notes move by _____

5. words sung in _____

6. Tunes are _____ — they do not follow the major or minor scales used today.

Gregorian chant was used during the Christian church service, which became known as _____.

Mass is divided into two parts:

_____ — the prayers that don't change

_____ — the prayers that do change according to the church calendar

The parts of the Ordinary that are sung:

1. _____ : a plea for _____.

2. Gloria: proclaims God's _____.

3. Credo: the _____ Creed.

4. Sanctus: proclaims God's _____.

5. Agnus Dei: proclaims the power of Christ's _____.

Music in
the Renaissance

During the **Middle Ages,** there was a tremendous power struggle between the church and the state. In the **Renaissance,** the **nobility** (class of persons distinguished by high birth or rank) gained the upper hand. When this happened, the royal courts became supporters of the arts, and secular music emerged as a strong force equal to that of church music.

We still have court songs from the twelfth and thirteenth centuries. This was the era of beautiful love poetry, which was often set to music. Sometimes these poems were specific messages to be delivered from one court to another—love letters in song rather than on paper. This was particularly effective, since not many people could read. This form of love poetry began in southern France, where the authors were known as **troubadours.** Although today people often think of troubadours as impoverished, this was not the case. They were often of noble birth, though they could be anyone who would learn and uphold the manners and ideals of the courtly love of which they wrote. Court songs grew and spread throughout Europe. In northern France, those who wrote in this style were called **trouvères**; in Germany, they were known as **minnesingers.** Troubadours, who wrote the poems, did not perform their works themselves, though they are often confused with those who did. Instead, they employed **bards** or **minstrels** (or, in the French, **jongleurs**), traveling performers who shared their songs from court to court.

During this period, musical notation was limited—as was literacy—and often just the words or sometimes the words and a simple melody remain. We also have a handful of dances that have been handed down from this same period, but still have only the melody. There's no way to know exactly how they were performed. We also don't know how early music sounded, because the instruments were very different from the instruments we have today.

Although Gregorian chant was the only music in churches through the early Middle Ages, this simple form could not last forever. The earliest form of **polyphony,** (more than one **musical line,** or voice, at a time) was called **organum** [pronounced organ numb]. Organum is a plainchant to which a composer or singer has added another line, sung at the same time, with the same words.

At first, the **harmony** moved along with the melody a certain distance from it—perhaps a fourth or fifth note above or below. Then, the harmony became more independent; sometimes it would go up when the melody went down, or vice versa. Later, more notes were added—there would be several notes sung at the same time as one chant note. Over time, another change was made, and composers began adding two lines of harmony, which all fit together to sound pleasant. Finally, **rhythm** became more structured, with more of a regular beat, like what we are accustomed to today. This transition took place between A.D. 900 and A.D. 1300.

Beginning about 1300, we have manuscripts of music from certain composers whom we remember for their contributions to the development of musical form and their lasting music.

- **Guillaume de Machaut**, c. 1300–1377, a Frenchman who wrote the first **ballades**, (secular songs sung in the courtly language—not Latin) accompanied by musical instruments. He also experimented with interesting rhythms. In the history of polyphonic music, Machaut is the first artistically important composer of polyphonic music to be known by name.

- **Guillaume Dufay**, 1397–1474, also French, brought many different styles together. He also wrote Masses for the church and helped to establish the form of the musical Mass.

- **Thomas Tallis**, 1505–1585, considered the "Father of English Cathedral Music."

- **Giovanni Pierluigi da Palestrina**, 1525–1594, an Italian composer considered the greatest representative of sixteenth century **counterpoint**. Counterpoint is the combination of simultaneously sounding musical lines according to a system of rules.

- **Orlando de Lassus**, 1532–1594, lived in Flanders. He was the most published composer of the age, with 1,250 works. Lassus was a well-traveled man and was able to write in the Italian, German, and French styles. He held the post of **Kapellmeister** (musical director) at the Bavarian Court Chapel in Munich.

- **William Byrd**, c. 1540–1623, is a well-known English composer. Though he was a Catholic living in sixteenth century London during the reign of Elizabeth I (a staunch Protestant), the queen loved music and gave him a post at the Chapel Royale. He was a bridge between the older musical sounds (**modal**) and the emerging newer sounds (**tonal**).

- **Giovanni Gabrieli**, c. 1553–1612, was a prominent Italian composer of church music who used musical instruments with choral music. (He is one of a number of composers named Gabrieli/Gabrielli during this time period.)

A Young Scholar's Guide to Composers

- **Carlo Gesualdo**, c. 1561–1613, was an Italian nobleman who did beautiful work with madrigals—using as many as five **voices**, or musical lines. **Madrigals** were songs that were written for several voices singing at the same time. They were always **secular** (not about God) and usually about love. Generally sung at a quick tempo, they were popular among the aristocracy of the time. Gesualdo was also important because he broke from the older modal sound.

- **John Dowland**, 1563–1626, was the finest **lute** player in England. He wrote primarily for a solo voice accompanied by the lute. Some musicians consider him to be the greatest English songwriter ever!

- **Claudio Monteverdi**, 1567-1643, was an Italian who linked Renaissance music to the **Baroque**, which is the next musical period we will be studying. By 1607, he had published five books of madrigals. With all his madrigal writing, he refined the Renaissance madrigal and then began to do new things with it—adding instrumental parts. This development helped to build the bridge between Renaissance and Baroque music.

Monteverdi worked to bring out emotions in his music. In 1624, he wrote in the "stile concitato," or "the excited genre," which he had read about in Plato's third book of *The Republic*. He said he wanted to "set about the rediscovery" of this music. In this new form, he used certain rhythmic patterns to attain the emotional effect he wanted. He also developed the stringed instrument techniques of tremolo and pizzicato. Both of these are common techniques today. In **tremolo**, the string player moves the bow back and forth rapidly on the strings. In **pizzicato**, the string player plucks the string with his finger instead of using the bow.

After Monteverdi's death, the madrigal form faded away as new forms arrived. However, Monteverdi's experimentation helped bring in the new Baroque era in his opera writing. At this time, opera was a new form. Just about a decade earlier, a group of intellectual Italians had decided that they would develop a new art form that would bring back the Greek tradition to the stage. Vincenzo Galilei wrote the theories of this new development in a book.

- **Vincenzo Galilei**, c. 1525–1591, the father of the scientist Galileo Galilei, felt that the music of his day was written only to sound nice to the ear. He said composers didn't consider "the expression of the words with the passion that these [words] require... Their ignorance and lack of consideration is one of the most potent reasons why the music of today does not cause in the listeners any of those virtuous and wonderful effects that ancient music caused." So Galilei challenged composers to consider the person who would be singing the line on stage—his age, his gender, what he was singing about—and the effect the composer would like this to have on the audience.

He also wanted composers to consider "the quantity and quality of sound, and the rhythms appropriate to that action and to such a person." In addition, he felt that the lines in this form should be simple and pure, without harmony.

- **Gregorio Allegri**, 1582–1652, the final composer we'll discuss in the Renaissance period, wrote *Miserere* (a setting of Psalm 1), a piece for nine voices in two choirs. It was so beautiful and sad that it was allowed to be performed only at the Sistine Chapel and only during Holy Week. The score was treasured so highly that it was a crime (punishable by excommunication) to copy the score. This law remained for several hundred years. The score was finally transcribed (written down and changed). Sadly, the version that is performed now is not even similar to this once-cherished score.

With these centuries of innovations, the road from plainchant to Baroque was built. This leads us to the Baroque masters. We'll give you an overview of the Baroque period and then on to our biographies, beginning with Antonio Vivaldi, the "Red Priest."

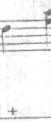

Music in the Renaissance *Note-taking Pages*

During the Renaissance, the _____ _____ became supporters of the arts.

Court songs: _____ _____ set to music.

Court songs were written by

_____ in southern France,

_____ in northern France,

_____ in Germany.

Court songs were sung by

_____ ,

_____ ,

_____ .

Because _____ _____ and _____ were limited, we don't know

how this music was performed.

Polyphony — music with _____ _____ _____ voice, or musical line,

at a time.

Organum — a type of polyphony in which a composer adds another line sung at the

_____ _____ .

Between A.D. 900 and A.D. 1300, several musical changes took place:

At first, harmony moved along with melody a certain _____ from it.

Then, harmony became more _____ .

Next, more _____ were added. Several notes were sung at the same time as one chant note.

Later, composers began to add two lines of _____ .

Finally, _____ became more structured.

Notable composers from this period:

_____ , who was French and wrote the first ballades

_____ , also French, who brought many styles together and helped establish the form of the Mass

_____ , considered the "Father of English Cathedral Music"

_____ , considered the greatest representative of sixteenth century counterpoint

_____ , the most published composer of the age

_____ , an English Catholic living in Protestant England who built a bridge between the older musical sounds and the new sounds

_____ , an Italian who used instruments with choral music

_____ , an Italian who wrote madrigals

_____ , the finest lute player in England, who is often considered the greatest English songwriter ever

_____ , who linked Renaissance music to the Baroque and added instrumental parts to the madrigal

_____ , the father of the scientist Galileo Galilei, who challenged composers to make music sound like the words it expressed

_____ , who wrote *Miserere*, a piece for nine voices, which was so beautiful it was allowed to be performed only at the Sistine Chapel during Holy Week

Ballad:

- _____ songs

- sung in _____ language

- accompanied by musical _____

Madrigal:

Song

- written for several _____ to sing at the same time

- always _____ (not about God)

- usually about _____

- generally sung at a _____ tempo

- popular among the _____ of the time

Counterpoint:

Describes the combination of simultaneously sounding musical lines according to a system of _____

The Baroque Period

The **Baroque period** is usually the period where people begin their study of classical music. This period began around 1600 and lasted until around 1750. This was a time of bold ornamentation, which was also expressed in art and architecture, as well as music. Instead of doing things simply, the artists at this time made their works as lavish and decorative as possible. The phrase "never one note when five will do" characterizes the music of this period well. This was a time of the rule of royalty and the nobility. Most wealthy households employed musicians (sometimes whole orchestras) and composers who wrote music for their patrons' parties, balls, and ceremonies. Because of the general public's appreciation for music as well, towns and churches also hired their own musicians.

Besides the great composers we will discuss shortly, there were other composers at this time who are not now as famous as those we will study. One of these is **Georg Philipp Telemann**, who was born in Germany. Telemann's parents tried to squelch his musical ambitions, but he was determined. When he went to Leipzig University, his mother wanted him to study law, but he continued to develop his musical abilities. He started a music group that did a lot of performing (and was later directed by **Johann Sebastian Bach**). In Telemann's lifetime, he held several major church and court positions and was extremely popular. He was a good friend of **George Frideric Handel**, who once said Telemann "could write a church piece in eight parts with the same expedition another would write a letter." He was also a friend of Johann Sebastian Bach's and became the godfather of his son.

Another lesser known composer is **Johann Pachelbel**, who was born in 1653 and moved to Vienna in 1673. From there, Pachelbel moved to Eisenach and finally to Erfurt, where he became **organ** teacher to Johann Sebastian Bach, as well as his siblings. His style is similar to that of Bach, and he is best known for his *Canon in D Major*. This famous piece is often played at weddings today.

Opera became a favorite form in the Baroque period. Like a play, an opera has scenery, actors, and costumes. Unlike a play, it is sung, not spoken, and is accompanied by an orchestra. The best-known operatic composers of this period were **Alessandro Scarlatti** and **Antonio Vivaldi** in Italy, **Jean-Baptiste Lully** in France, and Handel in England. As the period flourished, the oratorio became popular.

Oratorios, like operas, are sung, but they are usually about biblical stories and are unstaged—no acting, costumes, or scenery. At a time when church services were very formal and proper, oratorios were like operas that were acceptable to be performed in churches, and the people loved them. Oratorios tend to be long, like operas, sometimes lasting several hours. Another form that churches often perform is the cantata. **Cantatas** are like short oratorios which tend to fit within the typical length of a church service. Bach wrote many cantatas for his churches.

Instrumental music was also well liked. It was used for the many formal dances of the time. Suites from the Baroque period are still played. These **suites** are made up of many different dance movements, which are named for dance types: allemande, bourrée, courante, gavotte, gigue, minuet, sarabande, and waltz. The music written for dances tends to have a steady rhythm and is often repetitive—its melody may be repeated again and again. Bach and Handel wrote many of the Baroque suites that we hear today.

The concerto emerged as a common musical form. Vivaldi wrote many concertos for his students so that they could show what they had learned. **Concertos** are written for an instrumental soloist, usually accompanied by an orchestra, and they typically have three movements, first a fast one, then a slow one, then another fast one. So when you think of a concerto, think *fast-slow-fast*.

Another form you will hear when you listen to Baroque music, particularly organ music, is the fugue. In a **fugue**, usually the melody starts and then another line comes in, sometimes the same melody but played higher, or perhaps a different melody altogether. A fugue may have two, three, or four musical lines all going at the same time, and somehow it all sounds beautiful together.

During the Baroque period, people didn't have the same musical instruments we do today. The most common instruments were the organ, harpsichord, recorder, trumpet, and violin. These instruments have changed greatly since the 1600s, but they had the same basic form. A Baroque ensemble or group of instruments playing together may have included the recorder, violin, harpsichord, and viola de gamba or a small combination of the common instruments.

Other instruments did exist, however. We know that Vivaldi wrote for violin, flute, bassoon, guitar, mandolin, and piccolo. Louis XIV kept an orchestra that today we call a string orchestra. His consisted of six violins, twelve violas, and six cellos. Most Baroque orchestras were not as large. They often included a keyboard instrument—a harpsichord if the music was secular or an organ if the music was played in a church. The "festive" Baroque orchestra was used for special occasions—to celebrate a holiday or a victory. In addition to the string orchestra, it included the addition of woodwinds (a couple of oboes and a bassoon), brass (a few trumpets), and some percussion (a couple of timpani, or kettledrums). Looking at

artwork of the period and at the way music was arranged tells us quite a bit about the way Baroque instruments were combined and how they looked. Still, it is hard to know exactly what these instruments sounded like or how they were tuned. Some of these things we can only guess.

Summary of musical terms we have learned in the Baroque period:
- Opera
- Oratorio
- Cantata
- Suite
- Concerto
- Fugue

Summary of composers we mentioned from the Baroque period:
- Telemann
- Bach
- Handel
- Pachelbel
- Scarlatti
- Vivaldi
- Lully

The Baroque Period *Note-taking Pages*

During the Baroque period, music was characterized by the phrase,

"_____."

Musicians were employed by _____ _____.

Two composers we are introduced to in the Baroque period:

• Georg Philipp _____

• Johann _____ [besides Johann Sebastian Bach]

Musical Forms

Opera

Like a play, it has

_____,

_____,

_____.

Unlike a play, it is

_____ , not spoken, and is

accompanied by an _____.

Oratorio

Like an opera, it is _____.

Unlike an opera, it uses

_____ _____ and is not _____.

People liked oratorios because they were similar to operas but could be performed in

_____.

Cantata

Like oratorios but short enough to take up the same time as a _____ _____

Suite

Made of different dance movements, including:

1. _____

2. _____

3. _____

4. _____

5. _____

6. _____

7. _____

8. _____

Dance music tends to have:

• steady _____

• _____

Concerto

• written for an instrumental _____

• accompanied by an _____

• has three movements:

_____

_____

_____

Baroque Instruments

Most common:

- _____

- _____

- _____

- _____

- _____

Baroque orchestras were [larger - smaller] than orchestras we have today.

Antonio *Vivaldi*

b. 1678 d. 1741

The first Baroque composer we will study is **Antonio Vivaldi**, the "Red Priest." He was called that because of his bright-red hair and his venture into the priesthood. Antonio was born in Venice, Italy, in 1678. Because his father was the leading violinist of St. Mark's Chapel, Antonio was exposed to music from an early age. Although it is not clear that he actually wanted to become a priest, he was trained for the priesthood. In his day, becoming a priest was one of the few ways to obtain a free education.

At the same time that he was ordained as a priest at the age of 25, he was given a job as violin teacher at the Conservatory of the Ospedale della Pietà, an orphanage for girls. Musical training was very important at this orphanage. The girls learned to play many instruments—including the violin, flute, organ, oboe, cello, and bassoon—and also learned to sing. The children gave musical concerts every Sunday and on holidays. Vivaldi wrote more than four hundred concertos for these performances, in which the students were given a chance to show their musical skill. The audiences who attended were not allowed to applaud, so they would shuffle and stamp their feet, blow their noses, and cough to show their appreciation! Writing for the girls at the orphanage gave Vivaldi a wonderful opportunity to experiment with music without having to pay professional musicians. He could try different combinations of instruments and write solos for instruments that weren't usually thought of as solo instruments. Vivaldi was one of the first people to make use of the newly invented clarinet.

Vivaldi was an astonishing violinist; in fact, he was considered a better violinist than a composer. He claims that the pope himself asked him to perform for him. Vivaldi also had several **benefactors**—people who gave him money to play music or paid him to compose for them. These benefactors included the French king Louis the XV, for whom Vivaldi wrote *Festival on the Seine*. Vivaldi traveled in his native Italy and throughout Europe, to such cities as Rome, Florence, Amsterdam, and Prague. While performing his operas there he was also being influenced by other styles of music.

The orphanage continued to employ Vivaldi as their Master of Concertos as long as he sent them two concertos each month. Thus, he maintained his connection with the orphanage for most of the rest of his life.

Vivaldi never married, but he did have a good friend in his housekeeper, Anna Giraud, the daughter of a French wigmaker. Vivaldi taught her to sing. Both Anna and her sister lived in Vivaldi's home until he died.

Antonio Vivaldi wrote more than forty operas, which are rarely heard today. However, he is best known for his development of the concerto. A **concerto** is a piece for one solo instrument and an orchestra. In his work with this musical form, he created a standard for the concerto that is still followed. It has three movements: the first and the third are fast and the middle movement is slow. Vivaldi's concertos also had a great influence on **Johann Sebastian Bach**, whom we will study soon.

It is important to remember that the orchestra still hadn't developed into the large group of instruments we think of as an orchestra today. In Vivaldi's time, he often didn't know what instruments would be available when his compositions were played! The **solo concerto** is what we usually think of as a concerto. It features a solo instrument accompanied by an orchestra. Sometimes two, three, or four solo instruments would be featured within one concerto. The **concerto grosso**, or "grand concerto," used a small group of instruments— perhaps two violins or some other combination—playing together as the featured instruments, along with a larger group of instruments called a **continuo**. The continuo, therefore, is not some kind of instrument but is short for **basso continuo,** which means "continuous bass." The continuo was usually made up of a keyboard instrument (harpsichord or organ) along with a lower instrument (cello or bassoon). Its purpose was to provide the harmony for the featured instruments. Vivaldi wrote music for many instruments that we don't often hear today, such as the mandolin, lute, and classical guitar. He wrote such an enormous quantity of music that much of it was never published! Vivaldi was very popular in his time and was considered even then to be a musical genius.

Although ordained a priest in 1703, within a few years Vivaldi ceased to say Mass, giving up a much-needed income. At the time, he attributed this to physical complaints (possibly asthmatic bronchitis). Some have said that he would leave Mass to quickly jot down music and was simply thought of as an eccentric genius, but there isn't any real evidence to support this. However, he did fall under censure for "conduct unbecoming to a priest." Music, not Mass, was Vivaldi's passion.

Toward the end of his life, Vivaldi resigned from his job at the orphanage to move to Vienna to work for Charles VI, the Holy Roman Emperor. While Vivaldi was on his way to Vienna, however, Charles VI died from eating poisonous mushrooms. Vivaldi died the following year, in 1741, at the age of 63. We don't have any evidence that he was a believer in the Lord Jesus Christ. Sadly, he died a poor man and was buried in a pauper's grave.

Vivaldi was well known as a composer in Italy and in all of Europe in his day. A printer in Amsterdam even published many of his manuscripts. However, his works were quickly

forgotten and were almost lost to us. Fortunately though, in the early twentieth century, a Catholic boarding school was looking to raise money and found a large number of works from the sixteenth, seventeenth, and eighteenth centuries. These works were sold and then donated to the University of Turin, in Italy. When the professor of music there looked at all the works, he found that some of them didn't have endings so he thought there must be more somewhere. He was eager to find the endings of the compositions, and through careful sleuthing, he discovered who originally owned the music: Count Durazzo, once an Austrian ambassador in Venice. The professor contacted the descendants of the count to find the rest of the collection. He managed to locate it and was able to buy it through the generosity of two patrons who then donated it to the university. After World War II, this music began to be widely published. Long-playing recordings helped expose more people to his music. A new generation came to love Vivaldi's music.

After centuries of obscurity, Vivaldi is now often considered a Baroque composer equal to Bach and Handel. In fact, Vivaldi has perhaps become known to more people now than he ever was when he was alive. His most famous concertos are a set of four, entitled *The Four Seasons*, in which each concerto represents a different season. All four are often played in concert, and on the radio, and have been interwoven in many film scores. You may find that it's familiar to you when listening to "Spring" from *The Four Seasons*.

Antonio Vivaldi *Student Review*

1. Why is Vivaldi called the "Red Priest"?

2. With which place was Vivaldi connected for most of his life?

    a. church

    b. orphanage

    c. vineyard

    d. hospital

3. What is a benefactor?

4. How many movements does a concerto have?

    a. one

    b. two

    c. three

    d. four

5. Which famous composer was influenced by Vivaldi's concertos? _____

6. True or False: Vivaldi remained a devout priest all his life.

7. Vivaldi is best known for his development of the

    a. opera.

    b. fugue.

    c. concerto.

    d. clarinet.

8. True or False: Vivaldi's works were almost lost, but they were eventually recovered in the early twentieth century.

9. During which musical era did Vivaldi compose?
   a. Dark Ages
   b. Baroque
   c. Renaissance
   d. Classical

10. Vivaldi's most famous concertos belong to a set of four entitled

   The _____ _____ .

George Frideric *Handel*

b. 1685 d. 1759

George Frideric Handel[1] and **Johann Sebastian Bach** were born in 1685 in Germany and shared many similarities. Both were talented organists, masters at composing, and both went blind in their old age. Both even had unsuccessful eye surgery performed by the same surgeon! That is really where their personal resemblances end, though. Unlike the humble, homebody Bach, Handel was considered proud, a man of the world. Though he is thought to have been quite religious, he was also often arrogant and rude, with a temper to match. However, even his critics agreed that despite his temper, Handel was an honest, generous, and generally good-natured man.

Unlike Bach, Handel did not come from a musical family. His father wanted him to become a lawyer and tried to prevent him from becoming a musician. Still, Handel learned to play the **clavichord**—an early stringed instrument like a piano— and became very good at it. He did not become a full-time musician until he was 18, after his father had died.

Although Bach stayed in Germany throughout his career, Handel traveled all over Europe. He was born in Saxony, Germany, and went to Hamburg, Germany, where he began writing **operas**—dramas set to music—for the local opera house. He was offered a permanent position there, but he turned it down to go to Italy, where opera was very popular and he could learn the latest in writing opera **scores**—musical compositions. Handel's first major opera was performed in Florence in 1707, when he was only 22 years old. He left Florence for Rome, where he wrote sacred music for the Catholic Church—very appropriate in the city where the pope lived.

From Rome, he went to Naples and then to Venice, writing operas along the way. While in Italy, he gained a great appreciation for art, and he began an impressive art collection. An Italian composer named **Domenico Scarlatti** (also born in 1685) "discovered" Handel and his great talent. Others convinced these two to have a piano duel to see who was the greater musician. (Duels like this were very common among musicians at this time—similar to the "Battle of the Bands" today.) It was finally declared that on the harpsichord the men were equal, but on the organ, Handel was superior. The two men, surprisingly, became friends.

Handel went back to Hanover, where the Elector of Hanover appointed him **Kapellmeister**

(director of music for a monarch, nobleman, or church). He received a good salary and was allowed to take a one-year leave of absence, called a sabbatical. He took this time off right away, for he had been invited to London, England, to write more operas.

Operas were a fashionable form of entertainment for the people who lived there, and Handel immediately became popular in elite social circles. Back then, operas were not the serious events that they are now. People went to "see and be seen" and to hear their favorite opera stars. During the performance, people played cards, talked, walked around, hissed, and cheered! The performers on stage were not serious about what they were doing either. When they weren't singing, they would go out into the audience to chat or would stand on stage and talk to one another. (This was not too different from popular rock concerts today!)

Handel loved London and was very successful there, but after his sabbatical he thought he ought to return to his job in Hanover. He stayed at this job for a little more than a year, before his employer, the Elector of Hanover, let him go back to England. This time he stayed away two more years. Although the Elector of Hanover was paying Handel for a job, Handel was never there! Before he returned to Hanover, though, in 1714, a surprising thing happened. Queen Anne, the queen of England, died, and she didn't have any children to inherit her throne. So who should become the new king but Handel's employer, the Elector of Hanover. He became known as King George I. Fortunately, he forgave Handel for all his time away and even doubled his wages!

One popular story states that Handel decided to do something to make sure the new king wasn't too angry with him. He wrote what is now a very famous piece, called *Water Music*, for the king's procession up the Thames River. However, historians believe that the two had probably reconciled long before this procession took place.

Handel loved everything about London, particularly his popularity! He became a citizen of England, and the English were very proud of him. Most Europeans and Englishmen thought Handel was the greatest musician who ever lived. In 1719, the Royal Academy of Music was established in London to provide Italian opera as recreation for the nobility and gentry. (King George I understood Italian much better than he did English.) Handel was the director. An amazingly quick composer, he wrote many Italian-style operas that London society enjoyed. After George I died in 1727, Handel wrote four anthems for the successor's coronation, including *Zadok the Priest*, which has been sung at British **coronations**—the act or occasion of crowning—ever since. Handel was a knowledgeable businessman and, unlike most composers we will study, he fared very well financially.

By the mid 1720s, Italian operas became less popular in England, so Handel began writing English oratorios. **Oratorios**[2] are similar to an opera, but they are sacred works based on biblical themes, they are not staged (no actors or scenery), and they do not use costumes. Handel's most famous oratorio is *Messiah*, in which he set many verses from the King

James Version of the Bible to music, telling the story of Jesus from His birth in the stable to His resurrection. Many choirs probably sing *Messiah* in a town somewhere near you at Christmas or at Easter. This oratorio takes 3 hours to sing, and Handel wrote it in just 24 days, without ever leaving his house!

There are many stories about the writing of *Messiah*. It has been said that one day when Handel was writing the "Hallelujah Chorus," his servant brought him food, as he usually did, and found Handel with tears in his eyes. Handel said, "I did think I did see all of heaven before me and the great God Himself!"

A popular story about the "Hallelujah Chorus" relates that when King George II was in the audience, he was so moved by the "Hallelujah Chorus" that he stood up. It was the custom that when the king was standing, everyone must stand, so everyone stood up. Ever since then, people stand when they hear the "Hallelujah Chorus." (This is one of several plausible stories about the reason for standing—all are entertaining, but none has been verified.)

Handel wrote many, many sacred works of music, and his hope was to change lives with their message. Once, when a man told him how entertaining the *Messiah* was, he replied, ". . . I should be sorry if I only entertained them; I wished to make them better." His music, particularly *Messiah*, continues to change lives, because it proclaims the Gospel message.

In 1759, Handel knew he was dying, but he told his friends that he had only one desire left. "I want to die on Good Friday, in the hope of rejoining the good God, my sweet Lord and savior, on the day of His resurrection." Some say he did die on Good Friday, and some say it was the day before. He was buried in **Westminster Abbey**, a large, famous church in England, leaving behind a great legacy of music that glorified God.

Teacher Notes
[1]Handel adopted the spelling George Frideric Handel on his naturalization as a British subject, and this spelling is generally used in English-speaking countries. The original form of his name (Georg Friedrich Händel) is typically used in Germany.

[2]We'll be seeing the terms *oratorio* and *opera* throughout this course. This chart will help you remember the differences.

Opera	Oratorio
Secular—not specifically religious	**Sacred**—of, or relating to, religion
Scenery	**No Scenery**
Actors	**No Actors**
Costumes	**No Costumes**

1. Handel shares a birth year (1685) and some similarities with another famous composer named

    a. Beethoven.

    b. Vivaldi.

    c. Mozart.

    d. Bach.

2. True or False: Handel stayed in Germany throughout his career.

3. A Kapellmeister is the director of music for a _____ , nobleman, or church.

4. True or False: During the performance of an opera in Handel's time, people would play cards and talk.

5. In 1714, when Queen Anne of England died, the Elector of Hanover became King George I. What was his relationship to Handel?

    a. father

    b. son

    c. employer

    d. conductor

6. Which anthem did Handel write that has been sung at British coronations ever since?

    a. "God Save the Queen"

    b. *Messiah*

    c. *Zadok the Priest*

    d. *Water Music*

7. What are the differences between an oratorio and an opera?

Opera	Oratorio

8. What form of music is Handel's famous work *Messiah*? _____

9. At what part of *Messiah* do people usually stand? _____

10. True or False: Handel wanted to change lives with his music, not just entertain his listeners.

Johann Sebastian *Bach*

b. 1685 d. 1750

Born in 1685, **Johann Sebastian Bach** was the son of a highly regarded church organist, court trumpeter, and Director of Musicians in the small town of Eisenach, Germany. Sebastian (as he was called) was part of a rich musical heritage that ran deep in his family. He was the fifth of seven generations of musicians! Every year, the Bach family had a reunion and music was played all day and far into the night. What a joyful time for a little boy who dearly loved music!

Sebastian grew up in the same place as did the famous Protestant reformer Martin Luther, more than 100 years earlier! Have you ever heard of Wartburg Castle? Luther was hidden away in this castle in 1521 as he translated the New Testament into German. Wartburg Castle still sits on top of a hill in Eisenach. However, Sebastian and Luther shared something even more important—their attitude toward music, viewing it, above all, as a means of glorifying God.

Bach learned to play both the harpsichord and violin under his father's musical tutelage. His uncle, Johann Christoph (his father's twin), taught him to play the organ, too. Young Sebastian was very good at both of these instruments. He had such a musical genius, though, that he required very little in the way of formal training. Like a sponge, he soaked up music from any possible source.

Around the age of 9 or 10, Sebastian, one of eight children, was orphaned. He went to live with his eldest brother, Johann Christoph (named after his uncle). Johann Christoph was also an organist and the former pupil of **Pachelbel**. His brother wasn't thrilled to have another mouth to feed. Even so, he was a musician and Sebastian learned from him. Legend has it that his brother had a book of music that Sebastian wasn't permitted to handle, so the boy secretly copied it at night by the light of the moon. When his brother caught him about six months later, Sebastian had not only copied all the music in the book, he had memorized it! Sebastian also had an uncommonly fine voice, which earned him a place in the choir of a monastery at St. Michael's Church in Lüneburg, where he was paid to sing. While there, he also studied music.

Bach left the monastery at the age of 18 for a position as church organist in Arnstadt in southern Germany. The congregation loved him until he took a month's leave to walk 200

miles to Lübeck in northern Germany because he wanted to hear a famous organist named **Dietrich Buxtehude** play the organ. He stayed away four months instead of one, and when he returned, he used the new musical forms he had heard. The congregation didn't like this new music and they wanted him to leave. So he took a post as town organist in Mühlhausen, where he married his second cousin Maria Barbara Bach. There, he found success and approval, but he became frustrated by arguments within the church. Finally, he gave his letter of resignation, stating that in his position he would not be able to fulfill his ultimate goal, to establish church music "to the glory of God."

Bach's next post was in Weimar, where he served the Duke of Saxony-Weimar as a member of the chamber orchestra and Organist to the Court. Here, he matured as a composer and wrote many works for the organ. His duties expanded, and he became known as one of the greatest organists in Germany. There is an interesting tale about his skill at the organ. Although some thought he was the greatest organist, others thought the Frenchman **Louis Marchand** was better, so in 1717, arrangements were made for a contest. On the morning of the competition, after Marchand heard Bach improvising at the keyboard, he realized that Bach was the superior organist and left town!

Bach kept his job in Weimar for about nine years, but after a time, the important job of Kapellmeister was given to someone else, so Bach decided to leave. When he turned in his notice, the duke became angry and had him arrested. Bach was put in jail for a month! But even then, the always productive Bach made good use of his time by writing a group of **organ chorale preludes**—relatively short organ pieces used to introduce the hymn to be sung by the congregation. (Can you think of a New Testament apostle who also made good use of his time writing while in jail?)

In 1717, Bach took his family to Cöthen (also spelled Köthen), where he worked for Prince Leopold as Kapellmeister in the Cöthen court. Here, most of his work was secular, but Bach took advantage of the musical opportunities and composed much instrumental music. Prince Leopold also played in the orchestra that Bach directed. Sometimes Bach would accompany the prince on his travels. Sadly, after one of his trips, he returned to find that his wife, Maria Barbara, had fallen ill and died! During their 13 years of marriage, she had borne seven children. Five of them had survived their infancy.

After Maria Barbara's death in 1720, Bach married Anna Magdalena Wilckenin in December 1721. She gave up her career as a soprano to become a wonderful wife and mother to Bach's surviving children—and gave him 13 more! Of these, eight died in infancy or childhood. In all, Bach fathered 20 children.

Next, Bach applied for a post in Leipzig as the **cantor** (choir leader). He wrote the *St. John Passion* as an entry test for his employment. He got the job, but only because their first choice, **Georg Philipp Telemann**, didn't take the position. (This is ironic, because today

Bach is much more famous than Telemann!)

Bach was very busy in Leipzig. He was in charge of music for four churches, and he led Sunday morning services at two of them. He had to write a **cantata**—a piece for the choir to sing—every week, and he had to write a **Passion**—an oratorio based on a Gospel narrative of the suffering of Jesus Christ—once every year. In addition, he was the musical supervisor for the St. Thomas School, in charge of all the music teaching there and also did some of the teaching himself. While in Leipzig, he composed about 250 works for solo voice, chorus, and orchestra, including his Mass in B Minor. He continued writing for the keyboard and produced the famous *Goldberg Variations*.

When someone asked him about his remarkable talent, he gave this reply, "I was made to work; if you are equally industrious you will be equally successful." Bach struggled with his eyesight for years (which is very hard for a musician who needs to be able to read and write music). Some think that this problem started back when he lived with his brother and copied music by moonlight. Bach had an operation to try to fix his sight, but the operation failed and left him completely blind. He died in 1750, when he was 65 years old, after having written an incredible volume of music in every popular form except opera.

Bach's faith permeated his entire life, in the way he lived, the way he worked, and the way he wrote his music. He declared, "Music's only purpose should be for the glory of God and the recreation of the human spirit." At the end of his manuscripts, he always wrote the initials, S.D.G., or *Soli Deo Gloria*—"To God Alone the Glory." The front of his *Little Organ Book* holds the dedication, "To God alone the praise be given for what's herein to man's use written." These are just a few examples of the many faithful inscriptions found in his musical works, which include masses, cantatas, concertos, and orchestral suites.

Bach also wrote one of the most influential books in the history of Western classical music: *The Well-Tempered Clavier*. This is a collection of music composed, he said, "for the profit and use of musical youth desirous of learning, and especially for the pastime of those already skilled in this study."

Although he was a master composer of the Baroque era, the style he preferred— **polyphony** (more than one melody playing at the same time)—was falling out of favor. People were beginning to prefer what is known as the **homophonic** style (one melody with some accompaniment). Bach wasn't widely known as a great composer during his lifetime because most of his work had not yet been published or heard.

Even though a story is often told that "a famous composer named **Felix Mendelssohn** rediscovered his works 100 years later," this is an exaggeration. Bach's sons and a few other musicians kept his name and music alive. **Mozart** learned from Bach's music; **Haydn** was well acquainted with it; and **Beethoven** was brought up on *The Well-Tempered Clavier*.

Bach never gained wealth or fame in his lifetime but he left a legacy of faith, fathered several sons who became well-known musicians, and composed nearly 1,000 works, about three fourths of which were sacred music. Most importantly, he wrote his music for the glory of God.

Johann Sebastian Bach *Student Review*

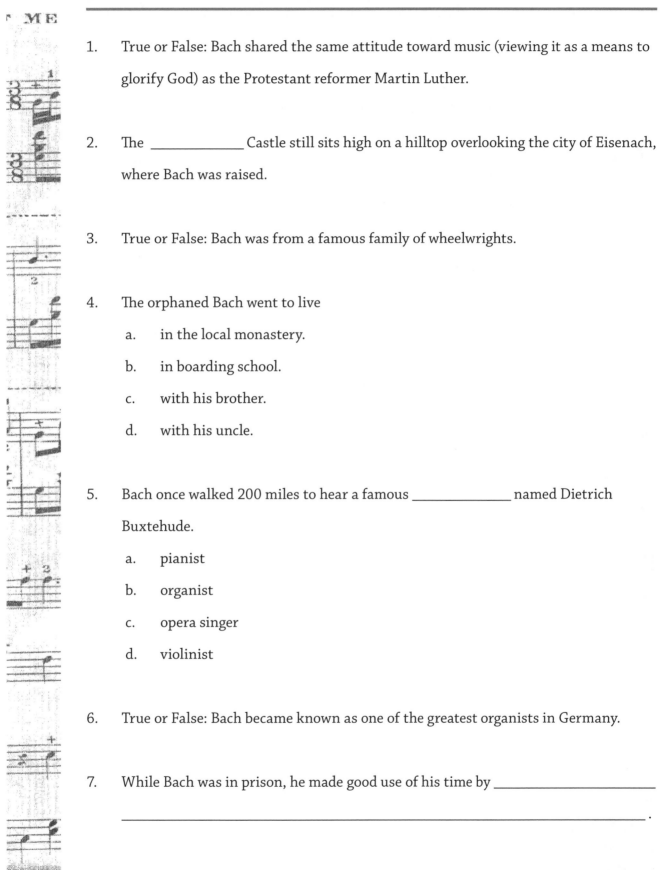

1. True or False: Bach shared the same attitude toward music (viewing it as a means to glorify God) as the Protestant reformer Martin Luther.

2. The _____ Castle still sits high on a hilltop overlooking the city of Eisenach, where Bach was raised.

3. True or False: Bach was from a famous family of wheelwrights.

4. The orphaned Bach went to live

   a. in the local monastery.

   b. in boarding school.

   c. with his brother.

   d. with his uncle.

5. Bach once walked 200 miles to hear a famous _____ named Dietrich Buxtehude.

   a. pianist

   b. organist

   c. opera singer

   d. violinist

6. True or False: Bach became known as one of the greatest organists in Germany.

7. While Bach was in prison, he made good use of his time by _____

   _____ .

8. Bach wrote at the bottom of all of his works the initials S.D.G. (*Soli Deo Gloria*).

What does that phrase mean? _____

9. Name one of Bach's compositions or books: _____

10. Which statements are true of Bach?

   a. He composed nearly 1,000 works.

   b. He was a master composer in the Romantic era.

   c. He wrote *The Well-Tempered Clavier*.

   d. He fathered 20 children.

   e. He was most famous for his operas.

   f. He left a legacy of faith.

The Classical Period

The **Classical period** emerged during the second half of the eighteenth century. Can you think of two major political events that were happening between 1750 and 1800? The American Revolution and the French Revolution! This was a time when people were daring to think differently and were wanting things to change. People were also challenging the established religions and the **monarchies**—monarchs, or kings—that ruled the country. People desired rights that included "life, liberty, and the pursuit of happiness." The Classical period is usually defined as being between 1750 and 1820.

Music reflected these changes as well, and the common people, not just the nobility, began attending public concerts. Because the audiences were different, composers began writing specifically for the enjoyment of the public—the common people instead of the nobility. This new era, therefore, called for less ornamentation. One way this was shown in music is that composers didn't write in counterpoint anymore. (Remember counterpoint? This music features two or more melodies working together at the same time within a piece.)

Instead, composers began writing in **homophony**, in which a work contains one melody. This melody was supported by harmony accompanying the melody in chords. A more straightforward era called for more straightforward music—and this was considered a clearer way of presenting a melody. As a result, music from the Classical era was easier to listen to—less taxing on the brain—than the Baroque music from the past.

New forms arose in this new era. Composers began to compose in the sonata form, minuet form, rondo, and theme and variations form. Music listeners of the time appreciated these forms—they were familiar with the structure. Within a few minutes of listening to a new piece, they would recognize the form and have an idea of what to expect. (This means they would then know when to expect to hear the theme again. They would also know how long the piece might last.)

The **sonata** form, a new favorite among composers, contains three sections: the exposition, the development, and the recapitulation. In the first section, called the exposition, a composer introduces listeners to a main theme. Later, he introduces a different, contrasting theme. In the second section, called the development, he develops the themes, playing with them and making them sound different. In the third section, called the recapitulation, the composer brings listeners back to the themes, making them sound very similar to the first time they

were heard. This is called ABA' format (said "A-B-A prime"), where A is the first section, B is quite different, and A' shows a return to the first, familiar sound—the ' is said "prime," and it means that although we can expect the theme to come back to the original A, it will be a little different from the first time we heard it.

The **minuet** is the one dance form that was carried from the Baroque period to the Classical era. One reason is that the dance itself continued to be popular in social circles. It also reminded people of the aristocratic courts in which orchestras first appeared. And it gave the newly established symphonic forms a nice contrast because of the way it used time and rhythm.

The **rondo** form takes a tune and repeats it—a lot, with some extra stuffing in between its appearances so that the listener doesn't get bored. It is light and especially easy to listen to. A rondo could be structured like this: ABACA or ABACABA (notice that A keeps recurring).

The **theme and variations** introduces a main theme. The theme is the melody. In this form, the melody is then repeated with several variations. (This isn't the only form that has a theme; most works have themes, or a main melody. But this is the only form that is structured with one theme and several different variations.)

During this period, the symphony also arose as a new form. A **symphony** is a longer piece of music that is made up of several **movements**, or parts. Each of these parts is usually written in one of the forms we just discussed. In a typical symphony (and remember that not all symphonies are typical), there are four movements. The first movement is a fast or moderate movement written in sonata form. The second movement is slow, and there is no standard form for it—sometimes it's written in sonata form, sometimes in rondo form, and sometimes in a variation form. The third movement is usually a minuet—the tempo is moderate and written in minuet form. The final, or closing, movement is fast and is written in either sonata or rondo form.

Although each movement in a symphony has its own themes and its own forms, they're written to go together. You cannot simply replace the second movement of one symphony with the second movement of a different symphony. Think of it like decorating a house. Usually, the rooms work together—the colors flow from one room to the next. They may not be the same, but there are elements that carry from one area to another. That is the way a symphony works.

Though the Classical period lasted only 70 years, it served a pivotal role in the development of "classical" music. The development of musical instruments, the growth of the orchestra, and the growing popularity of the newer **pianoforte** (which we now know as a piano) set the stage for the Romantic period that was to come.

The Classical Period *Note-taking Pages*

The Classical period took place between the years _____ and _____ .

Name two major political events that were happening in the world during this time:

1. _____

2. _____

What was different about concerts during this period? _____ .

What was different about the audiences attending these concerts? _____

_____

Composers began writing in _____ , instead of counterpoint.

Homophony occurs in a work that contains _____ melody.

This melody is supported by harmony, which accompanies the melody in _____ .

New forms:

1. _____   2. _____

3. _____   4. _____ and _____

Sonata form contains _____ sections.

Section #	Name	Music Contains	Format
1		theme	
2	development		B
3		theme is similar	

The _____ is the one _____ form that carried over from the Baroque period.

The _____ takes a tune and _____ it.

Some possible structures for a rondo:

_____ OR _____

The _____ and _____ form introduces a _____ and repeats it with

different _____ .

A _____ is made up of _____ movements.

These movements are actually other _____ .

Movement	Tempo (fast or slow)	Form
	fast or moderate	
second		any—sonata or rondo or variation
		sonata or rondo

(Franz) Joseph *Haydn*

b. 1732 d. 1809

Dubbed "Papa Haydn" by his dear friend **Amadeus Mozart**, **Haydn** was a man with strong principles, a strong work ethic, and a deep love for the Lord. Born in Rohrau, Austria (on the border of Austria and Hungary), in 1732, he was called Joseph by his family. The family loved music, though they were not musicians. In fact, his father was a wheelwright (made and repaired wooden wheels). Joseph was one of twelve children in this poor family. His father had hopes he would become a clergyman.

At the age of 6, he went to live with a relative who was a schoolmaster. There, he learned to read and write, studied the **catechism** (a brief summary of the basic principles of Christianity in question-and-answer form), and because of his unusual musical abilities, received music lessons as well. When he was 8, he went to St. Stephen's Cathedral in Vienna to be a choirboy, where he became a star pupil. Nine years later, at 17, his voice had changed, and he could no longer be a member of this choir. (After he left, his younger brother Michael became the new star pupil!)

Out on his own now, young Haydn labored to eke out a living by performing, composing, and giving music lessons to young people. Working hard to become a good composer, he was determined to better himself. He said, "I was never a quick writer and composed with care and diligence." Haydn was fortunate to learn the true fundamentals of composition from a famous composer living in Vienna at the time. He also claimed, "I listened more than I studied, but I heard the finest music in all forms that was to be heard in my time . . . thus little by little my knowledge and my ability were developed."

Certainly, they did develop. He ultimately became one of the best composers in Europe! Haydn was well respected and honored. His music reflects the life of a well-adjusted man, rather than that of a troubled man, as is often seen in musical genius. He was generous and industrious, with a good sense of humor and an even temper.

In 1760, Haydn married Maria Anna Alysia Apollonia Keller. He was not really in love with her, but with one of her sisters, and his marriage was not a happy one. Maria Anna did not appreciate music, and she was selfish and ill-tempered. Haydn once referred to her as "that infernal beast." They were married, however, for most of his life.

Haydn's career really began in 1761, when he was hired as musical director of the Esterházy household, working first for Prince Paul (for only a year, until the prince died), and then for Prince Nikolaus (Nicholas the Magnificent). Haydn was one of the last musicians who worked in a noble household—the age of nobility hiring court musicians was ending. The Esterházy home was one of the wealthiest in Hungary, and though Prince Paul's castle had more than 200 rooms for guests, Nikolaus, when he came to power, built a new castle in the country, known as Esterháza. This castle was the greatest palace in Europe (with the exception of Versailles), and Haydn served this family there for 29 years.

Esterháza was built with a special marionette theater and a 400-seat opera house! As Kapellmeister, Haydn was required to direct the orchestra, compose music, handle all the musical administrative duties, and oversee the personnel. His musicians loved him and, like Mozart, called him "Papa." He was always willing to take their part when necessary, and you can see his tact and easygoing nature in this story: One season, Prince Nikolaus stayed in Esterháza longer than was customary, and the musicians, longing for their families back in the city, began to complain. Instead of arguing with the prince, Haydn wrote a symphony in which, one by one, the members of the orchestra got up, blew out their candles, and left. When Prince Nikolaus saw this, he got the point, and the royal household left the next day to return to the city. This symphony is called the *Farewell Symphony*.

Not only was Haydn an excellent manager, he maintained an exceptional opera house. According to one report, German comedies and Italian opera alternated from day to day. "The Prince is always present, and six o'clock is the usual time. The delight for eyes and ears is indescribable. It comes first from the music, since the entire orchestra resounds as a complete entity: now the most moving tenderness, now the most vehement power penetrates the soul—because the great musician, Herr Haiden [Haydn], who serves the Prince as Kapellmeister, is the director."

Because Haydn's time was spent primarily in the country, he was able to hunt and fish when he wasn't composing. Although the other musicians didn't like being stuck far away from the city, Haydn enjoyed it. He said, in regards to being apart from the rest of the musical world, he was "forced to be original" in his compositions. Because composing did not come easily to Haydn, he set a regular time every day to write. Composing may not have been easy for him, but he certainly composed a lot of music! Often called the "Father of the Symphony," Haydn wrote 104 of them, as well as violin and keyboard concertos and other types of music. (A **symphony** is an extended piece for orchestra, usually in three or four movements.) He also wrote the music for a pair of two-hour weekly concerts, held on Tuesdays and Saturdays.

Haydn was a jokester when he was young (he said he received "more floggings than food"), and he still used this humor when he grew older and began to compose. He said, "God gave me a cheerful heart, so He will surely forgive me if I serve Him cheerfully." His cheerful heart shows in his music. In addition to the fun of the *Farewell Symphony*, Haydn wrote *Le Poule* (usually translated *The Hen*) *Symphony*. The nickname comes from the clucking second subject in the first movement, which reminded listeners of the jerky back-and-forth head motion of a walking hen.

In the *Surprise Symphony*, there is a loud drumroll during the quiet movement. Haydn said, "It will make all the women scream!" A diplomat at the Swedish embassy in Vienna once told this story, "[Haydn] showed me his Aria in D from *The Creation*, which depicts the movement of the sea and the rising of the cliffs out of the sea. 'Can you see,' he said jokingly, 'how the notes behave like waves? Up and down they go! Look, you can also see the mountains. You have to amuse yourself sometimes after being serious for so long.'"

This oratorio, *The Creation*, is one of Haydn's better-known sacred works. The words for it were taken from the Bible and from the writings of John Milton. Haydn also wrote an oratorio called *The Seasons*, which describes nature and man's enjoyment of the simple life. When asked about the two oratorios, he said he preferred *The Creation* because ". . . in *The Creation* angels speak, and their talk is of God. In *The Seasons* no one higher than Farmer Simon speaks."

Haydn met Mozart in 1781 when Mozart was 25. Haydn was in no way threatened by Mozart but rather deeply impressed by him—his only true competition—whom he considered "the greatest composer the world possesses now." The respect and influence was mutual with Mozart, who dedicated his important set of string quartets (nos. 14–19) to Haydn.

After Nicholas the Magnificent died, Haydn was free to travel and planned a trip to England. Before he left, Mozart wrote him a letter saying, "Dear Papa, you were never meant for running around the world, and you speak too few languages." Haydn wrote back, "The language I speak is understood by the whole world." With that, he went off to London. Sadly, his friend Mozart died while he was in England.

The people of London loved Haydn's music. While there, he wrote 12 symphonies, known as the *London Symphonies*. There, he also conducted an orchestra of 40 members while playing the piano. This orchestra was the largest he had ever conducted. One newspaper compared his musical abilities to Shakespeare's writing abilities!

After Haydn's second trip to England in 1794 to 1795, King George III asked him to stay, but Haydn chose to return to Vienna, where he lived and composed until 1809. His last words were, "Children, be comforted. I am well." His funeral was small and simple, owing to the war[1]. However, Mozart's **Requiem** was played later at a solemn memorial service. Likely, Haydn would have been pleased.

Teacher Note
[1]In April 1809, Austria rebelled against Napoleonic rule, announcing a "War of Liberation." This was part of the ongoing Napoleonic Wars.

(Franz) Joseph Haydn *Student Review*

1. Where was Haydn born?

    a. Hungary

    b. Germany

    c. France

    d. Austria

2. True or False: Composing did not come easily to Haydn.

3. Circle all of the following characteristics that describe Haydn and his personality:

    a. sense of humor

    b. stingy

    c. angry

    d. generous

    e. easygoing

    f. impatient

    g. respected

4. Haydn was one of the last musicians to work in a _____ household.

5. Was Haydn a Christian?

6. Define a Kapellmeister: _____

    _____

    _____

    _____

7. What part of Haydn's personality shows most strongly through his music?

   a. his cheerfulness

   b. his temper

   c. his generosity

   d. his love

8. Haydn is known as the "_____ of the Symphony."

9. *The Creation* is one of Haydn's well-known works. The words for it were taken from the writings of John Milton and from the _____ .

10. Haydn was a dear friend of another famous composer, _____ , who called him "Papa Haydn."

Wolfgang Amadeus *Mozart*

b. 1756 d. 1791

Wolfgang Amadeus Mozart, called a child prodigy and a musical genius, was born in the tiny independent city-state of Salzburg (in modern-day Austria) on January 27, 1756. His father was a talented violinist who began teaching his son keyboard and composition when Wolfgang was just 4. Because of the boy's extraordinary gift, his father took him on tour throughout Europe, along with his musically talented older sister, Maria Anna (whom he affectionately called "Nannerl"). They visited numerous cities over a period of years, playing in the royal courts of many nations. Young Wolfgang even performed for Marie Antoinette, who later became the queen of France. One advertisement for his performances claimed, "He will play a concerto on the violin, and will accompany symphonies on the harpsichord—the keyboard being covered with a cloth—with as much facility as if he could see the keys..." Wolfgang was popular everywhere he went, and as his fame grew, all the nobility wanted to have him play at their parties.

Mozart began his lifelong composing career at age 5, and at 6 he composed his first minuet. He wrote his first symphony when he was 8, his first oratorio when he was 11, and his first opera when he was 12!

When he was a young teen, he visited the Vatican, where he heard the papal choir sing. By law, this special piece of music (*Miserere* by Allegri) that he heard was allowed to be performed only at the Vatican, and the only copy of the music was kept there. Anyone who tried to copy it would be punished. Mozart loved the music so much that he ran home after hearing it and wrote down every note from memory! He had the amazing ability to memorize music after hearing it just once! Fortunately, the Vatican didn't penalize him for doing this.

One of the greatest influences on Mozart when he was a young man was **Johann Christian Bach**, whom Mozart met when his father took him to London. Johann Christian Bach was the youngest son of **Johann Sebastian Bach**. It was Johann Christian who first introduced Mozart to Italian music, still a strong musical influence of that time. When Mozart was a teenager, he spent three years in Italy, learning Italian and absorbing all he could about Italian music. As with **Handel's** music, Mozart's music is not in the style of his homeland; rather, it melds the different musical styles found throughout Europe yet is uniquely his own.

Whereas other composers we have studied enjoyed hobbies, for Mozart writing music was his best form of relaxation, though he also enjoyed playing pool and solving math problems. He gave his barber fits, because in the middle of having his hair done, he would leap up to write something down, saying that it was easier to compose than to sit still.

Mozart had a deep and living faith, evident in all he said and did. He once wrote to his father:

> *"Papa must not worry, for God is ever before my eyes. I realize his omnipotence and I fear his anger; but I also recognize His love, His compassion, and His tenderness towards His creatures. He will never forsake His own. If it is according to his will, so let it be according to mine. Thus all will be well and I must needs be happy and contented."*

In 1782, Mozart married Constanze Weber. She appreciated his music and his talent, and when he was composing late at night, she would help him stay awake by telling him funny stories and jokes and making his favorite drink. She also shared his faith. He once said, "I found that I never prayed so heartily, confessed or communicated so devoutly, as when by her side. And she feels the same." Wolfgang and Constanze had six children, though only two of them lived to adulthood.

The same year that Mozart married Constanze, he also met **Franz Joseph Haydn**, who became one of his dearest friends. Haydn was older than Mozart and was a mentor to him. In gratitude for all Haydn taught him, Mozart wrote six string quartets in Haydn's honor. Haydn himself heard a few of these in concert. It was after one such concert that Haydn wrote to Mozart's father, "Your son is the greatest composer known to me either in person or by reputation. He has taste and, what is more, the most profound knowledge of composition."

Unlike Haydn and other musicians of the era, Mozart held only short-term positions as a court musician. Many historians think all of the royal attention he received while he traveled with his father, performing at courts in other cities and countries, spoiled him. Because of this and after watching his father dealing with court politics, he chose to become a freelance composer. This meant that instead of a secure salary, he would receive payment only for works that were published. Because there were no copyright laws at the time, anyone who liked his music could copy it and perform it whenever they wanted, and Mozart wouldn't receive any profit from it. So although he was immensely popular, he never had much money.

Although Mozart was poor throughout most of his life, he had a giving heart. When a beggar once asked him for money, which he didn't have, he invited the man to follow him to a coffeehouse, where he quickly wrote down a piece of music. He sent the beggar to his publisher with the music manuscript and a note. The publisher then gave the beggar the

money that the composition was worth. Another time, one of his musical friends (Haydn's brother) was told by his employer to write six string duets. He became very ill after writing only four, so Mozart wrote the other two for him but didn't take credit for the work.

Mozart left us so much wonderful music and he so excelled in every type of music that it is difficult to know which pieces to list here. He wrote 22 operas, 3 of which are *The Magic Flute*, *Don Giovanni*, and *The Marriage of Figaro*. His sacred music includes Mass in C (the Coronation Mass), Mass in C Minor (probably written in celebration of his marriage), and the (unfinished) Requiem Mass in D Minor. He composed 41 symphonies, ending with no. 41, the *Jupiter Symphony*. Of his 27 piano concertos, his most popular is probably no. 23. There are so many other works—chamber music, violin concertos, instrumental music, and more—that one could spend years just listening to Mozart!

Mozart died at only 35 years of age, yet his short life was quite full. He was still composing even on his deathbed! The last work he created, one of his most famous, is a testimony to his faith. It's called Requiem. May we all be able to live with Mozart's faith, expressed when he said, "Let come what will, nothing can go ill as it is the will of God; and that it may so go is my daily prayer."

1. Mozart's father began teaching his son keyboard and composition when he was just

   _____ years old.

2. As a child prodigy, young Mozart performed all over Europe, even for Marie

   Antoinette, the future _____ of _____ .

3. Mozart had the amazing ability to memorize music after hearing it played just

   _____ .

4. Mozart relaxed by (circle all that apply):

   a.   writing music.

   b.   solving math problems.

   c.   gardening.

   d.   playing pool.

5. Were Mozart and his wife Christians?

6. Which of the composers that we've studied was Mozart's mentor?

   a.   Haydn

   b.   Bach

   c.   Handel

   d.   Vivaldi

7. True or False: Mozart was a famous court musician.

8. Once, when a beggar asked Mozart for money, he

   a. gave him cash.

   b. bought him lunch.

   c. wrote him music to sell.

   d. gave him a free concert ticket.

9. True or False: Mozart died young.

10. Which of the following of Mozart's compositions is a testimony to his faith?

   a. Requiem

   b. Piano Concerto no. 24

   c. Symphony no. 40

   d. *The Marriage of Figaro*

Ludwig van *Beethoven*

b. 1770 d. 1827

Ludwig van Beethoven was born in 1770, only 14 years after **Mozart**. He was the eldest surviving son born into a musical family in Bonn, Germany. At age 4, he began piano, violin, and composition lessons with his father. His father wanted Ludwig to be the next Mozart. Sadly, Beethoven's father was addicted to alcohol, so he sometimes forced his son to do crazy things, such as get up in the middle of the night and practice until morning. Fortunately, his mother was a gentle soul, and Beethoven often called her his "best friend."

Around the age of 10 Ludwig began lessons with the renowned musician **Christian Neefe**, a court composer and organist, who had some of Beethoven's first compositions published. When Beethoven was 11, he became assistant organist to Neefe. At the age of 12 or 13, Ludwig became a harpsichordist in the court orchestra through the efforts of Neefe. Around age 13 or 14, Ludwig became the assistant organist in the orchestra and received his first salary. At Neefe's suggestion, Ludwig went to Vienna, Austria, in 1787, where he took a few lessons with prominent composers of the day, including **Haydn** and, possibly, Mozart.

Sadly, young Beethoven returned to Bonn after just two weeks because his dear mother was dying. Although he always regretted not having any further studies with "the master" (Mozart), he knew he must go home. There, he took on the responsibility of becoming the head of the family, as his father was incapable. Then, he took the extraordinary step of petitioning the court for half of his father's salary and took on the support of his two younger brothers.

Ludwig remained the head of the family until the court sent him on for further study with Haydn in 1792. He studied with Haydn for about a year. One of his criticisms of Haydn was his "lack of thoroughness" in correcting his (Beethoven's) exercises!

This was a transitional period for Vienna and for music in general. Until this time, the main keyboard instrument was the **harpsichord**, but the new **pianoforte** was becoming increasingly popular. One of **Bach's** sons began to use it regularly, then Mozart, and finally Haydn followed the trend. As the pianoforte gained in popularity, Beethoven became well known as a gifted player of this new instrument.

Beethoven quickly found a patron, Prince Lichnowsky (although this relationship did not last throughout his career). Later, he was offered a position in a foreign court, but local nobility who recognized his talent wanted to keep Beethoven in Vienna. Some became patrons who paid him for compositions and for concerts. Beethoven also continued to support his brothers until they could support themselves. Beethoven had a strong personality, could be rude, and was not especially likable. But despite his bad manners, by force of will and talent, he was accepted into aristocratic circles. Where Bach, Haydn, and Mozart would have dined with the servants, Beethoven ate with the host!

Additionally, he sold music—at a decent profit in those days—by subscription. In a letter to a friend, he wrote, "my compositions bring me a good deal and I may say that I am offered more commissions than it is possible for me to carry out. Moreover, for every composition I can count on six or seven publishers—even more, if I want them. People no longer come to an arrangement with me. I state my price, and they pay."

Beethoven was not an attractive man. He was short—about 5' 4" with a large head, teeth that stuck out, and a round nose. Even he claimed he was unattractive. He was, however, highly confident in his musical abilities. In fact, he lived for his art, and perhaps because of this lack of balance in his life, his personality was rather grating. He was demanding, sullen, and arrogant (although he often followed his outbursts with reconciliations and scenes of penitence). He mistreated people—as a composer, he admitted that he "deliberately put trills at ends of compositions because of the desire to embarrass those Viennese pianists," some of whom were his sworn enemies. The famous French composer **Claude Debussy** said, "Genius can, of course, dispense with taste: of this Beethoven is an example. Mozart, on the other hand, his equal in genius, has, in addition, the most delicate taste." He was messy and disorganized and couldn't keep a servant (probably because of his temper) and according to many, his home was in a constant state of disaster. Yet he was also a genius of epic proportions!

Though Beethoven spent much of his time engrossed in his composing, he took many trips to the Austrian countryside to enjoy nature. He always kept a journal handy on his long walks, so he could jot down musical ideas. In fact, this love of nature inspired one of his famous works, the *Pastoral Symphony*, his Sixth Symphony.

Regrettably, Beethoven began to lose his hearing. This deafness began around age 30, when his career was at its height. He tried to hide this disability for a long time, but by the time he was 48, he was totally deaf. Musicians of Beethoven's caliber are gifted with both external and internal hearing. Although he lost his external hearing, he was still able to "hear" music within his head and place the proper notes on paper. Despite his continuing to compose, his deafness meant that he no longer could play the piano in public or conduct orchestras well, because he couldn't hear the music. He did continue to try, however. When he conducted, he never knew how the public was receiving a performance until he turned around and saw the applause and enthusiastic response. Sadly, Beethoven's deafness, in addition to his difficult personality, caused him to be a somewhat lonely, solitary man.

Beethoven's music is often divided into three periods based on style and chronology. (Years may vary depending on the source.)

The Early Period 1792–1802

He modeled his early work after other great composers, notably Bach, Haydn, and Mozart. (This is one of the best ways to become good at something yourself—to model what you do after the work of someone else who did it well.) During this time, he wrote six well-known string quartets, three (of six) piano concertos, and his first ten piano sonatas—of which two are very famous—the *Pathétique* (no. 8) and the *Moonlight Sonata* (no. 14).

The Middle Period 1802–1812

Beethoven's middle period coincided with the beginning of his hearing loss, in which he showed more of his emotions in his music. This period began with his Third Symphony, the *Eroica*, which broke previously accepted symphonic rules. During this time, Beethoven began to break away from many traditional musical rules to find his own writing style. This transition marks the shift from the Classical period of music into the Romantic period of music. In addition to the *Eroica*, he wrote three string quartets, two piano concertos, one violin concerto, five symphonies, more piano sonatas, a famous sonata for violin and piano, and his only opera, *Fidelio* (which was his favorite composition). His famous Fifth Symphony moves from sadness to hope and is thought to parallel his own struggles with his deafness. People around the world recognize its opening four notes! It's one of the most beloved symphonies of all times. His Sixth Symphony (also known as the *Pastoral Symphony*) has some of the earliest examples of **tone painting**—in which a composer tries to describe something with music, such as running water or tweeting birds.

The Last Period 1813–1827

During this period, Beethoven began to expand on traditional musical forms and patterns, making his music extremely unpredictable to the listener and quite unusual for his time. In his Ninth Symphony, Beethoven wanted a symphony with voices. He included the now-famous hymn "Ode to Joy" in the finale of the work. During this third period, he also wrote a Mass, *Missa Solemnis*, his last piano sonatas, and four string quartets. Those final sonatas show the change in his musical style and life. He became the predecessor to many other composers in the coming eras.

Because Beethoven's music was so unusual for his time, many people were unaccustomed to the new sounds and didn't like them. One Englishman said, "Beethoven always sounds to me like the upsetting of a bag of nails, with here and there also a dropped hammer." Still, much of the public enjoyed Beethoven's new music.

Beethoven's religious beliefs were unclear. Some people claim that he was a **humanist**—that he didn't believe in God but thought that people held the greatest power. Once he made a copy of a friend's composition. The man had signed it, "With God's help." Underneath it, Beethoven wrote, "O man, help your self." He was born a Catholic, but he didn't go to church, and he copied three Hindu passages to keep on his desk. Other people feel he did believe in God, saying that the journals he kept were full of references to God. For example, in one place he wrote:

> "Therefore, calmly will I submit myself to all inconsistency and will place all my confidence in your eternal goodness, O God! My soul shall rejoice in Thee, immutable Being. Be my rock, my light, forever my trust!"

In a letter to a friend, he wrote, "I have no friend. I must live by myself. I know, however, that God is nearer to me than others. I go without fear to Him, I have constantly recognized and understood Him."

Even though we can't know for certain whether Beethoven had accepted Christ, we can rest in the knowledge that God alone knows our hearts. And whatever Beethoven's religious beliefs, we know God gave him the gift of music. Beethoven was a great composer, and his music is some of the most beautiful ever written. Though he was a lonely man, he was highly esteemed by the public. Beethoven died in 1827 of pneumonia and other health issues. As many as 20,000 (or more!) people watched his funeral procession, and **Franz Schubert** was one of the torchbearers.

Ludwig van Beethoven *Student Review*

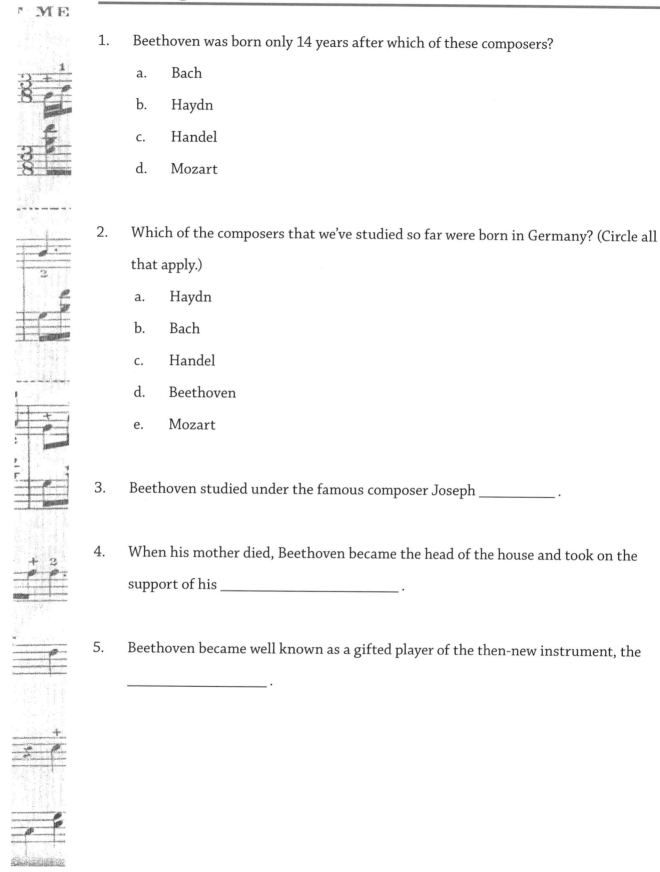

1. Beethoven was born only 14 years after which of these composers?

    a. Bach

    b. Haydn

    c. Handel

    d. Mozart

2. Which of the composers that we've studied so far were born in Germany? (Circle all that apply.)

    a. Haydn

    b. Bach

    c. Handel

    d. Beethoven

    e. Mozart

3. Beethoven studied under the famous composer Joseph _____ .

4. When his mother died, Beethoven became the head of the house and took on the support of his _____ .

5. Beethoven became well known as a gifted player of the then-new instrument, the _____ .

6. Beethoven wrote many famous pieces, including (circle all that apply):

   a. the *Pastoral Symphony*.

   b. the Fifth Symphony.

   c. the *Farewell Symphony*.

   d. *Moonlight Sonata*.

   e. "Ode to Joy."

7. How would you describe Beethoven's personality?

8. What was one of the biggest inspirations for Beethoven's music?

   a. God

   b. people in general

   c. his father

   d. nature

9. By the time he was 48, Beethoven was totally _____ .

10. True or False: Beethoven had an outwardly visible, obvious relationship with Jesus Christ.

Franz *Schubert*

b. 1797 d. 1828

One of Schubert's early teachers said, "The lad has harmony in his little finger." And that's how it seemed. Franz always had melodies going through his head. Once, when someone asked him about his composing, he said, "When I have finished one piece, I begin another."

Franz Schubert was born in 1797 in the musical city of Vienna and only left the city a few times. He was the twelfth of fourteen children, though just five of them lived to be adults. People could see his musical gifts when he was still very young. His father, a schoolmaster, taught him to play the violin, and an older brother taught him to play the piano. Together, Franz, his father, and his brothers played as a string quartet, with Franz on viola, his father on cello, and his brothers on violins.

Because of his beautiful voice, Franz was selected to attend the Imperial Court Choir School, where he was taught Latin, Greek, math, history, and science in addition to music, an important part of the curriculum and life there. Apparently, there wasn't a lot of food to eat at the choir school, because he wrote this letter to his older brother:

"You will know from your own experience that there are times when one could certainly do with a roll and a few apples, particularly when one has to wait eight and a half hours between a moderate-sized midday meal and a wretched sort of supper. . . How would it be, then, if you were to let me have a few kreuzer each month? You wouldn't notice them, and they would make me happy and contented in my cell. . . I rely on the words of the Apostle Matthew, especially where he says: Let him who hath two coats, give one to the poor. Your affectionate, poor, hopeful, and once again poor brother, Franz."

Because he was a reliable boy, he was given the privilege of leaving school to have music lessons with **Antonio Salieri**, who was the Court Musical Director, a friend of **Haydn's**, and one of **Beethoven's** teachers. Franz began composing when he was young—some say he was as young as 11, and by the time he was 21, he had written six symphonies, along with a lot of other music. When he came home from choir school for vacations, he assembled his family into a string quartet to try out the music he had written. His brother Ferdinand said, "family rehearsals were frequently interrupted by the young composer correcting the faults of his father with a gentle, 'Sir, there must be a mistake somewhere.'"

Schubert trained to be a schoolteacher, because his father didn't think he could make a living as a composer. Schubert worked as an assistant at his father's school for several years; he did a lot of composing during this time but didn't like teaching. He finally quit to compose full time. As his father predicted, Schubert was always poor. He didn't even have enough money to buy his own music paper! The only paper he had was given to him by friends. In fact, he totally relied on his friends. Schubert lived the lifestyle of a **Bohemian** (a person with artistic or literary interests who disregards conventional standards of behavior). He lived with one friend, ate with another, and relied on whichever of his friends had money to pay the bills. He was very popular, though. His friends were mostly other artists, writers, and performers. They loved to listen to his music and would get together in the evening for what they called "Schubertiads," where there was dancing, poetry reading, and improvisation, with Schubert at the piano or playing his latest compositions.

Although he wrote nine symphonies, he is most famous for his more than 600 songs for voice, accompanied by piano. These songs are called **lieder**—the German word for "songs." He wrote music for the poems of 91 different poets, including several song cycles—groups of songs that go together. Schubert's song setting of Goethe's[1] *Heidenröslein*, composed in 1815, has been called a "one-page wonder—a miniature musical miracle."

Schubert, who is probably the top Classical songwriter, is often considered, along with Beethoven, to be a bridge between music of the Classical period and music of the Romantic period. His music shifts between major and minor keys and back again. He also uses more **dissonant** (harsh and inharmonious sound) harmonies than were used before.

Until Schubert's lifetime, music was mostly for the **aristocracy** (wealthy, upper-class people). During the first two decades of the nineteenth century, music became more **bourgeois** (of, relating to, or typical of the middle class). Not only did Schubert write a lot of songs for all people, but during the early nineteenth century, Vienna was experiencing a great craze for waltzes, so Schubert wrote a lot of dance music. He also wrote six church Masses, several operas, and some chamber music. Schubert's operas didn't do well, primarily because Vienna was in the middle of an Italian opera craze, thanks to the famous composer **Gioacchino Rossini**. Schubert composed German operas. Although he admired Rossini, he chose not to compete with Rossini's Italian operas. Schubert did have some success with a couple of operas, but it was not a lasting success.

Schubert wrote constantly—it's said that he slept with his glasses on so he could begin composing as soon as he woke up! Once he told a friend, "The state should keep me. I have come into this world for no purpose but to compose." He was such a natural at composition that one music teacher wasn't able to teach him anything he didn't already know. He said, "This one's learned from God." Another teacher said, "If I wanted to instruct him in anything new, he already knew it. Therefore I gave him no actual tuition but merely talked to him and watched him with silent astonishment." His ability to compose almost-perfect works very

quickly became legendary, and today he is remembered as being one of the fastest writers in musical history! — spr —

He lived at a time in Vienna when other musicians and composers (like Rossini and Beethoven) were much more popular than he was, so his brilliance was overshadowed and somewhat overlooked. Still, there were some who realized his gifts. **Franz Liszt** called Schubert "the most poetic of them all." And after hearing Schubert's Ninth Symphony, **Robert Schumann** wrote to his future wife, Clara,

> *"Oh, Clara, I have been in paradise today! They played at the rehearsal a symphony of Franz Schubert's. How I wish you had been there, for I cannot describe it to you. The instruments all sing like remarkably intelligent voices: the scoring is worthy of Beethoven. Then the length, the divine length of it! It is a whole four volume novel, longer than the choral symphony. I was supremely happy, and had nothing left to wish for, except that you were my wife and that I could write such symphonies myself."*

Though some of his music did become famous, his first works were published for a very small commission. He later got the "going rate," but even that was very little. He sold 12 books of songs to one publisher for 800 florins, and from just one of these songs, "The Wanderer," the publisher made more than 36,000 florins in profit. No wonder Schubert was always poor!

One of his most famous symphonies was his Eighth Symphony, also called the *Unfinished Symphony*. Most symphonies have four movements, but this one has only two. In 1822, when Schubert was 25 years old, he was elected as an honorary member of a musical club in Austria. The story told is that he submitted these two movements as his membership initiation fee. Some say he never wanted to finish it; others say he did finish it, but it was lost. We may never know, but the first two movements are certainly worth hearing anyway! Also in 1822, he composed the Fantasie in C Major, popularly known as the *Wanderer Fantasy*.

Of all the musicians in Vienna, Schubert was most in awe of Beethoven. According to one acquaintance, Beethoven looked at about 60 of Schubert's songs and said, "Truly in Schubert dwells a divine spark!" Schubert had met Beethoven about five years before Beethoven died and was honored to be a torchbearer at his funeral.

We do not know for certain whether or not Schubert had a personal relationship with Christ. Some say he was religious—he was raised in the Catholic Church and wrote several Masses that are beautifully expressive of the love of Christ. And there are other letters from him that refer to God and his relationship with Him. On the other hand, Schubert's partying and casual lifestyle led him into poorly chosen friendships and immoral habits. (Some of these bad habits even directly contributed to his poor health.) A friend of his wrote, "Any one who knew Schubert knows he was of two natures foreign to each other, how powerfully

the craving for pleasure dragged his soul down to the slough of moral degradation." His biography should help us remember how important it is to live a life that speaks in all ways of our relationship with Christ.

After several years of illness (composing the entire time), he died in 1828 at the young age of 31, possibly from typhoid fever. He asked to be buried next to Beethoven. His tombstone is inscribed with: "The art of music has buried here a rich possession, but still fairer hopes." These fairer hopes were fulfilled, as more and more of Schubert's music was discovered in the homes of friends all over Vienna. Eleven years after Schubert died, Robert Schumann unearthed the Ninth Symphony when visiting with Schubert's brother Ferdinand, who had piles of Schubert's manuscripts. Schumann thought very highly of Schubert and raved about his compositions. Today, we remember Schubert as "The Poet of Music."

Teacher Note
[1]Johann Wolfgang von Goethe, famous German writer and philosopher, and author of *Faust*.

Franz Schubert *Student Review*

1. Franz Schubert was born in 1797 in the musical city of _____ .

2. Franz would often come home and join with his father and two brothers in a

   _____ _____ in order to try out new compositions.

3. The gatherings that Schubert's friends would have that included dancing, poetry

   reading, and Franz improvising on the piano were called

   a.   Franz parties.

   b.   Schubert days.

   c.   Schubertiads.

   d.   Franziads.

4. Schubert, along with Beethoven, is considered to be the "bridge" between the

   _____ period and the _____ period.

5. One of Schubert's most famous symphonies is his Eighth Symphony, which has only

   two movements. It is also called the _____ *Symphony*.

6. Schubert was most in awe of the composer _____ and asked to be

   buried next to him.

7. True or False: People were amazed at Schubert's ability to compose so quickly and

   perfectly.

8. Schubert was always poor. Which group did he rely on to support him?

   a. the government

   b. the church

   c. his friends

   d. his family

9. Schubert is most famous for his 600 songs for voice, also known as

   a. symphonies.

   b. operas.

   c. librettos.

   d. lieder.

10. True or False: His lifestyle showed his strong commitment to Christ.

The Romantic Period

The **Romantic period** of music is broad and stretches from **Beethoven's** later works in the 1820s through the early twentieth century. During the Classical era, which we have just studied, reason was supreme, rules were important, and everyone followed them. But beginning in the 1820s, artists and thinkers began to move away from this standard. Although we think of the word *romantic* as meaning "love," that's not what is meant when we speak of it in history. In history, people called "romantics" are people who were fascinated by the unknown; they relied on emotion and imagination. They were interested in what happened long ago or far away. They emphasized the way they felt, not necessarily what was true; they thought it was wrong to deny their feelings. They were particularly interested in nature and in man's struggle with nature.

In music, composers and musicians began to turn away from the musical "rules" that had been followed before. They tried new things. The melodies began to flow—more than those used earlier. The harmony became very rich; composers put together notes that people previously didn't think could sound nice together. Musicians say that Romantic music uses more chromatic notes. Let's discuss what that means.

At the beginning of this course, we looked at a piano keyboard. Look at one again. Before, we talked about scales—how each scale has natural half steps. A major or minor scale doesn't use *all* the notes in one octave—between one C and the C above it. From **Bach's** Baroque era music until now, composers began to use more and more notes that are not within the major and minor scales. This technique is called **chromaticism**, and the romantics used this technique a lot. The more "extra" notes a piece uses, the less predictable it is. It almost feels a little unstable. You can't imagine what's going to come next. As you listen to music from the Romantic period, see if you can get a sense of that unpredictability. Composers also played with a flexible tempo—speeding up and slowing down. Pieces became longer. There was greater contrast within the music.

The Romantic era also introduced a new form of music called **lieder**, art songs or poems set to music. (*Lied,* pronounced "leet," is the German word for "song" or "tune.") First, a composer would choose a poem and then set the poem to music. In the music, the composer would try to give the listeners a feeling of the emotion in the poem—helping the listeners to feel sad, angry, joyous or contented. One of the first composers to write lieder was **Franz Schubert**. As we discussed in his biography, he was part of the bridge into the Romantic era.

In instrumental music, there were some other new forms. Because romantics wanted to move away from the rules of previously established forms, they had to come up with some other types of works to take their places. Instead of rondos, sonatas, and other such forms, romantics wrote études, ballades, fantasias, and nocturnes.

- **Étude** is the French word for "study." An étude is a piece that is written to develop a certain technique on an instrument.
- A **ballade** is basically a ballad—remember that romantics liked things that happened long ago and far away. Ballads were popular during medieval times, so the romantics liked to think back to those idealistic times and write in the same form.
- A **fantasia** is like a fantasy—very imaginative.
- **Nocturne** is a word commonly used by **Chopin** for many of his beautiful songlike pieces. He took this word from a less famous Irish composer named **John Field**.

Composers still wrote dance music, but instead of composing short pieces that were part of a longer whole, they made the individual pieces longer and, again, used different forms. In the Romantic era, the dance forms were the mazurka, polonaise, and waltz. Composers wanted their music to sound as if it was free and spontaneous—made up at that moment. But this was also an illusion. They worked very hard to make their music sound that way!

Program music became popular. **Program music** is music that, without using words, describes specific nonmusical things—often parts of nature or feelings or people. One specific type of program music is the **tone poem**, or **symphonic poem**, a new type of orchestral composition that more or less followed an actual story or expressed a certain concept. Symphonic poems were shorter than symphonies and typically consisted of just one movement. A **program symphony** is very similar to a tone poem, except that there is more than one movement, as in a symphony! Often, the themes from a symphonic poem will appear in more than one movement in a program symphony.

During the Romantic era, the Industrial Revolution—a time of great change and many improvements and inventions—was in full swing. Not only were there great improvements in transportation and manufacturing, but there were also improvements in musical instruments. Valves were added to brass instruments, and keys were added to woodwind instruments. These improvements meant that the instruments had more flexibility, and they could play more notes! Some new instruments were developed—the contrabassoon, the bass clarinet, the piccolo, and the English horn were added to the woodwind section. More percussion instruments were added, such as cymbals, gongs, bells, and triangles. Orchestras got bigger—they had more types of each instrument and more instruments in each section. Therefore, composers during this era enjoyed writing for orchestras.

You may have noticed that we have not studied many women composers. There are two quite well-known women from the Romantic era. They are **Fanny Mendelssohn Hensel** (**Felix Mendelssohn's** sister) and **Clara Wieck Schumann** (**Robert Schumann's** wife).

We are fortunate to have these two women in our musical heritage. Until recently, it was difficult for women to receive musical training beyond simply playing an instrument—it was considered inappropriate for them to go to music school and learn about harmony or orchestration. It was also hard for any composer to get his work published—a composer had to have a certain reputation before a publisher would risk publishing his work. This made it particularly difficult for women. However, we know that Fanny Mendelssohn had some songs published under Felix's name! This makes us wonder how many other women may have published under the name of famous relatives or under a male "pseudonym"—a false name. We know that some female authors had their work published this way during this time.

In addition to the composers we are about to study, there is another composer whose name you should know. His name is **Richard Wagner**, and he lived from 1813 to 1883. He was not a nice man, and we are not going to devote a chapter to him. You should be familiar with his name, however, because he is famous for his operas. One of his particularly well-known operas is called *The Ring*. This opera is so long that it is often divided into four parts—the entire piece takes about 15 hours to perform!

The Romantic period was a time of great change and development, from new ideas to new sounds to new instruments. Of course, all these changes didn't happen at once, but you will begin to see the differences over time as we study this next group of composers.

The Romantic period took place between the years _____ and _____.

Romantics:

- Were fascinated by the _____

- Relied on _____ and _____

- Were interested in what happened _____ _____ or _____

   _____

- Emphasized the way they _____, not necessarily what was _____

- Were particularly interested in _____ and man's _____

   with nature

In Romantic Music:

- Melodies began to _____.

- Harmony became _____.

- Chromaticism, in which composers use extra notes outside the major and minor

   _____, was used.

- Pieces became _____.

- _____ within the music was greater.

New Forms of Music:

- Lieder— _____ songs or _____ set to music. (The composer tries to

   give the listeners a feeling of the _____ in the poem.)

- Étude—French word for "study"—develops a certain _____ on an

   instrument

- Ballade — a _____

- Fantasia — like a _____ — very _____

- Nocturne — commonly used by _____ for many of his beautiful _____ pieces

Romantic Dance Forms:

- _____

- _____

- _____

Program Music:

Tone Poem/Symphonic Poem

- Type of _____ composition

- Followed an actual _____ or expressed a certain _____

Program Symphony:

- Similar to a tone _____

- More than one _____

- Often, the themes of a _____ _____ will appear in more than one movement.

During the Romantic era, the _____ _____ was occurring and there were improvements also in musical instruments. Some new instruments even came into use during this period, such as the following:

_____

_____

_____

Two women who composed during this time:

_____

_____

Felix *Mendelssohn*

b. 1809 d. 1847

"**F**elix" means "happy man" in Latin, and that name fit **Felix Mendelssohn** perfectly. This man who ushered in the Romantic period was born into a distinguished Jewish family in Hamburg, Germany, in 1809, to a banker father and a refined and talented mother. Moses Mendelssohn, his grandfather, was a famous Jewish philosopher. Being well-to-do intellectuals, Felix's family ensured that he was well educated and well traveled.

When Felix was young, the Mendelssohns moved from Hamburg to Berlin, Germany. When the children were teased because of their Jewish heritage, Mendelssohn's father decided to convert to Christianity, and he had the children baptized. At this time, he also added the surname Bartholdy to the family name. Although the family's conversion didn't occur because his father became a believer, young Felix embraced his new faith and became a strong Christian, solid in his biblical knowledge and not afraid to share his beliefs with others.

A child prodigy like **Mozart**, Mendelssohn's talent emerged at an early age—not just in music, but in painting, writing, and languages as well. He loved literature, and it influenced much of his music, particularly the words of Goethe and Shakespeare. Mendelssohn first performed at the piano publicly at the age of 9, and he began composing at age 10. One of his teachers was so impressed with his abilities that he took Mendelssohn to meet the famous Goethe, then in his seventies. The precocious young boy and elderly poet/philosopher became friends.

By the age of 12, Felix was composing mature work. His loving parents even hired an orchestra so that he could hear his work played! Although he was very close to all of his family, his elder sister Fanny was especially dear to him his entire life.

In his teen years, Mendelssohn wrote the overture to Shakespeare's *A Midsummer Night's Dream*. You've probably heard part of it, even if you didn't know who composed it. The "Wedding March" from *A Midsummer Night's Dream* is the memorable music that has accompanied many brides down the aisle. One of Mendelssohn's greatest works, it has been said that this piece of music set the standard for all other Romantic overtures. It also set him up as one of the greatest composers of the time.

One of Mendelssohn's many gifts was his phenomenal memory. Several years after he wrote this piece, it was to be performed in England. He carelessly left the score in a coach one day, and it could not be found. Mendelssohn was not bothered by this turn of events. Instead, he sat down and rewrote the entire score from memory, which agreed, note for note, with the orchestra's parts!

Mendelssohn was very popular in England. He traveled there at least ten times. His success there was so great that he was invited to play privately for Queen Victoria and Prince Albert. The performance became rather informal: Queen Victoria began to sing while he accompanied her on the piano! They both had fond memories of the event.

In Leipzig, Mendelssohn married Cecile Jeanrenaud, in 1837, the daughter of a clergyman of the French Reformed Church, and together they had five children. As one would expect from a happy and godly man, his marriage was happy, too.

In 1841, the King of Prussia invited Mendelssohn to Berlin and offered him the difficult but prestigious role of Kapellmeister. Mendelssohn was honored and didn't want to offend the king by refusing, so he agreed. However, this position was very stressful to him.

Some of Mendelssohn's other great achievements are the founding and directing of the Leipzig Conservatory in 1843, which became one of the greatest conservatories of the time. He also wrote more than 200 works. He was a renowned pianist, conductor, and composer, and he was partially responsible for the renewed interest in **Bach's** music. Mendelssohn considered Bach's work the greatest Christian music in the world. Conducting Bach's *St. Matthew Passion*—the first time it was performed since Bach's death—was a key event in the Bach revival, as well as in Mendelssohn's career.

Mendelssohn's most famous symphonies are the Third Symphony (the *Scottish Symphony*), the Fourth Symphony (the *Irish Symphony*), and the Fifth Symphony (the *Reformation Symphony*), which ends with a setting of Luther's "A Mighty Fortress Is Our God," a hymn that is still sung today. Perhaps you've sung it in church? Mendelssohn composed much sacred music, and his oratorio *Elijah* is considered second only to **Handel's** *Messiah*.

Mendelssohn's great knowledge of Scripture was an outgrowth of his deep faith. Sometimes the words he was given to be set to music had been changed from what was written in Scripture. He said, "I have time after time had to restore the precise text of the Bible. It is the best in the end."

When in May 1847, he learned of the stroke suffered by his adored elder sister Fanny, he himself had a stroke from which he never fully recovered. Beloved by many, Mendelssohn's death after a series of strokes at just 38 years of age was mourned internationally. He left important works in every form except opera. This amazingly talented man used his gifts for God and remained cheerful, modest, and hardworking all his life.

Felix Mendelssohn *Student Review*

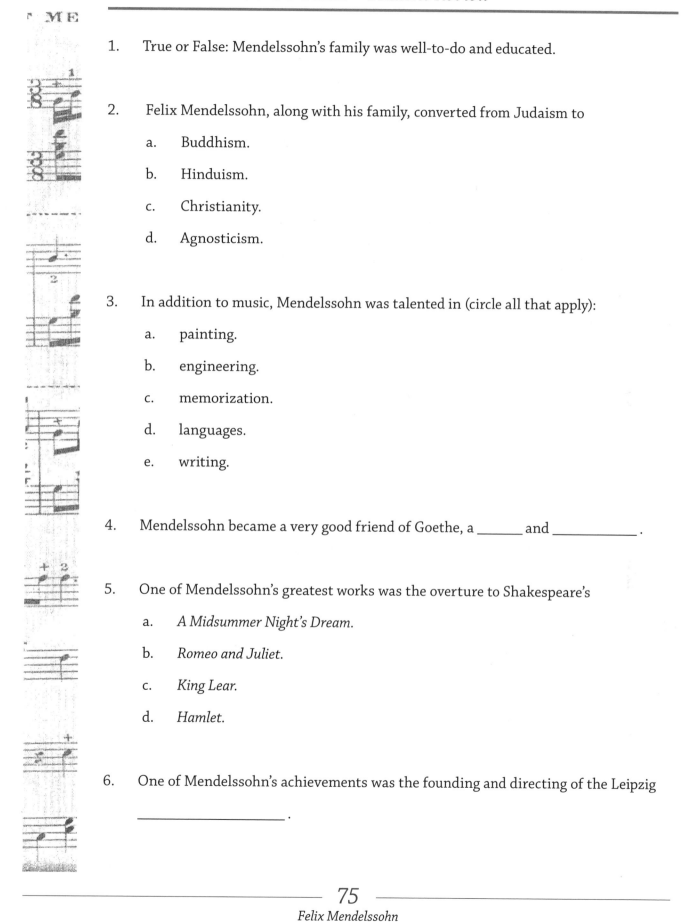

1. True or False: Mendelssohn's family was well-to-do and educated.

2. Felix Mendelssohn, along with his family, converted from Judaism to

   a. Buddhism.

   b. Hinduism.

   c. Christianity.

   d. Agnosticism.

3. In addition to music, Mendelssohn was talented in (circle all that apply):

   a. painting.

   b. engineering.

   c. memorization.

   d. languages.

   e. writing.

4. Mendelssohn became a very good friend of Goethe, a _____ and _____ .

5. One of Mendelssohn's greatest works was the overture to Shakespeare's

   a. *A Midsummer Night's Dream.*

   b. *Romeo and Juliet.*

   c. *King Lear.*

   d. *Hamlet.*

6. One of Mendelssohn's achievements was the founding and directing of the Leipzig

   _____ .

7. His Fifth Symphony (the *Reformation Symphony*) ends with a setting of Luther's

"_____," a hymn that is still sung today.

8. Mendelssohn died young, after composing important works in every form except

_____.

9. Do we have evidence that Mendelssohn loved the Lord? _____

10. True or False: Mendelssohn often rearranged words of Scripture to make the words

fit better into his music.

Frédéric (Fryderyk) *Chopin*

b. 1810 d. 1849

Frédéric Chopin was born near Warsaw, Poland, in 1810 to a French father and a Polish mother of poor but noble birth. Young Frycek (his nickname) had small, delicate hands and fingers that would later astonish all of Europe with their amazing dexterity. Frédéric's father was a well-educated, multilingual man who left France for Poland at age 16, never to return. (Later, Frédéric would leave his beloved Poland for France, never to return.)

Frédéric and his three sisters grew up in a loving home, in a city that was sophisticated and appreciated music. Their father was a tutor for aristocratic families and later a professor at a prestigious school. He brought up his children to behave with the refined manners his students possessed.

Music was an important part of the Chopin household. His father played the violin and flute, and his mother played the piano. She began teaching young Frédéric the piano, but he quickly surpassed her teaching skills. Before the age of 6, he could play every melody he had ever heard and had even begun to improvise!

Wanting to provide him with further training, his parents hired an older man by the name of Wojciech Żywny of Bohemia to tutor him. Some say that the wisest thing this teacher did was to recognize Chopin's natural genius and rather than attempt to improve it, he guided it instead. He didn't correct Frédéric's unusual and intricate piano fingering. Żywny introduced him to the music of **Bach**, which Chopin loved his entire life.

The slender, fun-loving boy made his public debut in Warsaw a week before his eighth birthday. He was hailed as their "Polish Prodigy." This earned him invitations into high society, where his charming manners and amazing talent made him a popular guest. In 1826, at age 16, Frédéric was enrolled in the Warsaw Conservatory, where he worked hard on his composing. The next year, his sister Emilice died of tuberculosis, the dreaded condition that Frédéric himself was to fight his entire life. (Remember **Beethoven**? He died the same year as well.)

Frédéric graduated from the conservatory after three years and then spent two weeks in Vienna, hoping to be noticed. The well-known composer and music critic **Robert Schumann** reviewed the unknown Chopin's set of Piano Variations, op. 2, and then wrote, "Off with your hats, gentlemen—a genius!"

Chopin returned to Warsaw and worked on two concertos that were strongly influenced by the rhythms of Polish folk music and dances, especially the mazurka. In 1830, he left Warsaw for the last time, taking with him a small urn of Polish soil. He landed in Paris, just a few weeks after his beloved Warsaw fell to Russia.[1] From then on, the 21-year-old made Paris his home.

He quickly became a popular piano teacher among the wealthy and powerful. Late at night, he was often found playing the piano at their glittering "salons." (Everyone who was anyone in the arts, letters, and sciences made their way to these fancy Parisian soirees.) A fastidious dresser who enjoyed a lifestyle he couldn't actually afford, Chopin always struggled with finances. His piano students provided some income, as did the sales of his sheet music and an occasional concert. During his lean times, rich friends and patrons helped to support him, especially later when his health declined and he could no longer teach or perform as he once did.

Paris in the early 1830s was a city teeming with people, ideas, business opportunities, and the arts. Its grandeur, virtues, vices, and vitality attracted many well-known figures. Chopin numbered among his friends and acquaintances the authors Victor Hugo and George Sand; the painter Eugene Delacroix; the composers **Rossini**, **Berlioz**, **Liszt**, and **Bellini**; as well as the famous banking family the Rothschilds.

Chopin preferred playing in small, intimate salons rather than in the large concert halls. This was probably because he was a bit of a snob and because his style of playing—refined and delicate—was much more suited to smaller gatherings.

In Paris, Chopin's health grew worse. Always susceptible to coughs and colds, he found it harder and harder to bounce back after each bout. In the meantime, he continued to work feverishly on his compositions, almost obsessively writing and rewriting each line and each page of music. Although he produced a relatively modest number of compositions in his lifetime, each one was chiseled and polished over hours, days, and months until it shone like a gem.

It has been said that while on his journey to Paris, Chopin heard that Warsaw had fallen. In his fury and despair, he composed a piece now known as *The Revolutionary Étude*. Because of his constant reworking of pieces, and because he rarely dated his manuscripts, it is impossible to determine just when and where this piece was written. Although this story is not likely to be true, Chopin was not known to have discouraged its telling!

Chopin is famous for his **études** (French for "studies"), which are instrumental pieces

designed to improve a player's technique. Most études are dull as dirt, despite their teaching value. But Chopin's études are exciting masterpieces in their own right, and for pianists around the world, they are the standard for technical excellence.

Do you remember we mentioned that when Chopin was a little boy his teacher didn't change his unusual fingering? This extraordinary ability enabled him to become especially proficient at playing a flexible tempo known as **tempo rubato** (literally, "stolen time"). This is a musical term for slightly speeding up or slowing down the tempo of a piece at the discretion of the soloist or the conductor, and it is especially common in piano music.

Chopin is also known for his **nocturnes**. (*Nocturne* is a poetic word for "music of the night.") These rather quiet, subtle, dreamlike pieces include melodies so incredible that some consider them the most beautiful in all of music.

The composer and pianist Franz Liszt introduced Chopin to a famous writer and feminist, a woman who went by the name George Sand. A year or so later, they became inseparable. She was older and supported him emotionally and financially and nursed him during his many bouts of illnesses. Nine years later she ended their relationship and left Chopin a broken man. He lived another two and a half years but composed no more.

In 1848, he played his last concert in Paris, just one week before the revolution[2] would depose King Louis-Philippe. Chopin left for the British Isles at the urging of an admirer, Jane Stirling. She paid for his quarters and arranged for him to play and tour the land. It is remarkable that he could manage to travel and play at all, as he was now in the final stages of tuberculosis.

During his time in England, he played for Queen Victoria and Prince Albert and met Charles Dickens. He had this to say of England: "Their orchestra resembles their roast beef and their turtle soup; it's strong, it's famous . . . but that is all."

He returned to Paris in late 1848, weighing barely 90 pounds! His beloved sister Louise came from Poland to be with him, as well as his old friend the Abbé Jelowicki. Although there are differing accounts of his last days, it is generally agreed that at the very end Chopin made a confession of faith with his dear friend the abbé present.

> The abbé later wrote: *"Day and night he held my hand, and would not let me leave him. . . . Soon he called upon Jesus and Mary, with a fervor that reached to heaven. He made the most touching utterances. 'I love God and man,' he said. 'I am happy so to die; do not weep, my sister. My friends, do not weep. I am happy. Farewell, pray for me!' . . . Exhausted by deathly convulsions he said to his physicians, 'Let me die. Do not keep me longer in this world of exile. Why prolong my life when I have renounced all things and God has enlightened my soul? God calls me; why do you keep me back? . . . Thus died Chopin, and in truth, his death was the most beautiful concerto of all his life."*

Chopin requested that **Mozart's** Requiem be played at his funeral. He died in October 1849. Thousands attended his funeral, and he was buried with his treasured urn of Polish soil. Although his body remained in Paris, his heart was sent to Poland. One writer said, "Paris never got the Polish out of the pianist."

Although Chopin lived during the time of the Romantic period, the influence of the Classical composers he so admired caused him to be, in some ways, like a few of the other composers we have studied, a bridge between the two styles.

Teacher Notes
[1]This was during the rebellion against the rule of the Russian Empire in Poland, called the "November Uprising" or the "Cadet Revolution."

[2]The February 1848 revolution in France ended the "July Monarchy" (a period of monarchy rule from 1830–1848).

Frédéric (Fryderyk) Chopin   *Student Review*

1. Chopin was born in _____ but lived his entire adult life in _____ .

2. True or False: Before age 6, Chopin could play on the piano every melody he had ever heard and had even begun to improvise.

3. Which of the characteristics below describe Chopin? (Circle all that apply.)

    a. "Polish Prodigy"   fun loving

    b. shy   sloppy

    c. mannerly   silly

    d. unintelligent   snobbish

4. From what disease did both Chopin and his beloved sister die?

    a. muscular dystrophy

    b. AIDS

    c. tuberculosis

    d. hepatitis B

5. True or False: Chopin preferred playing in large concert halls as opposed to small, intimate salons.

6. Match the following musical terms with their description:

    a. étude =   "music of the night"

    b. tempo rubato =   French for "studies"

    c. nocturnes =   "stolen time"

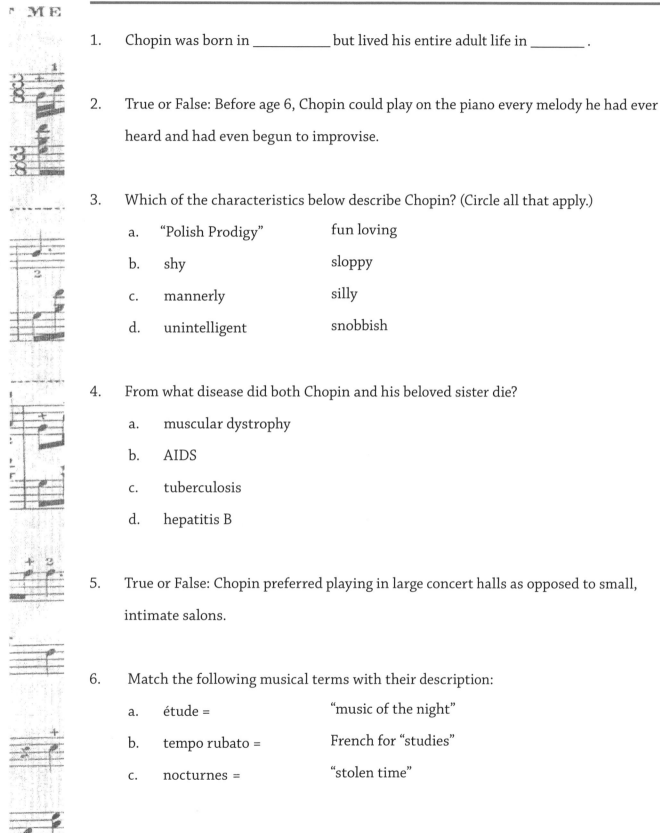

7. Chopin knew many writers, artists, musicians, and other famous people. Which of the following had he met? Circle all that apply.

Charles Dickens   Michelangelo

Victor Hugo   Mark Twain

Jane Austen   Georgia O'Keeffe

Queen Elizabeth   Franz Liszt

Eugene Delacroix   George Sand

8. What country was Chopin referring to when he said, "Their orchestra resembles their roast beef and their turtle soup; it's strong, it's famous . . . but that is all"?

_____

9. Chopin, along with some other composers, is considered a "bridge" between the _____ period and the _____ period.

10. Chopin requested that Mozart's _____ be played at his funeral, which was attended by thousands.

Robert *Schumann*

b. 1810 d. 1856

*I*n the last lesson, we learned about **Chopin**. Now we will hear about another man who was born in the same year as Chopin—**Robert Schumann**. Schumann, along with Chopin and **Mendelssohn** (who was born just one year earlier) all mark the beginning of the Romantic period of music.

When Robert was about 3, he was sent away for safety because his hometown of Zwickau, Saxony (in modern-day Germany),was overrun both by troops fighting in the Napoleonic Wars and by an epidemic. Later, as the son of a bookseller and writer, Robert was surrounded by literature. By age 10, he was immersed in the romantic, often morbid, works of the day. He also began to dabble in poetry and piano compositions. A likable, clever student, young Robert was an active member of his school's literary society. At age 12, he had formed his own orchestra. His love of both music and words would serve him well in his life as a composer and music critic.

In 1826, Robert's father died, leaving the 16-year-old with a comfortable inheritance (held until he was older) and a problem. He longed to study to be a musician, but his mother determined that he would go into law. He obediently enrolled at Leipzig University, although his heart wasn't in his studies. While he had a dreamy, romantic side, young Schumann also liked the party life as well. Studying law held no interest for him.

By then, he had taken some piano lessons from Friedrich Wieck, a leading piano teacher. Frustrated with the study of law, Schumann wrote to his mother, asking her to find out Wieck's opinion of Schumann's potential as a musician.

Wieck's reply to Mrs. Schumann was, "I pledge to turn your son Robert, by means of his talent and imagination, within three years into one of the greatest pianists now living." Thus began a new chapter in Schumann's life. He moved into the Wieck's house.

Life was not easy as a student in the Wieck home for Wieck was a hard taskmaster, driven to succeed. He'd already spent a huge amount of time training his young daughter Clara, a piano prodigy. She had, he believed, great prospects in earning money and in earning them both an entrance into high society.

Schumann loved children, and he enjoyed being with the young Clara and her siblings. But he also continued with his impulsive, reckless behavior, including wild partying. He also tended to be a difficult and stubborn student.

A sad thing happened to Robert during this time. He permanently crippled a finger, and this ended his hopes of becoming a concert pianist. However, it did not stop him from composing and writing. In fact, in 1834, he started a musical review newspaper with some friends. He was the editor for 10 years.

Schumann wrote to teach his readers about music, and this furthered his influence in the musical world of the time. He was an enthusiastic and knowledgeable writer. Generous and bighearted, Robert delighted in helping young talent. As we wrote in Chopin's biography, Schumann's review of one of Chopin's earliest pieces included this memorable line, "Off with your hats, gentlemen—a genius!" (This was written using one of his several pen names: Florestan and Eusebius.)

Once Schumann wrote this advice in his paper: "Diligently play fugues of Masters, especially those of **Johann Sebastian Bach**. Let the *Well-Tempered Keyboard* be your daily bread and you will certainly become a fine musician." Although he was generous to those he liked, he condemned the music of **Franz Liszt** and **Richard Wagner**. Like most music editors and critics, he wasn't always right!

Over the years, Robert and Clara fell in love. Clara's father, as you might imagine, disapproved. He knew of Schumann's instability and irresponsibility. Plus, he did not want to lose control of Clara's very promising career as a concert pianist. Nevertheless, despite Wieck's efforts to end the relationship, the young couple married in 1840, just a day before Clara's twenty-first birthday. (Happily, they reconciled with her father three years later.)

The Schumanns loved each other very much. They had eight children in their sixteen years of marriage. Robert was a kind and devoted father. Their family enjoyed playing chess and dominoes together. During this time, Clara continued her concert career and was their primary breadwinner.

Schumann wrote many piano pieces as well as chamber music and symphonies. He expressed a joy in song, composing beautiful vocal pieces. However, all was not well. He struggled mightily with depression, bouts of drinking, and mental instability.

In 1850, Robert Schumann accepted an appointment as the Düsseldorf Music Director in the hopes of furthering his career. This turned out to be disastrous. He was not suited to conducting, and his mental and physical health problems caused many difficulties. Meanwhile, Clara, considered the best female pianist of the nineteenth century, was struggling to fit in her piano practice because Robert needed their only piano for composing.

Clara was accustomed to practicing six to eight hours a day but between the children and Robert, that was not possible. Yet, it was Clara's concert tours that provided most of the family income.

In 1853, Schumann met the aspiring composer **Johannes Brahms**. Schumann quickly became mentor to 20-year-old Brahms, who was soon a close family friend as well. Schumann said this about Brahms in the last review he ever wrote, "I am convinced that he will create the greatest sensation in the musical world." Brahms greatly respected Schumann at a fragile time in Schumann's life.

Unfortunately, things went from bad to worse. Poor Schumann began hearing voices in his head. Sometimes, he described them as angelic; at other times, demonic. He was frightened by his mental condition. He begged Clara to find a safe institution for him where he might receive help.

Clara, still deeply in love with her husband, was gravely worried about him and sadly obliged. In 1854, Robert entered a private "Insane Asylum." While he was there, his young friend Brahms visited as often as he could. Two and half years later, on July 29, 1856, Robert Schumann died there. He was deeply mourned by his loyal and loving wife and children.

Robert Schumann is known today as a great poet-musician, a fitting description for a man who had always loved both. He is regarded as a master of the smaller forms, especially for piano and voice. He left behind some of the most beautiful melodies ever written.

Tragically, even though he composed incredible music (including an oratorio on the life of Luther and a Mass and a Requiem), from his letters and lifestyle it appears that Robert Schumann did not have a deep faith or relationship with Jesus Christ.

Clara Schumann continued to perform until she was 71. She played her husband's music and was one of the most influential pianists of her time. She died in 1896, 40 years after her beloved Robert.

1. Schumann's works (along with Chopin's and Mendelssohn's) mark the beginning of the _____ period of music.

2. When Schumann's father died, Schumann's mother wanted him to study

    a. medical science.

    b. music.

    c. art.

    d. law.

3. What happened to Schumann that forced him to give up his dream of being a concert pianist?

4. Because of his love for literature, Schumann, along with being an excellent composer, was also an excellent

    a. novelist.

    b. English teacher.

    c. librarian.

    d. editor.

5. Schumann and another composer we've studied, named _____ , were born in the same year.

6. True or False: Schumann married his piano teacher's daughter and they had eight children.

7. In 1853, Schumann became a mentor to and a great friend of the composer _____

_____ .

8. True or False: Schumann died at home of tuberculosis.

9. Who provided most of the income for the Schumann family?

10. Clara Schumann was considered the best female _____ of the nineteenth

century.

Franz *Liszt*

b. 1811   d. 1886

Born in rural Hungary, **Franz Liszt** (pronounced "List") lived with his parents on the estate of the richest family in Hungary, the Esterházy family. (You might remember that this was the same family for whom **Haydn** worked.) Franz's father, Adam, was a musician and quickly recognized his young son's incredible talent. Although he was only a poor steward working for the Esterházy family, the elder Liszt did all he could to train young Franz.

By the time the boy was 9, he was already performing. Several wealthy noblemen noticed his talent and paid for him to go with his father to Vienna. There, he studied piano under **Carl Czerny** (a noted pupil of Beethoven) and composition under **Antonio Salieri**. These men helped to spread the news about the charming lad who was just an amazing prodigy. By age 12, he was already a veteran of the concert stage.

Having grown up with devout Catholic parents and being very interested in spiritual matters, Franz began talking and writing of entering the priesthood. His parents discouraged this, though, as they felt his musical gift was from the Lord and should be used in a wider arena. His sixteenth year was a sad one for Franz, as his father—and constant companion—died. Franz began suffering from nervous exhaustion.

His education as a child had focused on music and little else. When he grew up, he decided he wanted to become an educated, cultured man. He feverishly embarked on a self-improvement course. He said:

"My mind and fingers have been working like two lost spirits—Home, the Bible, Plato, Locke, Byron, Hugo . . . Beethoven, Bach, Hummel, Mozart, Weber are all around me. I study them, meditate upon them, devour them with fury. Besides this, I practice from four to five hours [daily]. . . . Ah! Provided I don't go mad you will find an artist such as you desire, such as is now required."

His piano skills, already extraordinary, became astonishing! There have been few other pianists in all of history who could perform as Liszt could on the piano. His fingers flew fast and furious, and his technical skills were practically flawless. Before Liszt, pianists kept their hands close to the keyboard, playing from wrist and finger rather than arm or shoulder. Liszt played with such movement and zeal, he practically assaulted the piano. Astonishingly, he often played his complete recitals from memory!

His long, flowing hair and his commanding presence contributed to his effect on the crowds. People were awed whenever they saw him perform. Women even swooned and hoped he would toss one of his velvet gloves! He was treated almost like a modern-day "rock star."

Liszt also had an ego to match his talent. Up until Liszt came along, a concert consisted of several different artists and perhaps an orchestra. Each musician played for a portion of the concert. However, Liszt decided he wanted to be the sole performer, so he "invented" the solo performance. He called them **recitals**.

Chopin, who lived at the same time and often saw him in Paris, admired Liszt, although he was perhaps a little jealous of him, as well. After hearing Liszt play one of his études, Chopin wrote to another pianist, "I should like to steal from him the way to play my own études." Nevertheless, Chopin later dedicated his first Twelve Études to "Mon ami, Franz Liszt."

Liszt was also a generous and kind man, if he received the admiration he felt was due him. He supported, encouraged, or taught literally hundreds of musicians, giving freely of his time and money. His support certainly helped the careers of many important musicians, including **Schumann**, **Chopin**, and, later, **Richard Wagner**. Outliving many of his musical contemporaries, and having such a major impact on both music and musicians, Liszt was called the "Grand Old Man" of European music.

His generosity was apparent also when he heard of the terrible flooding in his homeland of Hungary. In about six weeks, Liszt gave eleven charity concerts in Vienna. All the proceeds went to the victims of the flooding. (This was probably the beginning of concert benefits, or relief projects, which are still done to this day.)

Sadly, Liszt's personal life was filled with the immorality of a man who was a slave to his fleshly desires. He was a well-known womanizer who had more than a few children outside of marriage. All knew his vanity and conceit; he even expected the aristocracy to treat him as an equal. (Because of his temperament and talent, he was!)

Liszt claimed to be religious all of his life, and in his fifties, he decided to become an abbot in the Catholic Church. His lifestyle does not appear to reflect a repentant heart and a love for Christ. On the other hand, only God knows our hearts. We will leave Liszt now, knowing that he was one of the most talented men ever to live, although certainly not one of the meekest or humblest.

Among his many talents and innovations:
- almost perfect sight-reading skills
- ability to learn anything quickly

- made music more accessible to common people
- introduced recitals
- introduced the **symphonic** (or **"tone"**) **poem**
- played to the audience, was a showy dresser and performer; some call him the first superstar
- possibly the greatest pianist of all time
- first to play an entire program from memory

1. Franz Liszt was born in rural

   a. Germany.

   b. England.

   c. America.

   d. Hungary.

2. Franz's father died when Franz was

   a. 9.

   b. 4.

   c. 16.

   d. 18.

3. True or False: Franz could perform his complete recitals from memory.

4. Because he wanted to be the sole performer in concerts, Liszt "invented" the

   _____ .

5. Circle all the following characteristics that describe Franz Liszt:

   a. humble

   b. kind

   c. discouraging

   d. moral

   e. vain

   f. generous

   g. slow to learn

6. Which composer that we've studied was an admirer of Liszt and possibly even a little jealous of him? _____

7. True or False: Liszt was probably the originator of charity concerts, or benefits.

8. Liszt was called the "Grand Old _____" of European music.

9. True or False: Liszt had weak performance skills.

10. Liszt introduced the symphonic or _____ _____.

Giuseppe *Verdi*

b. 1813 d. 1901

Verdi was one of the most celebrated composers of the nineteenth century. He was born around the same time as the German opera composer **Richard Wagner**. Although Verdi's operas reigned supreme in Italy, Wagner reigned supreme in all the rest of Europe.

Giuseppe Verdi was born in Roncole, about 3 miles from Busseto, in the province of Parma, Italy. This little village consisted of about 200 impoverished, uneducated laborers. His parents scraped by, being poor keepers of an insignificant inn as well as a tiny shop where they sold coffee, sugar, pipes, and such.

At that time, the French (under Napoleon) occupied all of Italy. Parma is a flat region with rich soil and a strong agricultural community—but supporting the French armies took a heavy toll on the land. The war years were difficult for the people there.

Music enthralled young Giuseppe. When the organ-grinder passed through his little village, he could not be kept at home. Even though his family wasn't musical, Giuseppe showed musical talent at an early age. His parents somehow managed to give him a little **spinet** (a small piano) of his own. He remained attached to this first instrument and kept it all his life.

At age 10, he became the organist of the little church in Roncole. Up until this time, Verdi had received no schooling. His father decided it was now time for him to get an education. An arrangement was made for Verdi to board with a cobbler in Busseto, attend school, and walk home every Sunday to play the organ at the church. During the next two years, he worked hard and learned reading, writing, and arithmetic.

While in Busseto, the largest and most famous merchant in the city, Antonio Barezzi, befriended Verdi. Barezzi loved music and had the local **philharmonic** orchestra society play often in his home. Here, for the first time, Verdi was led into a serious study of music. Barezzi became Verdi's mentor and a great influence in his life. Verdi said later, "I owe absolutely everything to him."

When Verdi was 19, Barezzi encouraged him to apply to the Milan Conservatory. However, this soon-to-be-famous musician was denied admission to the school! But the serious, shy Verdi didn't let this stop him from pursuing his music. He decided to go to the city of Milan anyway to study privately under **Vincenzo Lavigna**, a successful composer of his day. Unfortunately, Verdi couldn't make enough money working as a musician, and he returned to his hometown.

Back in Busseto, conflict arose. There was an opening for the town Music Director. The person in this position would be in charge of all music within the town, including all the church music. Verdi wanted the job, but he soon learned that music and politics were always intertwined. Some wanted him to be the town music master, including a few in the church. But the local head of the church and others preferred Verdi's rival because that man was respectful of authority and the church. (Verdi had a strong dislike of priests, which he made no attempt to hide. He was also considered stubborn and unforgiving.) Until a selection could be made, the authorities solved the problem by temporarily banning all church music in Busseto! Finally, a competition was held in Parma in 1836, and a creative solution was found. Verdi would be the director of secular music, and his rival would be the director of church music! So now Verdi had a paying job as the head of the Busseto Philharmonic Society and the town marching band.

In 1836, Verdi married his mentor's daughter, Margherita Barezzi, a gifted musician herself and a lively, bright, and pretty woman. He had known her for a long time. Their daughter, Virginia, was born the next year. Their son, Icilio, followed in 1838. During this time, his first opera, *Oberto*, was introduced to the public, becoming a modest success. Even though *Oberto* was full of sad music, this was a happy time in Verdi's life.

Sadly, though, what followed was a series of unfortunate events: By 1840, his wife and both his small children were dead from various illnesses. During this dark time, he was under contract to compose a comic opera. Imagine trying to write an upbeat, happy piece while so sad and alone! Not surprisingly, this opera—*Un giorno di regno*—was a failure. At its premiere, Verdi (according to custom) had to sit in the orchestra pit in full view of the audience, who responded to his opera with hissing!

This experience was so discouraging that Verdi decided to stop composing. However, at the determined insistence of his publisher, Verdi persevered. He was rewarded for his efforts when his next opera, *Nabucco*, made him famous. It was an opera based on the biblical tale of Jewish captivity. It had beautiful, long melodies and emotional choruses. It is said that after the opera was performed, people were singing the songs in the streets! Imagine writing a song and hearing a stranger sing it out loud as you walked by. Such was the fame that Verdi gained.

During the next 10 years, Verdi became more and more famous, composing and producing

about 12 more operas in Italy. For some, the most original and important opera that Verdi wrote is *Macbeth*, based on the play by his favorite dramatist, William Shakespeare. Another of his famous operas, premiering in Venice in 1851, was *Rigoletto*.

In 1859, Verdi married his longtime companion, Giuseppina Strepponi, a singer who had performed in his opera *Nabucco*. After that, he entered the world of politics. In 1860, he was elected to the first national Parliament, but he withdrew five years later. Then, he was named senator in 1875 by the king, who later offered to make him a marquis in 1893. However, Verdi decided not to take the position. He did not enjoy politics very much and wanted to focus more on his music.

In 1871, before he had become a senator, Verdi wrote *Aida*, which was followed by 15 years of very limited output. The most noteworthy composition that he made during that time was called Requiem. In 1887, his opera *Otello* was performed, and this made him world famous!

He wrote his last opera, *Falstaff*, in 1893. A few years later, his second wife died. He spent his remaining years in Milan, a wealthy and charitable man, beloved and honored by the nation. He died in 1901; 28,000 people lined the streets to pay their respect. The Italians had lost their grand master of opera.

Despite the fact that Verdi produced biblically themed operas, we know he did not have a good opinion of Christianity. Though he did not compose from a Christian worldview, Verdi was still a significant composer in the world of opera. His music was well respected then, has stood the test of time, and is just as famous today.

Giuseppe Verdi   *Student Review*

1. Verdi was born in which European country? _____ .

2. Like Richard Wagner, Verdi was known for his

    a. symphonies.

    b. jazz music.

    c. operas.

    d. All of the above.

3. True or False: Verdi came from a wealthy, educated family.

4. Verdi's first instrument was a

    a. flute.

    b. spinet.

    c. organ.

    d. clarinet.

5. What relationships did Antonio Barezzi have with Verdi?

    a. mentor

    b. employer

    c. uncle

    d. father-in-law

    e. priest

6. True or False: Verdi was not very respectful toward the church.

7. True or False: Verdi's first opera, *Oberto*, was written during a happy time in his life.

8. What personal tragedies did Verdi live through?

9. Besides music, Verdi was involved in

    a. politics.

    b. science.

    c. art.

    d. the church.

10. Which of the following operas were composed by Verdi? (Circle all that apply.)

    a. *Aida*

    b. *Rigoletto*

    c. *The Pirates of Penzance*

    d. *Otello*

    e. *Nabucco*

    f. *Macbeth*

Anton *Bruckner*

b. 1824 d. 1896

Anton Bruckner was born to musical parents in a rural village in Austria. Although most of his ancestors had been poor farmers, his mother was a choir vocalist and his father was a schoolmaster and an organist. The large Bruckner family, deeply religious Roman Catholics, were hardworking people, as were most of the people of that area. When Anton was 10, his father fell ill, and young Anton helped him carry out his musical responsibilities.

Three years later, his father died, and Anton was enrolled in the nearby St. Florian Monastery as a choirboy. This old baroque monastery had one of the greatest organs in continental Europe. This wonderful exposure to fine organ music helps explain Anton's love of and marvelous proficiency at the organ all his life. While at St. Florian, he received a general education as well as a musical one. These were hard years, during which he came down with typhoid fever. He wrote home to his mother, "I cannot describe how sick I am. Only the thought that all God does is for the best keeps me going."

Anton's voice changed in 1839, so he could no longer sing in the boys' choir. However, because of his exceptional violin playing, he was allowed to stay for an additional year. Afterward, he began training to become a schoolmaster-organist like his father before him.

Throughout the period from 1841 to 1855, Bruckner held a variety of jobs. He was a teacher while still continuing his own music studies for higher teaching posts. From 1856 to 1868, he was an organist (a significant post), and he still continued his music studies. He stayed more steadily employed than many composers we have studied. Much later, he became a professor at the Vienna Conservatory, and later still, at the University of Vienna. However, there was little money in teaching, and Bruckner struggled with poverty for most of his life. Eventually, he settled in Vienna, where he continued to take music classes as well as teach them.

By all accounts, Bruckner was something of a social misfit in the sophisticated world of musical Vienna. Though he had a quiet self-confidence about his work, many considered him a "country-bumpkin"—a poorly dressed, socially awkward sort of man. It didn't help that he had very odd habits. For example, he counted everything in sight: buttons, church crosses, windows, and so on. In addition, in his vain attempts to marry, he proposed (unsuccessfully) to many young ladies, most of whom he barely knew. He was sent off to "rest and recover" for a period of time at a sanatorium in 1867. He loved beer, the polka, **Richard Wagner**, and God.

Bruckner had some very fine character qualities. Devout, he dedicated and composed his music for God, not for man and not for money. He stuck to his beliefs, no matter how old-fashioned they appeared to others. He also doggedly stuck to his music, despite little success or recognition.

Bruckner worked hard teaching and composing while living in Vienna. He had a small group of admirers, including young **Gustav Mahler** (who today is considered a great Classical composer) and a few well-respected conductors. Mahler said of him: "Bruckner: half simpleton, half God."

Unfortunately, there was a feud in full swing in Vienna, and Bruckner got caught in the crossfire. Very simply, there were two factions involved: **Johannes Brahms** and his followers and Richard Wagner and his followers.

You'll remember Brahms from a previous lesson; however, we won't be spending a lesson on the equally famous Richard Wagner. Wagner was considered to be the finest composer of opera in all of Europe (except in Italy, where **Verdi** reigned supreme). Wagner was one of the most powerful personalities of the time. A difficult man who loved himself above all things, he was lauded by many for his amazing music. Bruckner adored Wagner's music as well as the man himself.

Brahms despised Wagner, his music, and anyone who supported Wagner. At this time, Brahms, too, was influential, and his open hostility toward Bruckner (for preferring Wagner's music) was extremely damaging to Bruckner's career. In addition, one of Brahms's biggest supporters in this feud was an influential music critic, Eduard Hanslick, who took many malicious swipes at Bruckner in print.

Bruckner was a simple man, unable to play the game of politics necessary to overcome this type of attack. As a result, he was in his sixties before his reputation and fame began to grow and his talent was appreciated.

Of course, it didn't help that the first three symphonies he submitted to the Vienna Philharmonic Orchestra were rejected as "too wild and daring," "nonsense and unplayable," and "unperformable." (Ironically, today his works hold an important place in this same orchestra's musical repertoire!)

One of the saddest tales in music is the story of the debut of his Third Symphony. Bruckner

himself conducted it (only because the scheduled conductor fell ill). It should be noted that Bruckner was generally considered to be a terrible conductor. Most of the audience, unknown to him, departed during the performance. Naively unaware, he proudly turned at the end to accept the applause and was shocked and tearful to find only a handful of supporters left (including a young Mahler). The good news, though, was that a publisher was in the audience who agreed to publish the Third Symphony.

Despite this kind of setback, which might have destroyed a more sensitive soul, Bruckner kept on writing. It certainly helped that he felt called by God to compose. In fact, he once said this, "When God calls me to Him and asks me: 'Where is the talent which I have given you?' then I shall hold out the rolled-up manuscript Te Deum and I know He will be a compassionate judge."

Te Deum is a choral work that is praised to this day. He wrote other religious music as well, Masses, a requiem, and several hymns. Modern-day author and music critic Harold C. Schonberg wrote this about Bruckner and the music born of his deep faith: "Even unbelievers can find themselves carried away by the simple conviction of the man." His most popular works today include Symphony no. 4 (*Romantic*) and no. 8, although many believe no. 7 to be his finest. His main influences were **Beethoven** and Wagner.

Happily, Bruckner received a bit of recognition and appreciation for his works in his later years. Before he died in October 1896, the University of Vienna gave him the honorary degree of Doctor of Philosophy. Additionally, the Habsburg emperor Franz Josef so appreciated Bruckner's music that he gave him an apartment and a pension and told Bruckner to name any wish. Bruckner shyly asked if the Emperor could "please stop Herr Doktor Hanslick from insulting me in print?"

Bruckner was foremost a religious composer. His compositions speak of a humble reverence for life and reveal his unswerving devotion to God above. Despite his inadequacies as a man, God gave him talent and he used it to glorify his beloved Maker.

Anton Bruckner *Student Review*

1. True or False: Anton Bruckner was born to an aristocratic family in Vienna.

2. Anton wrote to his mother "Only the thought that all God does is for the best keeps me going." What difficulty that he experienced might he have been referring to?

3. Why did Bruckner feel out of place in Vienna?

4. Some of Bruckner's character qualities were (circle all that apply):

    a. his devotion to God.

    b. his outgoing personality.

    c. his idleness.

    d. his willingness to keep working on his music despite little success or recognition.

5. True or False: Bruckner preferred Wagner's music to that of Brahms.

6. Anton Bruckner was in his _____ before his reputation and fame began to grow.

7. One of the composers who appreciated Bruckner's work was _____ .

8. Circle the names of the composers who influenced Bruckner.

    a. Wagner

    b. Mozart

    c. Paul McCartney

    d. Beethoven

9.   Toward the end of his life, Bruckner received financial support from

     _____ .

10. Bruckner will always be remembered

     a.   for his operas.

     b.   as a religious composer.

     c.   for his innovative use of new instruments.

     d.   as a lyricist.

Stephen *Foster*

b. 1826 d. 1864

Stephen Foster is the first American composer we study in this course. His childhood was quite different from the Europeans we've learned about. Stephen[1] was born on the fourth of July in 1826. This particular fourth of July was especially significant because of three events:

1. It was the fiftieth anniversary of the signing of the Declaration of Independence.
2. Thomas Jefferson died on that day.
3. John Adams died on that day as well.

In the home of William and Eliza Foster, however, there was great joy that day as the eighth child was welcomed into the family. Stephen's mother was a kind, loving woman. His father was a businessman and had some political connections. He was considered well educated for the time and place. However, due to business difficulties, the Fosters were often in financial need.

Stephen spent most of his life in Pittsburgh, Pennsylvania. It was a lively place, a busy frontier town where three great rivers converged. (The Monongahela and Allegheny rivers meet in Pittsburgh, where they form the Ohio River.) These water highways transported men, women, children, animals, and cargo up and down the Ohio River valley to the Gulf of Mexico. This was an era and a place in which business ruled, and the arts were not as developed or as appreciated as they were in Europe during that time.

Stephen was closest to his brother Morrison, or Mit, as he was often called. Mit was three years older and understood his brother in a way none of the rest of the family did. Steve was born with a deep love of music, but unlike many of the other composers we've read about, Stephen grew up in a time, place, and family that did not think highly of musical talent (at least not in boys). At best, it was an acceptable hobby for a young man, but it wasn't a satisfactory occupation. As you might imagine, Steve did not receive much support for this musical gift. He was occasionally indulged with a musical treat—a night at a concert, a flute or clarinet to play—but generally he had to keep his passion for music in check. In fact, Mr. and Mrs. Foster spent much time trying to arrange things so that Stephen would follow a proper career choice.

Besides briefly attending boarding school and a local (private) grammar school, Steve was also privately tutored. His formal schooling ended in his early teens. During this time, he and Morrison and their friends formed a secret all-male club called Knights of the S.T. (probably standing for "Square Table"). They met at the Fosters' home and spent much of their time singing. Some of Steve's earliest works were composed during this time. When he was 18, his first song was published.

Stephen also had a gift for performing and mimicking. He was influenced by minstrel performers and "**Ethiopian**" music, in which white men imitated and exaggerated black music and stereotypes of the times. As a child, he played "theatre," performing Ethiopian songs for friends and neighbors. He loved the soulfulness of the **Negroes** (a term, like "colored," used during this time to refer to African Americans), whom he heard singing on the wharves where the boats arrived from New Orleans and other points south.

Additionally, he was exposed to Negro music because of his relationship with the Fosters' **bound** (similar to an indentured servant) servant, Olivia Pise. Morrison wrote about "Lieve," as she was called, as "she was a devout Christian and a member of a church of shouting colored people. Stephen was fond of their singing and boisterous devotions. She was permitted to often take Stephen to church with her. . . . "

When Foster was 20 or 21, he moved to Cincinnati to work for his elder "brother" William. (William was actually a young relative of Stephen's father who was taken into the family and treated as a son.) Stephen worked as a bookkeeper for William. It was while in Cincinnati that Stephen had his first musical success. "Oh! Susanna," a rollicking, fun song he penned, caught the public's imagination and spread like wildfire. Not only did it appear immediately in every minstrel show, it quickly became the theme song of the forty-niners on their way to the California Gold Rush.

The commercial success of this song (and another of the same period, "Uncle Ned") gave Foster the means with which to show family and friends that he could make as good a living in music as he could in commerce. Unfortunately, even though these songs stormed the nation, Foster actually earned very little from them. It is thought that the publishing firm that Foster sold "Oh! Susanna" to profited a quick $10,000 for this song that Stephen sold them for $100. By 1850, at least ten of his pieces had been published, and he quit bookkeeping and moved back to Pittsburgh.

There, in 1850, he proposed to Jane Denny McDowell, the daughter of a well-regarded physician. Jane was later described by her granddaughter as "buoyant and sunny in disposition, attractive and loveable and full of the joy of living to the last day of her life." She and Stephen loved each other, but theirs was not always an easy marriage.

The year 1850 was a busy one for Foster. He published 11 songs, including the well-known

"Camptown Races" (originally called "Gwine to Run All Night") and another popular work, "Nelly Bly." During this time, Foster also began a relationship with E. P. Christy, the minstrel performer (whose name later became a generic word for minstrel shows). These so-called "Plantation Melodies" sung at the minstrel shows were highly popular, and Foster provided a number of them over the next few years.

One of his most popular, enduring songs was written in 1851—"Old Folks at Home," often called "Way Down Upon the Swanee River." Despite the crude dialect, this song has an appeal that has crossed race and class and cultures. It speaks of the yearning for home in a simple, yet haunting melody.

A funny (and true) story about this song is that the river he initially used was the Pee Dee River, but his brother Morrison related that Stephen was looking for a better name. They pulled out an atlas, and found the Suwanee[2], a little river in Florida. "That's it! That's it exactly!" said Stephen, and so it was. "Old Folks at Home" is the state song of Florida, but Foster never visited Florida! In fact, he most likely visited the South only on one occasion.

Jane and Stephen's only child, Marion, was born in 1851. Her father was devoted to her. She, as an adult, said, "I was his pet. He took me everywhere with him, and I was the only one allowed to invade the sanctity of his den where he wrote his songs. . . . He could not bear the slightest noise or interruption in his work. . . . "

Although a kind man who loved his family, and a musical genius, Foster did not have a successful family life or a financially successful musical career[3]. Although there are many myths surrounding Foster's last years, the truth is somewhat difficult to determine. To sum up a complicated history, his lack of money led to hard times for his family. And, sadly, drinking became a problem for Foster, as well. His wife, though she loved him, had to live apart from him during two different periods. There are any number of stories regarding his last months, but this is what we read from his wife, who was writing to his beloved brother Morrison concerning Stephen:

> *"Sept. 30th, 1861*
>
> *"Dear Mit:*
>
> *"I have been spending a couple of months here, and I am now beginning to feel very uneasy about Steve, and he has not at present the money to send me. I concluded to ask you to lend me ten dollars as I wish to go back to him immediately, and indeed it is very necessary that I should be with him."*

A week later she again wrote:

> *"I received your letter yesterday, enclosing ten dollars and I assure you that I am very much obliged indeed. When I arrive in New York, I will deliver your message to Steve."*

Jane was probably with Stephen during the winter and spring of that year, 1861 to 1862. She wrote Morrison again in June 1862:

> "I received a few days ago your very kind letter. You have my best and warmest thanks for your kindness. I left Steve in New York; he was well, and publishes once in a long while. The clothing you sent him he was very much obliged to you & told me that he would write and thank you."

This last letter from Jane was written about three months before Stephen died:

> "You do not know, dear Mit, how much relieved I felt about Steve when I read your letter. If you can persuade him to return to Cleveland with you, I am sure that all will soon be well with him again."

Unhappily, whatever Morrison's plan was, it was not to be. In this letter sent to him by Foster's young associate and collaborator, George Cooper, we read this:

> "Your brother Stephen, I am sorry to inform you, is lying in Bellevue Hospital in this city very sick. He desires me to ask you to send him some pecuniary assistance as his means are very low. If possible, he would like to see you in person."

Two days later, Cooper sent the following telegram to Morrison (which probably reached him before the letter did):

> "Stephen is dead. Come on."

Part of the legend surrounding Foster's last days is the tale of possessions. His wallet contained 38 cents and a little piece of paper with five penciled words—"Dear friends and gentle hearts." This is true. However, stories of his dying a "friendless bum in a sordid room" are greatly exaggerated. This letter from his brother Henry should be taken into account: "We found everything connected with Stevey's life and death in New York much better than we expected, he had been boarding at a very respectable hotel [or boarding house] and did not owe the landlord a cent or any one else that we knew of. . . ."

Thus ends the life of Stephen Foster. Although we don't know whether he knew the Lord, we do know his music lives on. His compositions have survived more than a century and have a solid place in the annals of American composers.

Teacher Notes
[1]You will find his childhood nickname(s) spelled various ways; spelling rules were so much more relaxed then and it depended on who was writing it and when it was written, including:
- Steve
- Stevey
- Stephy

- Stevie
- Stevy

[2]The Suwannee River—also spelled Suwanee River—is a major river of southern Georgia and northern Florida. Foster spelled it "Swanee" to better fit the melody. (We call this "poetic license.")

[3]It is not that Foster was a bad businessman as some have supposed. The laws and regulations regarding music copyright at this time were virtually nonexistent.

1. Stephen Foster grew up in

   a. Vienna, Austria.

   b. Cincinnati, Ohio.

   c. Atlanta, Georgia.

   d. Pittsburgh, Pennsylvania.

2. True or False: As a child, Foster received much encouragement from his family to become a musician.

3. In his family, Stephen was closest to _____ .

4. Foster's music was influenced by (circle all that apply):

   a. Beethoven.

   b. minstrel performers.

   c. jazz.

   d. "Ethiopian" music.

5. Foster's first musical success was the song _____ .

6. The song "Oh! Susanna" was the "theme song" for the _____ on their way to the California _____ _____ .

7. True or False: Foster never married.

8. Which of Stephen Foster's songs is the state song of Florida?

9. True or False: In spite of publishing many popular songs, Foster did not make much money from his musical career.

10. True or False: Stephen Foster leaves a legacy as a great American composer and a strong spiritual leader.

Johannes *Brahms*

b. 1833 d. 1897

One of three children, **Johannes Brahms** had a difficult childhood. He was born in 1833, in a poor and filthy section of Hamburg, Germany. His father, an unstable man, was a musician who played mostly at local dance halls. Johannes's mother was a seamstress. Their marriage was not a happy one.

When his father began teaching young Johannes, it quickly became apparent that the boy, who had **absolute pitch**, was gifted. Although they lived in poverty, his parents scraped together the money to provide Johannes with music lessons. His father hoped he might develop into a child prodigy who would become a financial asset to the family.

The boy's first piano teacher realized his potential as a composer. After two years of lessons, he sent Johannes to the distinguished pianist and composer **Eduard Marxsen**, who gave him lessons in music theory and taught him the music of **Bach** and **Beethoven**. Brahms remained loyal to these teachers and kept in touch with them throughout his life. He continued to love the works of Bach and Beethoven all the rest of his days.

When he was 13, family friends invited him to their home in the country to teach their daughter the piano during the summer. Brahms enjoyed two wonderful summers with these friends. He enjoyed the fresh air and the countryside, and he had time to compose. After this experience, he began teaching piano and arranging dance music in order to make a living.

In 1847, **Mendelssohn** passed away. Brahms's revered teacher Marxsen wrote, "A great master of the musical art has gone, but an even greater one will bloom for us in Brahms."

An extreme perfectionist throughout his life, Brahms, as he composed, destroyed all but the best of what he had written. By age 18, he had finally composed the first work that he didn't later destroy. By then, he had already burned about 100 compositions!

Brahms was discovered by Eduard Reményi, a Hungarian violinist who took him on tour as his accompanist. While they were on tour, they played for Queen Victoria's first cousin, George V, the blind king of Hanover. A young man on the household staff at Hanover, Joseph Joachim, had been a student of Mendelssohn. At the age of 22, Joachim was already becoming a famous violinist. The two became lifelong friends, and Brahms later composed a violin concerto for him. Through Joachim, Brahms was introduced to **Franz Liszt**, who was already a well-known composer and performer. In 1853, Brahms and Reményi went to visit him. There are conflicting stories about this first meeting between Liszt and Brahms. Some say Brahms was nervous; others say he fell asleep while Liszt performed. All that we know for sure is that they did meet.

Also through his friend Joachim, Brahms got to know the composer and critic **Robert Schumann** and his pianist wife, **Clara**. He played some of his compositions for them, and they were amazed. Schumann wrote about Brahms in a musical journal. His praise was so great, other musicians were jealous, and Brahms had trouble living up to people's expectations of him. Still, Schumann helped launch Brahms's career.

Brahms lived with the Schumanns for a time and returned to their home to help Clara when Schumann asked to be admitted to a mental institution. Brahms kept track of the family's finances, taught the older children to read, and handled their correspondence. Brahms and Clara became very close, and they remained friends for the rest of their lives. Brahms always sent new compositions to Clara for her review before he sent them to his publisher. He never married.

From 1857 to 1859, he spent his autumns in Detmold, Germany, where he led the court orchestra and taught the family of Prince Leopold III. He enjoyed his time there, and directed a choir, too, which gave him the chance to work on his choral technique. He also decided his counterpoint technique needed improvement and exchanged exercises with Joachim by mail. Brahms continued to learn.

Because of Schumann's praise, Brahms's work was always anticipated. However, this does not mean his work was immediately appreciated. In fact, in 1858, when he finished his Piano Concerto no. 1 in D Minor, the audience hissed him off the stage! Writing to his friend Joachim, Brahms said, "I am only experimenting and feeling my way," adding sadly, "all the same, the hissing was rather too much!" Two publishers turned the work down before he could get someone to publish it. Now it is one of his most famous and frequently performed pieces.

Around this same time, one critic coined the term "New German School"[1] for the "progressive" music composed by the German composer **Richard Wagner**, as well as that of Franz Liszt and **Hector Berlioz**. Joachim and some of Brahms's other friends convinced Brahms to "object publicly to the claim that everyone who mattered in music had accepted the principles adopted by this 'progressive school.'" Brahms did object, but at the time he was only 26, and the first public performance of his work hadn't been well received. He was not particularly influential, but he never did care for Wagner's work; instead, he remained true to his Classical roots.

Brahms was not the easiest person to have as a friend. He was prickly, tough, and often bad-

tempered, although people usually agreed that beneath that exterior he had a heart of gold. Brahms was aware of his personality. His pupil Gustav Jenner wrote, "Brahms has acquired, not without reason, the reputation for being a grump, even though few could also be as lovable as he." Brahms once said, "I let the world go the way it pleases. I am only too often reminded that I am a difficult person to get along with. I am growing accustomed to bearing the consequence of this." His stubborn and blunt manner cost him many friends.

From the 1860s onward, when his works sold widely, Brahms became financially successful. He continued to prefer a modest lifestyle, however, living in a simple three-room apartment with his housekeeper. He even gave away much of his money to relatives and anonymously helped support a number of young musicians.

Brahms is considered one of the world's most extraordinary composers of symphonies. His Symphony no. 1 in C Minor premiered in 1876. With great respect, Hans von Bülow called it "Beethoven's Tenth Symphony"!

The Violin Concerto in D Major, first performed in 1879, was dedicated to his dear friend Joseph Joachim. It stands out as one of the greatest of all concertos.

The work that cemented Brahms's fame was his German Requiem. It was different from traditional requiems because instead of using a standardized Latin text, Brahms derived his text from Martin Luther's German Bible. Although a traditional Requiem Mass begins with prayers for the dead, Brahms began his with "Blessed are they that mourn: for they shall be comforted." About this work, Brahms once said that he would have gladly called it A Human Requiem.

What, then, are we to make of his religious beliefs? Although Brahms often referred to God and attributed his creative ability to Him, he evidently had some peculiar beliefs, as well. Some quotes lead us to believe he knew Christ; others would have us think he had no relationship with Him! Although it is impossible for us to know whether or not he did have a personal relationship with Christ, we do know that God gave him his talent.

Shortly after his cherished friend Clara Schumann died, Brahms passed away in 1897 from cancer and was buried in Vienna. Brahms never wrote an opera, nor did he ever write a tone poem. He preferred instead to compose **absolute music** (music that stands alone, needing no words to describe it). In a time when Wagner's operas and the shocking works of **Richard Strauss** were all the rage, Brahms stayed true to his calling. He composed serious, "pure" music in the manner of Beethoven and Schumann; music that is highly regarded to this day. Lovers of his music consider Brahms on a par with Bach, **Mozart**, and Beethoven.

Teacher Note
[1]New German School has to do more with a type or genre of progressive music of that time, not with a composer's nationality. Although Wagner was German, Liszt and Berlioz and others were not.

Johannes Brahms *Student Review*

1. How would you describe Brahms's childhood?

2. Two of Brahms's favorite composers were _____ and _____ .

3. What did Brahms do with his compositions that he didn't think were good enough to publish?

4. _____ helped to launch Brahms's career by writing about him in a musical journal.

5. Brahms gave music lessons to the family of
   a. Queen Victoria.
   b. Prince Leopold III.
   c. Henry VIII.
   d. All of the above.

6. True or False: Brahms was a part of the progressive "New German School."

7. Brahms's personality could best be described as
   a. shy.
   b. outgoing, the life of the party.
   c. self-centered.
   d. difficult yet lovable.

8. Brahms is remembered best for composing _____ .

A Young Scholar's Guide to Composers

9. How was Brahms's German Requiem different from a traditional Requiem Mass?

10. True or False: It is difficult to know exactly what Brahms believed about God.

Pyotr Ilyich *Tchaikovsky*

b. 1840 d. 1893

You have most likely heard the music of **Tchaikovsky** at Christmastime at the ballet, on television commercials, or at the mall. The music was written for the famous ballet *The Nutcracker*, which is tremendously popular at Christmastime. But Tchaikovsky wrote many other pieces of music as well: three famous ballets, eleven not-so-famous operas, an extremely well-known piece called the *1812 Overture*, six symphonies, and a variety of other works. Unlike most of the composers we've studied who were European, Tchaikovsky was born in Russia.

Pyotr was born in 1840 to a family that was not particularly musical. He did take piano lessons from the age of 5, but at the age of 10, it was decided that he would begin training for a career in civil service, to serve his country in law. He had to study away from home. When he was 14, his mother, with whom he was very close, died of cholera. He took this sad news very hard.

He continued his training and took a job with the government. But after two more years, he decided that music was what he loved the most. He especially loved the works of **Rossini**, **Bellini**, **Verdi**, and **Mozart**. His decision to leave his job was cemented when he heard Mozart's opera *Don Giovanni*. In fact, his time as a **civil servant** (public employee) was so unfulfilling to him that later in life he said he didn't have any memories of it at all!

A year after he began studying music theory, he enrolled in the new St. Petersburg Conservatory. It was run by Anton Rubinstein, with whom he developed a friendship. When he enrolled, he told his sister, "I have entered the newly-opened conservatory. . . . Do not imagine I dream of being a great artist. I only feel I must do the work for which I have a vocation. Whether I become a celebrated composer or a struggling artist—it is all the same." He did very well at the conservatory, and Rubinstein recommended him to his brother Nikolai, who had just opened a conservatory in Moscow. There, Tchaikovsky taught harmony for many years and composed while he wasn't working.

The Piano Concerto no. 1 in B-flat Minor is the most famous of Tchaikovsky's three piano concertos. He dedicated it to his friend Nikolai Rubinstein, but when he showed it to him during the Christmas of 1874, he was bitterly disappointed, for Rubinstein thought it was terrible! He refused to play it in public unless Tchaikovsky made many changes. Tchaikovsky said, "I shall not change a single note. . . . and I shall publish the concerto exactly as it is now." And he did. He crossed Rubinstein's name off the dedication page and, instead, dedicated it to **Hans von Bülow**, the German pianist and conductor who was an admirer of Tchaikovsky's music. Von Bülow played it in Boston, and the people liked it. Now it is often played.

In 1876, Tchaikovsky composed *Marche slave*. There is a sad story behind this piece. In June of that year, during the Serbo-Turkish War, Turkish soldiers slaughtered a large number of Christian Slavs. Nikolai Rubinstein asked Tchaikovsky to compose a piece for a benefit concert to aid the kingdom of Serbia. In an outburst of patriotism, he wrote what was first known as the *Serbo-Russian March* (later called *Marche slave*) in just five days!

Tchaikovsky was very close to his family and wrote many letters throughout his lifetime. He also struggled throughout his life with certain ongoing sins and fears. He told his nephew, "I suffer, not only from torments that cannot be put in words, but from a hatred of strangers and an indefinable terror—though of what, the devil only knows."

In 1877, Tchaikovsky married one of his students at the conservatory who had written him many love letters. It was a hasty decision on his part, and after a few weeks they no longer lived together. Struggling emotionally for many reasons and bordering on a nervous breakdown, he fled to St. Petersburg.

Then, a wealthy widow named Nadezhda von Meck fell in love with his music. She told Tchaikovsky she didn't ever want to meet him, but she did become his **patron** (this means she provided money for him to live on), so he could spend his time writing. Soon, he was able to quit teaching and spend his time composing and traveling, including conducting at New York's Carnegie Hall during its opening. Von Meck and Tchaikovsky developed a strong friendship through their letters. This friendship lasted 13 years and resulted in more than 1,200 letters between two people who never met! Suddenly, however, she ended it. Tchaikovsky was heartbroken. Around this same time, his sister died. As Tchaikovsky often did when he was emotional, he threw himself into his music, and he wrote *The Nutcracker*.

His Sixth, and final, Symphony, which his brother called the *Pathétique*[1], was written to describe life, with the last movement depicting death. Ironically, Tchaikovsky died just nine days after its premiere, at the age of 53. This symphony is now considered one of his best and most popular works.

Despite his many struggles, we can admire Tchaikovsky for his beautiful music and for his strong work ethic. He wrote, "I have some very low moments, but an insatiable thirst for work consoles me. . . . If one lacks the right mood, one must force oneself to work, otherwise nothing will be accomplished." He also wrote, "Without work, life has no meaning for me."

Although Tchaikovsky did not appear to be a believer, he thrived on routine, which included a daily Bible reading. He was searching for spiritual truth and once wrote, "on one side my mind refuses to be convinced by dogma. . . . on the other hand, my education, and the ingrained habits of childhood, combined with the story of Christ and His teaching, all persuade me, in spite of myself, to turn to Him with prayers when I am sad, with gratitude when I am happy."

His passion for his homeland was evident in his music, where he tended to use Russian folk melodies and harmonies. He wrote, "In short, I am Russian in the fullest sense of the word." We can remember Tchaikovsky for his stunning melodies, exceptional orchestrations, and desire to rise above his troubles by creating timeless music.

Teacher Note
[1]Pathétique—means "passionate" or "emotional," not "arousing pity."

Pyotr Ilyich Tchaikovsky   *Student Review*

1.   In which country was Tchaikovsky born?

2.   True or False: Tchaikovsky's family was very musical.

3.   True or False: It was decided that Tchaikovsky, at the age of 10, would begin training for a career as an architect.

4.   True or False: Throughout his life, Tchaikovsky suffered from many torments and fears.

5.   Tchaikovsky was a friend and an associate of two brothers in the music field, Anton and Nikolai _____.

6.   There is a sad story behind *Marche slave*. He composed it for a benefit concert to give _____ to the kingdom of Serbia.

7.   What is a patron?

8.   Did Tchaikovsky ever meet his patron, the widow Nadezhda von Meck? _____

9.   Tchaikovsky wrote the music for a ballet that we often hear at Christmastime. What is the name of this ballet? _____

10. Tchaikovsky's Sixth, and final, Symphony, which was written to describe life and death, was called the

   a.   *Pathétique.*

   b.   *Marche slave.*

   c.   *1812 Overture.*

   d.   Piano Concerto no. 1 in B-flat Minor.

Antonín *Dvořák*

b. 1841 d. 1904

Antonín Dvořák (pronounced "duh VOR zhahk") was the eighth son of a butcher and innkeeper in a little village of 400 people, 20 miles north of Prague, Czechoslovakia (now known as the Czech Republic). His father played the violin and **zither**, and young Antonín began playing songs on the violin when he was five years old. When he was little, a railroad line ran very close to his house. This fascinated him, and he was interested in trains for the rest of his life. Often, even as a grown-up, he would go to train stations just to watch the trains.

In his early teens, Antonín went to a nearby town to live with his uncle and learn German. His family felt that learning German was important if he wanted to be a successful innkeeper. But while he was living there, he became a friend of an organist, who encouraged his interest in music and taught him to play the piano, organ, and violin. His new friend, along with his uncle, encouraged his father to allow Antonín to study music in Prague at the Organ School there. Finally, his father gave in, and Dvořák went to Prague in 1857, when he was 16 years old. His work at the school was good, but it wasn't remarkable. In 1859, he joined a band, playing the viola, and this band became the core of the orchestra of the new Provisional Theatre. Not long after the group started, Bedřich Smetana, another Czech composer, became the conductor of this orchestra, and Dvořák played under him for about a decade.

Dvořák was determined to compose. He spent a lot of time studying other composer's works, particularly **Beethoven's**, and then he would try to write his own work. Usually, he ended up burning his compositions in the stove and trying again. Although he left the Organ School in 1859, he didn't see any public success until 1873.

Shortly after this first public success, he married a woman named Anna Čermáková, the daughter of a goldsmith. Anna had a lovely contralto voice and sang in the chorus of the National Opera. Dvořák loved family life and was devoted to his family. Together, he and Anna raised six children. After eating dinner with them once, **Tchaikovsky** said, "His wife is a simply charming woman and an excellent hostess."

In 1874, Dvořák took a job as a church organist. Not long after starting this new job, he met **Brahms**, who became his mentor and lifelong friend. When Dvořák was 33, his Third and

Fourth symphonies won a state grant from Austria. Brahms was one of the judges! Brahms was obviously impressed with Dvořák and recommended Dvořák's *Moravian Duets* to his own publisher. Dvořák was a wise man, and he was careful not to upset his relationship with Brahms. He was sure to give credit where it was due. Dvořák won more awards in 1876 and 1877. Brahms continued to encourage him.

In 1878, at the age of 37, Dvořák conducted his first concert with a program entirely of his own works. This public appearance served as a springboard to his career. Because of his new status, his publisher began to pay him more for his works, and he had the confidence to quit his job as organist to compose fulltime.

Dvořák's influence spread outside Europe. He visited England, where his music was very successful. Brahms encouraged Dvořák to move to Vienna, but Dvořák saw himself as a nationalist—someone who is very devoted to his own country. He didn't want to change that perception. He did travel, though, including a trip to Europe, where he played concerts that had been set up by Tchaikovsky.

In 1892, he took a job in New York City at the new National Conservatory of Music. He traveled to the United States with his wife and two children. The other children stayed in Europe with family until nine months later, when they joined him and the family was reunited. Dvořák's three years in the United States were difficult for him—he was homesick for Prague. However, the Americans and the American lifestyle fascinated him. He had a tremendous appreciation for the music of the African Americans, particularly, Negro spirituals. In fact, he considered "Go Down, Moses" to be "as great as a Beethoven melody." He befriended a man who had learned many spirituals from his grandfather, a former slave. This man became Dvořák's personal assistant and a family friend.

Dvořák was a visionary—he said in an interview with a reporter for the *New York Herald* that black music would play a role in future American music. He was so right! The beginnings of jazz were right around the corner.

Besides being fascinated with spirituals, Dvořák developed an interest in the Native American culture after seeing a performance of Buffalo Bill's "Wild West" show. Dvořák spent much of his vacation time in a Czech community in Spillville, Iowa. While he was there in the summer of 1893, he spent two weeks getting to know members of the Kickapoo Medicine Show, who were camping nearby.

Dvořák did a tremendous amount of composing while he was in the United States, and much of his music was influenced by African American and Native American cultures. In fact, one melody from his Ninth Symphony, the *New World Symphony*, was turned into the spiritual "Going Home" by one of his students. This symphony was first performed in Carnegie Hall. Dvořák also composed the *American String Quartet*, a suite for piano, and a cello concerto,

before funding at the conservatory began to run out and he was overcome by homesickness. Once he returned to Prague, he devoted himself to writing operas. Dvořák died suddenly in Prague in 1904 at age 62. At that time, Dvořák was the most celebrated Czech in any field.

Though Dvořák was known as eccentric and stubborn, he was a happy and well-adjusted man. His good friend Brahms claimed, "He is strange, but his heart is in the right place." The famous composer **Edvard Grieg** claimed, "It was amusing to meet Dvořák; he is quite original, to say the least, but very likable all the same."

Most importantly, when others spoke of his genius, he always pointed them back to his Creator, noting that it was "the gift of God." He usually concluded a composition with the notation: *"Bohu díky"* ("Thanks be to God").

Antonín Dvořák *Student Review*

1. Besides the violin, what else did Dvořák become interested in at an early age?

2. Which composer's works did Dvořák study the most?

    a. Bach

    b. Tchaikovsky

    c. Beethoven

    d. Chopin

3. Which composer was Dvořák's lifelong mentor and friend?

    a. Brahms

    b. Joplin

    c. Haydn

    d. Mozart

4. True or False: Dvořák's first concert consisting entirely of his own works went so well that it became the springboard for his career.

5. Dvořák wouldn't move to Vienna because he was a

    a. homebody.

    b. nationalist.

    c. patriot.

    d. paraplegic.

6. Dvořák told a reporter for the *New York Herald* that _____ music (which he was personally fascinated with) would play a role in future American music.

7. This prediction was correct, because just around the corner were the beginnings of _____ music.

8. Dvořák was born and died in _____.

9. Besides being influenced by black culture, Dvořák was also influenced by

    a. European culture.

    b. South American culture.

    c. Native American culture.

    d. Eskimo culture.

10. True or False: Dvořák was a Christian.

Gabriel Urbain *Fauré*

The youngest of six children, little Gabriel was sent to live with a nurse until he was about four years old. About his childhood in France, **Fauré** had this to say, "I grew up a rather quiet, well-behaved child in an area of great beauty. But the only thing I remember clearly is the **harmonium** (similar to an organ) in the little chapel at the college. Every time I could get away I ran there—and I regaled myself . . . I played atrociously."

At a young age, Gabriel was heard improvising on the chapel harmonium and piano. It was suggested to his father that he had real musical talent. So, at the age of 9, Gabriel traveled 500 miles to Paris to board at the École Niedermeyer. His talent was such that after he played the organ for the school director, he was given a full scholarship. Fauré said about his experiences at the Niedermeyer: "I was there for many years; it was a hard life, but what a delightful one! . . . we made music."

During the next 11 years at boarding school, Gabriel excelled at the piano. **Camille Saint-Saëns**, one of the instructors, took special note of Fauré, and the two began a lifelong friendship. Saint-Saëns introduced him to the music of contemporary composers like **Robert Schumann**, **Franz Liszt**, and **Richard Wagner**, as well as the author Gustave Flaubert. A generous friend, Saint-Saëns also helped him find jobs and also publishers for his work.

After graduating with first prize in several areas, Fauré took the first of several jobs as a church organist. Although he was a charming and friendly person, he was not known to be religious; in fact, he called himself an "incorrigible religious defaulter." His lifestyle was considered unbecoming of a church organist, and he was fired at least once. (Smoking during the sermons didn't help, either.)

Then, in 1870, France declared war on Prussia, beginning the Franco-Prussian War. Fauré served his country in the Imperial Guard, acting as a messenger and liaison officer. In between battles, he often gave spur-of-the-moment concerts in abandoned houses! France lost to Prussia, and in 1871 the German Empire was proclaimed (with the kingdom of Prussia as its largest constituent).

After the war, Fauré returned to the École Niedermeyer, this time as a professor of composition. Later, he taught at the famous and popular Conservatoire de Paris. In 1905,

he became the director of the Conservatoire—despite vehement opposition from many of the staff. They did not want the changes he wished to make. Fauré wrote this, comparing the École Niedermeyer to the Conservatoire, "In 1853 the masterpieces of **J. S. Bach**, which constituted our daily bread [at the Niedermeyer] had still not found their way into the organ class at the Conservatoire."

Fauré was an efficient and capable administrator, and he worked hard to improve the quality of teaching at the Conservatoire. He made many reforms and hired new teachers, including **Claude Debussy**. And he continued writing and composing his own music. (Several of his students there, including **Nadia Boulanger** and **Maurice Ravel**, later became famous musicians in their own right.)

Fauré is considered the master of the French art song—he had a special talent for setting words to music. He composed about 100 songs, including *Clair de Lune* and the song cycle *La Bonne Chanson*. He is perhaps known best for his Requiem in D Minor, op. 48. Most of his work he composed for the piano, his favorite instrument.

We have discussed other composers who have written requiems, including **Mozart**, **Verdi**, and **Brahms**. What is a requiem, and why did composers write them? A Requiem Mass (from the Latin *requiescere*, "to rest") is a specific type of service performed in Catholic, Anglican, and some Lutheran churches immediately preceding a burial. The common basis of requiems is prayer for the salvation of the soul of the departed. Requiem is also a title for the musical composition for this service (or mass). Eventually, composers began to write requiems for the beauty and drama of the music and not just for specific burials, creating a new genre of music.

Even though Fauré wrote this beautiful piece of religious music, in his own words he tells of his lack of faith after reading an article on salvation. "How nice is this self-assurance! How nice is the naiveté, or the vanity, or the stupidity, or the bad faith of the people for whom this was written, printed and distributed."

Chopin was a major influence on Fauré. Both musicians had the same delicate sensibility, refinement, and excellent workmanship. One of Fauré's piano pieces was especially intricate. Supposedly, he sent it to Liszt (the man who could sight-read and play anything on first glance) who returned it with a curt note saying it was "too difficult."

Despite being "deeply moved" by a Wagner performance in Munich, Fauré did not in any way emulate Wagner's style. And despite living through a number of different musical styles, he remained true to his own music, not following any passing fads but rather growing and maturing in his compositions with each passing year. But even while he was true to his own style—he truly nurtured younger composers and encouraged them to compose in their own way, a gift not always found in teachers.

Of his personal life, we know that his first love, Marianne Viardot, broke his heart after first accepting, then rejecting, his proposal of marriage. People considered Fauré a fine-looking man with agreeable manners, and he was popular at the Paris salons of the day. Here, his friends encouraged and helped him in his music career. They also attempted to help him recover from his huge disappointment in the loss of his betrothed.

Years later, wanting to be wed, Fauré agreed to an arranged marriage with Marie Fremiet. Their marriage took place in 1883, and their first son, Emmanuel, was born nine months later. Philippe was born in 1889. (Sadly, theirs was not a happy marriage, and Fauré spent less and less time with his family and more and more time with friends, both male and female.) Fauré taught music lessons to provide for his family, but, as with so many musicians, money was always tight. Then, times got worse: In the 1880s, both of his parents died and his own health deteriorated. Just as things were looking quite grim, a princess who enjoyed his music sent Fauré and several of his friends on a vacation to Venice.

There, in this magical city, Fauré's vitality and musical inspiration returned. He began a new era in his compositions. His career took off:
- 1892—appointed Inspector of provincial conservatories
- 1896—became organist of the L'église Sainte-Marie-Madeleine[1] and teacher of composition at the Conservatoire de Paris[2]
- 1905—appointed Director of the Conservatoire

Then, in the early 1900s, Fauré began to have hearing difficulties. As time went on, his hearing grew worse and worse. Although he attempted to keep his hearing loss a secret, eventually he could hide it no longer. In 1920, at age 75, he had to step down from his post at the Conservatoire. But even during his years of hearing impairment, Fauré continued to compose beautiful music! In fact, some of his most enduring works came from this time: Second Cello Sonata, Piano Trio, and String Quartet.

His health (he was a heavy smoker) and hearing continued to deteriorate, and he died from pneumonia in 1924. The government accorded him a state funeral in which Fauré's own music, including his Requiem Mass, was played.

Teacher Notes
[1]L'église Sainte-Marie-Madeleine; (less formally, just La Madeleine) is a church in Paris. It was designed originally as a temple to the glory of Napoleon's army. Now, however, the Madeleine is affiliated with a Benedictine abbey, and Masses and the most fashionable weddings in Paris are still celebrated there. It is home to one of the best pipe organs in Paris. The composers Camille Saint-Saëns and Gabriel Fauré were both organists at the Madeleine, and the funerals of Frédéric Chopin, Saint-Saëns, Fauré and others were held there.

[2]Conservatoire de Paris is an institution of higher learning in Paris, founded in 1795, but built upon the foundations of an earlier school, École Royale de Chant.

Gabriel Urbain Fauré *Student Review*

1. True or False: Fauré was a noisy, ill-behaved child who loved to make music.

2. Fauré was sent to boarding school because

    a.   he had talent.

    b.   he was a great student.

    c.   he drove his parents crazy.

    d.   he was orphaned.

3. Where was Fauré's boarding school located?

    a.   Prague

    b.   Germany

    c.   Austria

    d.   Paris

4. Saint-Saëns took special note of him because he excelled at which instrument?

    _____

5. Was Fauré a "model" church organist? _____

6. Fauré served his country in which war? _____ – _____

7. Fauré is considered the master of what type of song? The _____ _____ song.

8. A Requiem Mass is a specific type of service performed in some churches

    immediately preceding what event? _____

9. Which two composers/teachers had a strong impact on Fauré? _____ and

    _____

10. Fauré lost his _____ in later life, similar to _____ , another

    composer we have studied.

Sir Edward *Elgar*

b. 1857 d. 1934

England was suffering a "drought," a drought of composers, that is. Ever since the famous English composer **Henry Purcell** died in 1695, English music had languished. This 200-year dry spell was finally broken with the arrival of the English composer **Edward Elgar**.

He was born in a tiny home of red brick, known as "The Firs," in a small village just outside the city of Worcester, England. As a child, young Edgar loved to roam out-of-doors. There, he explored the twists and turns of the old town, fished in the Severn River, and soaked up the atmosphere of the quiet countryside that he found soothing all his life. Looking back on his childhood, he later wrote, "I am still at heart the dreamy child who used to be found in the reeds by the Severn with a sheet of paper trying to fix the sounds and longing for something very great."

Worcester was a cathedral city, about 130 miles from London. It was one of the famous "Three Choir" cities. It shared with Gloucester and Hereford a famous annual music festival where composers and conductors of world renown came to participate.

Edward's mother, Anne, was a remarkable woman. A farmer's daughter of no means, she had "the unmistakable air of good breeding." (Although she was the granddaughter of a Major-General—so she did have some stature socially.) She loved nature, books, writing, and sketching. She passed her love of learning on to Edward, for whom she wrote this little verse:

"Nervous, sensitive & kind
Displays no vulgar frame of mind."

Edward had an outstanding memory, and as a youth he memorized "Hyperion" by John Keats and "The Saga of King Olaf" by Henry Wadsworth Longfellow, for which he later wrote a cantata.

His father was a "jack-of-all-trades" musician. Along with his brother, he owned the local music store, he played the organ for the cathedral, he was a piano tuner, and he taught music lessons.

Although Edward was not formally trained in music as so many of the other composers were, he certainly absorbed music as part of his family's lifestyle. His father and uncle's music store was his "school." There, he had access to all the latest books on music, musical scores by the great composers, and instruments to play. He read scores as eagerly as some children read books! By age 12, he was playing the violin along with the adults in the local music club. He played the organ and the piano as well.

Edward once said in a magazine interview: "I read everything, played everything, and heard everything that I possibly could. . . . I am self-taught in the matter of harmony, counterpoint, form, and, in short, the whole of the 'mystery' of music."

With seven children and little income, money was always tight in the Elgar household. Although Edward wanted to train formally as a musician—and especially to study abroad—this was just not financially possible, so at age 15, he was apprenticed to a lawyer. As you might imagine, this was not the best job for an artistic, sensitive, dreamy youth. Although he tried for a year, it did not work out and he came back to Worcester, determined to support himself as a musician. While working on his own violin skills, he also taught organ and did some basic composing. After a while, he realized he did not have what it took to become a concert violinist, so he concentrated on his composing. In the meantime, he accepted a job as a band conductor at the local insane asylum, where he worked for five years. During this time, he saved enough to take a trip to Paris, where he was delighted to hear **Camille Saint-Saëns** play. Edward took every opportunity to improve his playing, composing, and knowledge of music.

A major turning point in Elgar's life came when he fell in love with one of his piano students: Caroline Alice Roberts. They wed in 1889 when she was 40 and he was 31. At this time of rigid class distinctions, her family strongly disapproved of their union because of his family's lower middle-class standing and his Roman Catholic religion. (Her family was both upper middle class and Protestant.) They were so displeased that several of her family members cut Caroline out of their wills.

Caroline and Edgar received, as a wedding gift, a copy of Cardinal Newman's poem "The Dream of Gerontius." (This was later to become the basis of one of Elgar's best pieces, for which he is still known today.) This same year Elgar composed his first significant work, the *Froissart Overture*.

Caroline loved Edward and passionately believed in his talent and ability. She was a wonderful source of inspiration and encouragement. Her presence in his life unleashed his talent, and his compositions took on a new maturity and depth, which had been lacking until then. She was always his biggest supporter and admirer. Their only child, a daughter they named Carice Irene, was born in 1890.

Elgar's big musical break, and his first claim to fame, came 10 years later when the

celebrated conductor **Hans Richter** came across Elgar's composition Variations on an Original Theme and chose to perform it in London. This piece, commonly known as *Enigma Variations*[1], has a mystery attached to it. Dedicated to "my friends pictured within," he gave each of the themes in it (similar to chapters in a novel) the nickname of one of his friends. But the main theme itself is said to have a counterpart, a theme that is not heard—the so-called "silent theme." Musicologists have poured over his scores looking for this "silent theme" but have thus far been unsuccessful in identifying it. Elgar enjoyed this little puzzle that he told only to his wife and his publisher.

After Richter conducted *Enigma*, *The Dream of Gerontius* was performed at the Birmingham [England] Festival in 1900. About this piece Elgar has said, (himself quoting from author John Ruskin's *Sesame and Lilies*) "This is the best of me. For the rest, I ate, I drank, I slept, I loved, I hated, like as another. My life was a vapour, and is not. But this what I saw, and know. This, if anything of mine, is worth your memory." Sadly, it was poorly performed, and Elgar was depressed over the initial lack of enthusiasm and understanding of what was later considered to be a masterpiece. In one letter, Elgar bemoaned the terrible performance and wrote these distressing words, "I have worked hard for forty years and at the last, Providence denies me a decent hearing of my work: so I submit—I always said God was against art and I still believe it."

But his reputation continued to grow. When Richter saw the partial score to Elgar's *Falstaff*, he wrote, "What themes! Unmistakably and genuinely Elgar! . . . Admittedly I can only imagine it, for . . . even one's boldest imagination proves to be far from reality."

Then, war loomed and the world changed. World War I, 1914 to 1918, was a very difficult time for Elgar emotionally. The war profoundly affected him, as it did most Europeans. During this time he wrote mainly patriotic pieces. His most famous is *Pomp and Circumstance* March no. 1 (also known as *Land of Hope and Glory*) which was first publicly performed at the coronation of King Edward VII in 1902. It has since become a second national anthem for the English (and very familiar to Americans as a popular graduation song).

He also composed one children's piece and a ballet. During 1918 to 1919, he wrote his last four masterpieces: the Violin Sonata, the String Quartet, the Piano Quintet, and the great Cello Concerto. These are quiet works, moving and melancholy. Then, in 1920, his beloved wife, Caroline, died. From that time on, even though he lived another 14 years, Elgar did very little composing.

This poor, uneducated composer left a huge impression on all of England, finally becoming Sir Edward Elgar[2] and a national institution. Elgar left behind an amazing body of work and gave to England a composer uniquely hers.

Teacher Notes

[1]Enigma—a saying, question, picture, and so on, containing a hidden meaning; riddle.

[2]Sir Edward Elgar: In 1904—Elgar was made a knight bachelor. This allowed him the title of Sir Edward Elgar. In 1928—Elgar was created a Knight Commander of the Royal Victorian Order, becoming 'Sir Edward Elgar OM KCVO.' In 1931—Elgar was made a baronet, becoming 'Sir Edward Elgar Bt OM KCVO.'

1. Elgar was born near this large cathedral city, which was one of the famous "Three Choir" cities.

    a. Worcester

    b. London

    c. Athens

    d. Dover

2. Elgar's appearance as a composer ended a 200-year "drought" of music in which country? _____

3. True or False: Elgar was from a rich upper-class family.

4. True or False: Elgar was formally trained in music and composing.

5. Elgar married one of his piano students, Caroline Roberts, whose family opposed the union because of Elgar's _____ _____ religion and his _____ _____ social status.

6. What is an enigma, and how did Elgar use it in his music?

7. Which piece of music did Elgar consider "the best of me," despite its poor debut?

    a. *Enigma Variations*

    b. Violin Sonata

    c. *The Dream of Gerontius*

    d. *Falstaff*

8.   During which war did Elgar compose *Pomp and Circumstance*? _____

9.   Elgar's *Pomp and Circumstance* is commonly played at what type of American event?

_____

10.   How were Elgar's last four masterpieces described?

Claude *Debussy*

b. 1862 d. 1918

Claude **Debussy** was born into a nonmusical family in St.-Germain-en-Laye on August 22, 1862. This small village was about 13 miles from bustling Paris, and there his parents owned a small crockery (china) shop. His father held many jobs over the years, trying to make ends meet. Due to politics, he ended up in jail for about a year during the Franco-Prussian War. At that time, Claude's Aunt Clementine took young Claude and his sister to live with her.

Claude's musical talent was recognized, and his aunt arranged for Claude to have piano lessons. At the age of 10, he was accepted into the prestigious Paris Conservatoire. At this very early age, he was already exhibiting a love of unorthodox harmonies and a disdain for the "rules of music," for which he would become famous.

His life there was not easy. He was poor, wore shabby clothes, and did not get along well with the other students or the professors, probably because of his disregard for musical forms and his unconventional ideas. It seems, too, as if young Claude really wasn't especially interested in anyone else's opinions. A fellow student described him as "uncommunicative, not to say surly; he was not attractive to his friends."

While still enrolled in the Conservatoire, Claude was recommended for a summer job with a wealthy family (and **Tchaikovsky's** patrons). They hired him during two summers to accompany them to Russia as their personal pianist and as a piano tutor for their children. This opportunity exposed him to Russian music.

In 1884, after about 11 years at the Conservatoire, Debussy won the prestigious Prix de Rome, which allowed him three years of study at the French Academy in the Villa Medici in Rome. He didn't especially appreciate this opportunity. Once there, he complained about the food, the weather, the city, and the accommodations. He spent only two years there, although the prize allowed for another year of study and the privilege of playing the piano with **Liszt**. But as usual, Claude was still at odds with everyone over his musical style. Once, he said this: "Generally speaking, I feel more and more that music, by its very essence, is not something that can flow inside a rigorous, traditional form. It consists of colors and rhythmicized time."

After a bit of travel, Debussy returned to Paris in 1887. France during this time was not very stable. Government after government rose and fell, the rural economy was bad, banks failed, and there were rumors of war. For a time, things seemed to get better. Improvements such as public telephones and mass transit appeared. The Eiffel Tower opened as part of the Universal Exhibition in celebration of the French Revolution; construction began on the Panama Canal;, and France was energetically expanding her colonial holdings.

Attending the 1889 Exhibition, Debussy was exposed for the first time to the **Javanese gamelan**—an Indonesian orchestra comprised of bells, gongs, and percussion instruments. He was fascinated by this music, and it influenced his compositions.

During this time, Debussy was composing a bit, hanging out with his friends—mostly poets, writers, his current girlfriend, and a few musicians. He was always short of cash and relied on others to help pay the bills. His private life was not happy. Debussy was a man of few friends and an unpleasant demeanor.

After a 10-year relationship with one woman, he left her and married another; then in 1908, he married Emma Bardac. They had a daughter—his much-beloved Claude-Emma, nicknamed "Chouchou." Although Debussy tended toward depression and discontent, his young daughter always cheered him up. For her, he wrote the charming *Children's Corner* suite for piano and a children's ballet, *The Box of Toys*.

Debussy admired **Frédéric Chopin** and **Igor Stravinsky**. He wrote to Stravinsky once and said, "It is a special satisfaction to tell you how much you have enlarged the boundaries of the permissible in the empire of sound." He also loved the works of the American writer Edgar Allan Poe. In fact, he began (but never completed) an opera based on Poe's "The Fall of the House of Usher."

Debussy spent 10 years writing his only completed opera, *Pelléas et Mélisande*. It debuted in April 1902. Many in the audience found it totally incomprehensible. They were confused by the opera's formlessness, unusual harmonies, and absence of the traditional arias and dance. This opera produced strong opinions, both for and against it. The liberals declared it was genius; traditionalists said it was not opera and, in fact, was not much of anything. The French writer Marcel Proust, Debussy's friend, was enthusiastic about it.

Pelléas et Mélisande launched a very prolific period for Debussy, in which he wrote several pieces, including two that are still popular today [titles listed here in English], *The Sea* and *Prelude to the Afternoon of a Faun*. The latter may be his most famous composition. His music is called by some "impressionistic," after the famous French Impressionist painters of the time. Although Debussy did not like that description, he really did "paint with music." He broke many of the musical rules of the time and created new music, more about feelings and images than form. One of the most creative of artists, he dealt in "colors and shadows and mist." He was influenced by non-Western music and incorporated that influence into Western musical styles.

In 1909, Debussy was diagnosed with cancer. While the political climate in Europe was growing more and more tense, his health was growing worse and worse. War broke out in Europe, and France was quickly embroiled in the Great War, World War I. Soon, German planes were dropping bombs on Paris itself, and Debussy was torn over the destruction of his favorite place on Earth. The Debussy home was a tense place, with the constant air raids and his rapidly declining health. Even then, he managed to write a few more compositions, most notably his études. But, eventually, his body was so wasted away that he was unable to compose. He said then, "Music's completely abandoned me."

Just as it seemed Paris was about to fall to the Germans in early 1918, Debussy died. Although there was no public outpouring of sympathy and grief from a nation that was itself losing millions to war, Debussy's 12-year-old daughter Chouchou wrote this remarkable note to her half-brother, Raoul:

> "Thursday arrived, the Thursday when he was to be taken from us for ever! I saw him one last time in that horrible box—lying on the ground. He looked happy, so happy and then I could not control my tears. I almost collapsed but I couldn't embrace him. At the cemetery Mama, naturally, couldn't have behaved better and as for me, all I could think of was, "I mustn't cry because of Mama." I summoned up all my courage. Where did it come from? I don't know. I didn't shed a single tear. Tears restrained are worth as much as tears shed, and now it is night for ever. Papa is dead. Those three words. I don't understand them or rather I understand them too well."

We know nothing of Debussy's spiritual life, except by what we can see from his actions. From these, there isn't any reason to suppose that Debussy loved the Lord. Of his musical life, we can say that Debussy influenced almost all later twentieth-century composers, including **Béla Bartók** and Igor Stravinsky, the minimalists **Steve Reich** and **Philip Glass**, and even the jazz composers **Thelonious Monk** and **Duke Ellington**. He helped to establish a new concept of tonality in Western music, expanding the tonal palette for later composers and listeners. Many consider him the most important composer of piano music in the twentieth century.

1. At age 10, Debussy was accepted into the prestigious _____ Conservatoire.

2. True or False: Debussy was a model pupil, conforming to his professors' ideals of music.

3. When Debussy returned to Paris after studying in Rome, much was happening. Which of the following events were going on when Debussy returned?

    a. There were rumors of war.

    b. Mass transit appeared.

    c. The Eiffel Tower opened.

    d. The rural economy and banks were doing well.

    e. Construction began on the Panama Canal.

4. Which American writer/poet did Debussy admire? (He even started an opera based on one of his/her works.)

    a. Edgar Allan Poe

    b. Emily Dickinson

    c. William Wordsworth

    d. Henry David Thoreau

5. What is Debussy's most famous composition?

    a. *Pelléas et Mélisande*

    b. *The Sea*

    c. *Prelude to the Afternoon of a Faun*

    d. *Children's Corner*

6. Debussy's music is called by some _____ , after the famous French painters of the time.

7. True or False: Debussy died during World War I.

8. Debussy's daughter, who was 12 years old when he died, had an unusual nickname. What was it? _____

9. On which twentieth-century composers did Debussy have a strong influence?

10. True or False: We can tell by his lifestyle that Debussy was a believer.

Richard *Strauss*

b. 1864 d. 1949

You would never imagine that the beautiful little boy with a head full of curls was from a wealthy family. He lived above a brewery in a small apartment with no running water or electricity. Eating chocolate wasn't allowed except as a special treat at Christmas. The young boy's father was the most famous (and outspoken!) horn player in Germany. He had severe views on raising his son, including living within a strict budget and listening to and playing only conservative music. He made certain that his boy was not "contaminated by **Wagner**, **Liszt**, or any other music of the future." He was, by most accounts, a short-tempered, bossy man.

However, this little boy, whose name was **Richard Strauss**, did not have an entirely unhappy childhood. His younger sister Johanna wrote of their childhood holidays: "Excursions to lonely valleys among the peaks, then coffee with whipped cream and little cakes. . . . There were innumerable joys and freedom which ever remained in Richard's heart."

Richard exhibited fine musical talent from a very early age. He played the piano beautifully at 4, the violin at 5, and was composing polkas at 6! In fact, some thought he could easily be another **Mozart**, touring Europe as a child prodigy.

Though his father took it for granted that Richard would become a musician, he wanted him to have a well-rounded education. Therefore, Richard attended **gymnasium** (grammar school) and then went on to the university for awhile, where he studied philosophy and art history but not music.

Even if Richard didn't study music formally, he was surrounded by the best of teachers: his talented father and his father's musical friends. Richard played in a small orchestra conducted by his father, and his natural ability to compose music began to attract attention. His early compositions were well regarded, and some considered him to be a "budding **Brahms**."

After he left the university, he spent some time in Berlin. A fast-growing city, alive with activities, it was an exciting place for a young man who came from the quieter atmosphere of Munich. Unfortunately, young Richard fell in with a fast crowd, and he spent much of his time partying, performing at parties, and playing a card game called "Skat" (which he remained obsessive about the rest of his life).

In Berlin in 1884, the famous conductor **Hans von Bülow** decided his orchestra would perform one of Richard's compositions. The piece was very well received, and von Bülow asked Richard to compose another one. Then, in a kind gesture, von Bülow allowed Richard to conduct the world premiere of this piece in his home city, Munich. With such a powerful and famous patron as von Bülow, young Strauss quickly became a well-known conductor and composer.

Richard Strauss married soprano Pauline de Ahna in 1894. She was famous for being strong-willed, ill-tempered, and outspoken, but the marriage was evidently a happy one. He told people that she was good for him. She would yell at him to stop playing cards and to "Go compose!" which he dutifully did. His private life was solid and scandal-free.

Then, Strauss became a friend of **Alexander Ritter**, a composer and poet who greatly admired Franz Liszt and Richard Wagner (those same composers from whom Richard's father had worked so hard to shield him!). Ritter, married to Richard Wagner's niece, now greatly influenced Richard Strauss, as did the works of Wagner. As you might imagine, Richard's compositions changed dramatically from a traditional, Classical style to something much more modern. Strauss himself said this of Ritter: "His influence on me was in the nature of the storm-wind." Ritter's **anti-Semitism** (hostility toward the Jewish race) was especially strong, but Strauss himself had grown up with these same views.

The showy pianist and composer Franz Liszt coined the term **symphonic poem** around 1850 to name a new type of orchestral composition that more or less followed an actual story or expressed a certain concept. Symphonic poems were shorter than symphonies and typically consisted of just one movement.

Strauss took the symphonic poems to new levels. He wrote music to match particular works of literature—first *Macbeth* and then *Don Juan* (which launched him to international fame). These were followed by other pieces, such as *Death and Transfiguration*, *Thus Spake Zarathustra*, and then *Don Quixote*. Strauss's reputation as a conductor and composer soared.

Unlike almost all the other musicians we have studied, Strauss was a good businessman, known for driving a hard bargain. He never apologized to those who muttered that music was art and not meant to be a moneymaker. (Ironically, despite his great financial success in the late 1800s and early 1900s, Strauss died virtually destitute.) He was also a hard-working man who didn't just wait for inspiration—he charged ahead and wrote prolifically.

Many loved his works, but many hated them. Almost all of his works were controversial, and each added to his fame. As a composer, he wrote larger-than-life, flamboyant pieces utilizing huge orchestras. (Interestingly, though, as a conductor he used very small movements and showed no emotion.)

Strauss became best known for his outrageous, scandalous operas. Beginning with his third opera, *Salome*, Strauss shocked the world with his strident music and dreadfully immoral story line, borrowed from Oscar Wilde. As much of an uproar that *Salome* caused, it was nothing compared to the next opera, *Elektra*. Not only was it a most difficult opera to sing, the experimental music with its jagged and discordant harmony was painful to hear! The riots and public outrage made headline news. Strauss always caused a sensation!

After *Elektra*, Strauss appeared to enter a new phase. He began working with a different collaborator, and his works settled down to become well liked but not necessarily loved.

During this time, the Nazis came into power. Strauss, famous and living in Germany, needed to either align himself with them or leave the country. He was appointed their Music Director without even being consulted. He decided to keep the job but to remain **apolitical** (politically neutral). The Nazis didn't like him, but they wanted him for the prestige they thought he provided. For his part, he did not seem to share their political views, but he did nothing to oppose their regime, either. Like so many, he preferred to look the other way. Perhaps part of the reason for keeping a position of this sort was to help protect his daughter-in-law, who was Jewish. He did, in fact, protect her from much harassment on at least a few occasions.

Richard Strauss was a bridge between the late Romantics and the Modern composers, embracing the tone poem form instead of the Classical symphonic form and employing harsh dissonances in his later works. He followed in the footsteps of Richard Wagner and was one of the last of the late-Romantic composers.

You might wonder what sort of religion Strauss practiced. Well, it doesn't appear from what we can see that he had any kind of relationship with the Lord Jesus Christ. In fact, he once said this in reference to the Eastern European composer **Gustav Mahler**, "Mahler is always seeking Redemption. I don't know what I am supposed to be redeemed from." For all we know, that statement may sum up his spiritual life.

Richard Strauss *Student Review*

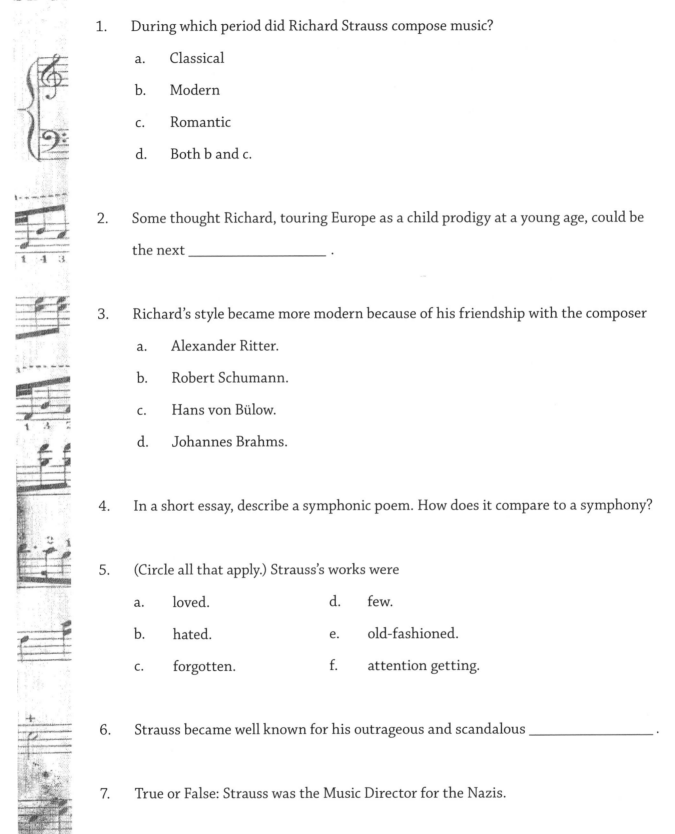

1. During which period did Richard Strauss compose music?

    a.   Classical

    b.   Modern

    c.   Romantic

    d.   Both b and c.

2. Some thought Richard, touring Europe as a child prodigy at a young age, could be the next _____ .

3. Richard's style became more modern because of his friendship with the composer

    a.   Alexander Ritter.

    b.   Robert Schumann.

    c.   Hans von Bülow.

    d.   Johannes Brahms.

4. In a short essay, describe a symphonic poem. How does it compare to a symphony?

5. (Circle all that apply.) Strauss's works were

    a.   loved.   d.   few.

    b.   hated.   e.   old-fashioned.

    c.   forgotten.   f.   attention getting.

6. Strauss became well known for his outrageous and scandalous _____ .

7. True or False: Strauss was the Music Director for the Nazis.

8. For which of the following works of literature did Strauss write music?

   a. *Don Quixote*

   b. *Don Juan*

   c. *Macbeth*

   d. All of the above.

9. Unlike the other musicians we've studied, Strauss was a good _____, known for driving a hard bargain.

10. True or False: Strauss made headline news with his controversial opera *Salome*.

The Contemporary Period

1910 to Present

The **Contemporary period** of music was ushered in by three significant events that took place during the end of the nineteenth century and the beginning of the twentieth century. First, a scientist named Charles Darwin developed some theories that led people to believe that what the Bible says about Creation isn't true. He wrote a book called *On the Origin of Species*, which suggested that the world, and its animals and people, might have evolved from one species to another. Until then, most people in Western civilization believed that God had created the world and everything in it. It was a big shock to their faith to even consider the idea that something else could have happened. Unfortunately, evolution is a theory that is still popular today. The second thing that happened is that a man named Sigmund Freud began to study people's behavior. He came to the conclusion that people are guided by their subconscious thoughts. He said that people didn't know why they did things and that they couldn't control their behavior. This was very shocking, because suddenly people began to think that maybe they weren't responsible for things they did or might not be able to control the things they did. The third thing that happened is that Albert Einstein, a brilliant mathematician, came up with the Theory of Relativity. This theory is very complicated and hard to understand, and most of us who are not great scientists don't even have to think about it. But it was an important discovery, and people who didn't understand it decided that it meant that everything is relative—that nothing is absolute, or absolutely true. Again, this stunned the world, because until that time, all people had thought that there were things that they could definitely count on. Now they thought that might not be true.

Therefore, during the twentieth century, people, especially artists and musicians, began to react to these ideas. Because suddenly it seemed that many things people had counted on might not be true, they slowly stopped paying attention to the rules that had been established.

In music, this meant that they started composing some strange pieces. Instead of using the regular major and minor scales that had been used for centuries, musicians made up new scales. They gave up composing melody and tried writing music without it!

You might wonder how someone could do that, but one musician, named **Arnold Schoenberg**, invented a musical form commonly known as serialism. In **serialism**, each note is assigned a numerical value and, instead of following a melody, the music is based on mathematical formulas! This led many other composers to do other unique things.

157

In the 1960s, a man named **John Cage** took music to another level. Not only did he leave the idea of melody, but he abandoned the idea of music using traditional instruments. He wrote a famous piece called *4'33"*. This piece is unique because it's different every time you hear it. It begins at a certain time and ends 4 minutes and 33 seconds later, and it consists of whatever sounds are heard during that period of time, perhaps outside traffic, the shuffling of someone's feet, birds singing, or someone coughing. It was certainly a very different idea for music!

It is often said that the Romantic era has extended through the twentieth century. This is because not everyone during this time experimented with the new type of contemporary music that completely abandoned traditional musical ideas that included melody and harmony. So much of the music during the twentieth century was written in a developing Romantic style. The composers that we will be learning about during this period fall in the latter category—although their sounds may be new and different, you will still recognize melody and harmony in their work.

As believers in Christ, we know that although people may come up with new theories such as we learned about at the beginning of this chapter, God's Word is true and unchanging. We know that He did create the world, and everything in it, out of nothing. We know that we are responsible for our actions and that although we have a sinful nature, God can save us from our sin through Jesus's work on the cross. Then, He lives in our hearts and helps us to resist temptation. We also know that although there may be parts about our physical world that are relative, His Word, His laws, and His love are always true and unchanging. It is comforting to know that although some people are easily influenced and may react to new thoughts in radical ways (writing music that is hard to understand and appreciate), many continue to believe in the world as God's Word tells us He created it. Those who recognize and appreciate the natural laws and order that God created continue to write music that we can appreciate and enjoy.

The Contemporary Period *Note-taking Pages*

The Contemporary period took place between the years _____ and the _____ .

Three important events happened during this era:

Who	What	Why It's Important
1. Darwin	Wrote _____ _____	People thought maybe _____ was not the creator.
2. Freud	Studied _____ _____	People thought maybe they couldn't _____ their behavior.
3. Einstein	Theory of _____	People thought maybe nothing was absolutely _____ .

During the twentieth century, composers made up _____ _____ .

They tried writing music without _____ .

Serialism

• Invented by Arnold _____

• Each note is assigned a _____ _____

• Music is based on mathematical _____

John Cage wrote a piece called _____ . He did not use traditional _____ .

Much of the music in the twentieth century is still written in the _____ style.

Although man may come up with new _____ , God's Word is _____

and _____ .

Scott *Joplin*

b. 1867 or 1868[1] d. 1917

Scott Joplin, the first African American composer in this study, was born sometime between July 1867 and January 1868[1] in Texas into a musical family. Information about Scott's childhood and teen years is very sketchy and poorly documented. His father was a former slave. His mother cleaned homes and supported his love of music. There is a plausible anecdote that young Scott gained access to a piano in a home where his mother worked. He taught himself the rudiments of music, and by age 7 he was so good that a local German immigrant musician offered him free piano lessons and taught him theory and an appreciation of European music. He also introduced Scott to composers such as **Bach**, **Mozart**, and **Beethoven**.

While he was still a young child, his family left the farm on which his father worked as a laborer. They moved to the newly established town of Texarkana (which straddles the Texas-Arkansas border).

In the 1880s, the teenaged Joplin lived for a while in Sedalia, Missouri, where he attended an African American high school. Unconfirmed anecdotes tell of his starting a musical career in the 1880s and then traveling to St. Louis.

During the summer of 1891, Joplin moved back to Texarkana, where he worked with a minstrel troupe. In 1893, he was in Chicago at the World's Fair, leading a band and playing the cornet. After the fair, he returned to Sedalia and played with a local ensemble of black musicians. After playing with this band for only about a year, he formed his own band. He also attended music classes at an African American college.

Joplin played a type of rhythmic piano music called ragtime. **Ragtime**, defined as "syncopated piano music," is a unique type of music that was popular from 1899 to 1918. It is the music that brought in the Jazz Era, although it's quite different from jazz itself. In it, piano players try to copy fast banjo solos with **syncopated** (stress on a normally unstressed beat) rhythm with one hand and strong, steady beats with the other hand. It isn't like the jazz we hear today. Joplin became the most famous ragtime pianist and composer ever.

Joplin traveled with his music; he also gave music lessons and worked on composing. His first published piano rag was entitled "Original Rags." However, the piano rag that Joplin is most

famous for is "Maple Leaf Rag," which sold hundreds of thousands of copies by 1909 and earned Joplin a steady income for the rest of his life.

Right on the heels of the publication of the "Maple Leaf Rag," Joplin completed *The Ragtime Dance*, a stage work for dancers, with a singing narrator. This ballet was unique in that during the show, narrators told the audience the types of dances being performed. A group of talented young locals from the Black 400 Club performed the work in Sedalia in 1899.

Most people in Joplin's time didn't consider ragtime music an art. Many people disapproved of it. This was extremely frustrating to Joplin, because as an African American, he wanted to write classical compositions that would increase respect for his race. In addition to his rags, he also wrote marches, waltzes, and two operas, but prejudiced music critics who wouldn't recognize his hard work and talent dismissed his music.

In 1901, he married his first wife, Belle. Early in 1903, he filed a copyright application for an opera, *A Guest of Honor*. Newspapers of the time disclosed that the opera was about the African American leader Booker T. Washington's dinner at President Roosevelt's White House in 1901. This was a controversial event for many white people, but, naturally, African Americans were honored. Joplin paid tribute to Roosevelt with his piano rag "A Strenuous Life" and later tried to celebrate the event with the opera *A Guest of Honor*.

He formed a large opera company and began a tour. Early on, someone stole the box office receipts, ruining the company's financial position. The tour ended with Joplin unable to meet his payroll or to pay for the company's bills at a boardinghouse. His possessions, including the music from the opera, were confiscated. Sadly, the music was never recovered.

In June, his marriage to Belle having ended, Joplin returned to Arkansas and married Freddie Alexander in Little Rock. The couple traveled by train to Sedalia, stopping at towns along the way so that Joplin could give concerts. Early in July, they arrived in Sedalia. Freddie developed a cold that worsened, and she died at the age of 20—just 10 weeks after their marriage.

Joplin's admirers describe him as intelligent, mannerly, and articulate. He was also a quiet, modest man who was generous with his time, assisting and instructing younger musicians. All his life he had an intense belief in the importance of education.

When Joplin moved to New York City in 1909, he wrote his second opera, *Treemonisha*. He was so passionate about it that when he couldn't find a publisher, he attempted to publish it himself. He trained musicians to perform it and wrote a piano-only version so that if audiences heard it and liked it, they might give him money to produce this huge project. The opera was important to music history because it was the first example of popular music combined with classical music in a classical music form. Unfortunately, Joplin was not able to get *Treemonisha* published while he was alive.

In 1913, Joplin, along with his new wife, Lottie, began his own music publishing company. During the next two years, he composed several new works, including rags and a musical. Sadly, he became ill with a disease that caused him to lose his mental abilities. He spent the last six months of his life in an "Insane Asylum", where he died in 1917.

Throughout his musical career, Joplin faced an audience that wasn't quite ready to truly appreciate his compositions. Ragtime was popular for less than 20 years, until 1918, when jazz and blues took over. Fortunately for Joplin's reputation, there was a ragtime revival in the 1960s and 1970s. The year 1970 marked the first performance of *Treemonisha* on Broadway. The film *The Sting* also featured his music. These events brought Joplin's music to the public's awareness and it quickly became incredibly popular! In piano recitals and rock concerts, the public universally loved ragtime music. Joplin would have been so pleased.

Although he was somewhat underappreciated during his lifetime, Joplin is an inspiration. Despite the prejudices he endured, he continued to compose great music. His publisher John Stark said at his funeral, "Here is the genius whose spirit was filtered through thousands of cheap songs and vain imitations." At that time, of course, no one realized that Joplin would someday rank as one of America's finest composers. In 1976, he was awarded the Pulitzer Prize for his contributions to American music.

Teacher Note
[1] His exact birth date is unknown.

1. (Circle all that apply.) Scott Joplin lived in which of the following towns during his lifetime?

    a.   Texarkana

    b.   New Orleans

    c.   New York City

    d.   Pittsburgh

2. By age _____ , Joplin was taking piano lessons from a German immigrant.

3. For what style of music is Scott Joplin famous? _____

4. Ragtime music can be described as: _____ _____ _____ .

5. True or False: Ragtime is the style of music that led to today's rock music.

6. Joplin's most famous rag is called _____ _____ _____ .

7. (Circle all that are true.) Scott Joplin wrote

    a.   waltzes.

    b.   opera.

    c.   a ballet.

    d.   a requiem.

    e.   marches.

8. One of the reasons that Joplin's work was not respected as art during his lifetime was probably because:

9. *Treemonisha*, Joplin's second opera, was performed for the first time in what year?

    _____

10. True or False: Joplin was awarded a Pulitzer Prize in 1976 for his contributions to American music.

Charles *Ives*

b. 1874 d. 1954

Charles Ives grew up in Connecticut, the son of George Ives, the town band director. Charles's father had served as the youngest bandmaster in the U.S. Army during the American Civil War. (In fact, his band had been called the best band in the army.) Charles received much of his musical education from his father, who felt that "man as a rule didn't use the faculties that the Creator had given him hard enough." As a result of this belief, his music lessons were quite unusual, stretching Charles's musical abilities. These lessons included having Charles sing "Swanee River" in the key of E-flat while he accompanied him in C Major. Always stretching musical convention, George Ives experimented with the use of quarter tones—tones that exist midway between those we are accustomed to hearing next to each other. George said:

"If the whole tones can be divided equally, why not half tones? That is, if one has twelve notes in an octave, why not more or less. If you can learn to like a consonance (so called) why not a dissonance (so called)? If the piano can be tuned out of tune to make it more practicable (that is, imperfect intervals), why can't the ear learn a hundred other intervals if it wants to try?"

To experiment with these smaller intervals, George used such "instruments" as a slide cornet, glasses (filled with water), a retuned piano, and violin strings stretched over a clothespress. This experimentation with music not only influenced his son Charles's interest in music, but it also affected his later compositions.

George Ives also gave Charles a unique perspective on music. Because George Ives had spent a lot of time with soldiers, singing sentimental tunes, and with communities where simple marches and camp songs were woven deep into the emotional fabric of the people, he believed that it was the importance of this emotion that surpassed the music itself. This may help explain why Charles Ives once wrote, "What has sound got to do with music!?" Amazingly, he was able to separate the intent of the composer, the passion of the performer, from the sound he heard. Charles had been thinking "out of the box" before he even started composing.

Besides Charles's close relationship with his father, not much is made of his youth. He did seem to be a musical prodigy, and his father taught him as much as he could before he sent him to someone else for piano lessons. Though his father thought he might become a concert pianist, Charles focused on the organ and began work as a church organist at the age of 14—the youngest salaried church organist in Connecticut. His father (the most influential musician in the region) was, needless to say, a major influence in his music and his life. Charles began composing at age 13—marches, simple tunes, and hymns. When he was 17, he wrote *Variations on "America,"* which became one of his more popular pieces.

Charles also excelled at sports. He was the captain of both the baseball and football teams at his high school; he pitched a winning ten-inning game against the Yale freshmen, and soon after he made the Yale football team. This love of sports appeared later in his notes for an unfinished composition: Giants vs. Cubs, August 1907, Polo Grounds.

In 1893, Charles went to New Haven to prepare for college. He entered Yale in 1894 and immediately became the organist at one of the most prestigious churches in town. His success at Yale was not so much in his studies as it was in his extracurricular life. Charles was a popular boy who could often be found playing at parties and theaters—sometimes sharing his own compositions. He was a prolific composer throughout his college years. But during Charles's freshman year, his father died suddenly. This was a great blow to Charles, and he missed him all his life.

In response to his father's earlier advice, Charles decided against a profession as a composer, feeling that the kind of music he wanted to write would not be popular to the general public or allow him to properly support a family. Instead, he went into the insurance business, where he became quite successful. His first job out of college was for Mutual Life Insurance Company of New York, where he earned $15 per week. He continued working as a church organist in churches in New York City, as well as in Connecticut and New Jersey. Composing continued to be a very serious hobby for him. He was right—his music was not popular, but he continued to write as his heart directed, without changing styles to fit conventional standards.

It's amazing that Ives was able to compose as much as he did during this period, because he also thrived in the insurance industry. In 1907, he formed Ives and Co. along with his friend Julian Myrick. This company, which became Ives and Myrick, was ultimately one of the largest agencies in the country. This same year, Ives suffered his first heart attack. No one is sure if these "heart attacks" were physical or emotional, but they continued to be a problem to him throughout his life.

In 1908, he married a nurse, Harmony Twitchell. She was the daughter of a prominent minister and the sister of a college friend. Though they had met 10 years earlier, the romance didn't flourish until later. They moved into their own place in New York City, which remained their primary residence, but they also kept a weekend home in Connecticut. Charles obviously found a soul mate in his wife. He once gratefully said this about Harmony, "She never told me to be good and write something nice that people would like."

After his first heart attack, he began to write a tremendous amount of music. In fact, much of his work was composed between 1907 and 1918. By 1917, Charles and Harmony had adopted a daughter, Edith. Charles had another new interest: working to support the American war effort (despite his earlier outspoken objection to the war). With the stress of parenthood, campaigning for war bonds, demands of both a full-time business and a rigorous musical life plus the disappointment of steady rejection from the music world, Ives's health collapsed. In October 1918, just before his forty-fourth birthday, he had a serious heart attack. Sadly, neither he nor his work ever completely recovered.

His composing ended entirely when in 1927, he told his wife, with tears in his eyes, "I can't seem to compose any more. I try and try and nothing comes out right." *Sunrise*, written in August 1926, turned out to be his final piece. Though he didn't compose anything new for the rest of his life, he did tweak and alter his other pieces until his death. In 1930, he resigned from his insurance company and spent the rest of his life fine-tuning his compositions and overseeing their editing, distribution, and performance. However, considering that he had composed only on weekends and evenings, Ives produced a substantial body of music over the course of his lifetime.

Ives's compositions are an eclectic group. They range from songs and hymns (inspired by his work as a church organist) to symphonies. He wrote some works in which he clearly stayed with traditional forms. Other pieces were entirely experimental. Eventually, he settled into his own style, merging both traditional forms and experimental ideas. He wrote one piano sonata that mimics the opening of **Beethoven's** Fifth Symphony and also contains a "cluster chord"—which the performer is supposed to play by hitting the keys with a 14¾-inch piece of wood!

Often when you listen to Ives's music, you can hear a common Ives technique—he borrowed themes or melodies from other musicians and worked them into his own compositions. For example, in the end of his Second Symphony he has fragments of "Columbia, the Gem of the Ocean," some barn fiddling, and **Stephen Foster's** "Camptown Races" all going on in different keys at once! He also continued his father's work by incorporating George's earlier experiments into his pieces. Some of these musical innovations are known as

- **polytonality** —music played in two different keys at the same time
- **microtones**—notes that fall between the notes that are on the piano
- **polyrhythm**— two different rhythms played at the same time

Ives will always be considered a pioneer in twentieth-century music, because these new techniques appeared in his music decades before any other composers used them.

The sounds he used were new to people's ears, and his music wasn't performed often. However, some influential musicians championed his cause, and even **Aaron Copland** performed his music, which began to receive great reviews in the 1930s and 1940s. When someone asked the famous composer **Igor Stravinsky** to give his definition of a musical

masterpiece, he said simply, "Decoration Day." (This is the second movement of a symphony entitled *New England Holidays*.) Ives received the Pulitzer Prize for his Third Symphony in 1947, 43 years after he had completed it! From that point on, Ives's music has become an important part of the American classical repertoire.

Ives the composer spoke a different language from the composers before him. Many consider him a symbol of daring, uncompromising, independent genius, years ahead of his time. Ives the person is hard to know. He was a private man; he only ever granted one newspaper interview, and he rarely attended events. He was brought up on Ralph Waldo Emerson and we're told he idolized the man and his philosophy of Transcendentalism. We have no evidence to suggest that he had a personal relationship with Christ. Ives died on May 19, 1954, in New York City.

Charles Ives *Student Review*

1. In what part of the United States did Ives live?

   a. Northwest (Oregon, North Dakota)

   b. South (Georgia, Alabama)

   c. Southwest (New Mexico, Texas)

   d. Northeast (Connecticut, New York)

2. Charles Ives received much of his musical education from _____ , who was the _____ .

3. Charles's music lessons with his father could be described as _____ .

4. Besides music, as a young man Ives enjoyed (circle all that apply):

   a. soccer.

   b. football.

   c. lacrosse.

   d. baseball.

5. What kind of industry did Charles work in as his career?

6. True or False: Ives lived in conflict with his wife, who wanted him to write a different kind of music.

7. What health problem did Ives have?

8. True or False: Ives's music was popular in his day.

9. What was a common technique of Ives?

    a. borrowing melodies from other composers

    b. borrowing themes from other composers

    c. incorporating his father's experiments

    d. All of the above.

10. What kind of prize did Ives receive for his Third Symphony?

    a. the Nobel Prize

    b. third place

    c. the Pulitzer Prize

    d. a new car

George *Gershwin*

b. 1898 d. 1937

George Gershwin holds a special place in the development of American music. He brought classical music to ordinary people by bringing together popular sounds and a classical format in the same piece of music. In addition, his life exemplified the "American dream."

George's parents were Russian Jewish immigrants who met and married in New York City. When George's father, Moishe Gershowitz, came through immigration in Ellis Island, he Americanized his last name, changing it to "Gershvin." George changed it further to the more American "Gershwin."

George was the second of four children in a family with no known musical heritage. As a child, George was fascinated by **ragtime** (a style of jazz) music, which was popular at the time, and by the **player pianos** (mechanically operated pianos), which often could be heard in his new neighborhood. When George was 12, his parents bought a piano for his older brother, Ira, expecting him to be the musician in the family. George quickly took it over and played it constantly, especially when the family had company.

His teacher, Charles Hambitzer, introduced him to a variety of different classical musicians—**Chopin**, **Debussy**, **Ravel**. . . . Among his favorite musicians were **Liszt** and an American composer of popular music, **Irving Berlin**. Hambitzer didn't care for George's great interest in popular music, but he did recognize his talent, saying, "I have a pupil who will make his mark in music if anybody will. The boy is a genius, without a doubt."

In 1914, when Gershwin was 16 years old, he quit school and began working for a music publisher on **Tin Pan Alley** (the theatrical section of Broadway in New York City that housed most publishers of popular songs). As a **song plugger** (a piano player employed by music stores in the early twentieth century to promote new music), he made only fifteen dollars a week. However, this meant playing the piano for a living, and with all this playing, he became very good! Soon, he toured the vaudeville circuit as a pianist and also as an accompanist for the popular singer Nora Bayes. All the while, he continued to compose.

His first song, "When You Want 'Em, You Can't Get 'Em," was published in 1916. Although this song was not very successful, later that year another of his songs was used in a Broadway show. **Al Jolson** heard Gershwin's song, "Swanee," and added it to his own show. It was an immediate success, and in 1918 more than two million records were sold! Gershwin earned more than $10,000 in **royalties** (money paid to an artist for each copy of his work sold in a year) just for that one song!

La, La Lucille is considered Gershwin's first musical. It ran for a hundred performances and received good reviews. He wrote music for a number of musicals in the early twenties. Then, in 1924, he wrote the music for the musical *Lady, Be Good!*, with lyrics by his brother Ira. This show included the now-classic songs "Oh, Lady Be Good!" and "Fascinating Rhythm." It also began a series of successful musicals by the George and Ira Gershwin team, including *Oh, Kay!*, *Funny Face*, *Girl Crazy*, and *Of Thee I Sing*.

Because of the success of the Gershwin musicals, the well-known band leader Paul Whiteman asked Gershwin to write a jazz piece for piano and orchestra to premiere at a future concert he was planning. Gershwin agreed—he wanted to write more classical music. He didn't think much more of it until his brother Ira showed him an article in a January 4, 1924, newspaper claiming that Gershwin was "at work on a Jazz concerto which would premiere in his concert February 12th at Aeolian Hall." This was news to Gershwin, who then put together his *Rhapsody in Blue* (named by Ira) in three weeks' time!

Supposedly, he was inspired by the regular rhythm of the train and other sounds he heard as he traveled to Boston. Having composed it so quickly, the written piano part still had gaping holes in it. Gershwin told Whiteman that when he conducted the orchestra, he should watch Gershwin during his solo parts and Gershwin would nod when the orchestra was supposed to come in again. Gershwin improvised these parts, or played them from memory, and didn't write them down until after the performance. The concert was a huge success! *Rhapsody in Blue*, which has become one of Gershwin's most famous pieces, opens with a **clarinet slide**[1]. Ironically, Gershwin did not write this himself—he had simply written a long scale. The slide was a joke by the clarinetist during a lengthy rehearsal. But Gershwin loved it and decided to include it.

Rhapsody in Blue was Gershwin's first classical piece. Not only did it inspire composers everywhere to try their hand at jazz, but it fused classical and jazz together, bringing the jazz style into more cultured musical arenas. Though he continued to write popular songs for movies and musicals, he also wrote more classical pieces throughout his short lifetime, including Piano Concerto in F (commissioned by the conductor of the New York Philharmonic), Three Preludes for Piano, *An American in Paris* (penned after he returned from a trip to Europe in 1928), and ultimately, the folk opera *Porgy and Bess*, about African American life. In fact, Gershwin was quite affected by African American music. DuBose Heyward, author of the book on which *Porgy and Bess* was based, told this story:

"The Gullah[2] Negro prides himself on what he calls 'shouting.' This is a complicated pattern beaten out by feet and hands as an accompaniment to the spirituals and is indubitably an African survival. I shall never forget the night when, at a Negro meeting on a remote sea-island, George started 'shouting' with them. And eventually to their huge delight stole the show from their champion 'shouter.' I think he is the only white man in America who could have done it."

George and Ira Gershwin went back and forth from California to New York, writing for both Broadway musicals and Hollywood movies. George struck up a great friendship with the composer **Arnold Schoenberg**, his Hollywood neighbor and tennis partner. Gershwin always felt that the technical skills of his composing were lacking. He asked Maurice Ravel, Schoenberg, and **Igor Stravinsky** for lessons. Ravel told him, "I would only make you a bad Ravel, and you're such a good Gershwin already." Another of these famous composers is said to have asked Gershwin how much money he made. When Gershwin answered, "Oh, I guess around a half million," the composer suggested, "How about you give me some lessons?"

In 1937, at the height of his career, Gershwin began to have serious headaches and seemed to smell burning rubber. While in Hollywood, he collapsed, fell into a coma, and died on July 11, 1937, of a large brain tumor. Though his life seems short, his contributions were tremendous and long-lasting. He combined previously separate genres—such as African American folk music and opera—breaking some traditional rules and bringing newfound creativity to American music.

Teacher Notes

[1]Clarinet slide: Rather than actually playing distinct notes, the clarinet can make a noise that starts at one pitch and ends at another higher or lower pitch, smoothly hitting every pitch in between.

[2]Gullah: A unique Creole language spoken on the coastal islands and adjacent mainland of South Carolina and Georgia. The "Gullah Negro" is probably so called because he descended from slaves from the country of Angola.

George Gershwin   *Student Review*

1. George Gershwin's parents were Jewish immigrants from what country? _____

2. Gershwin brought popular sounds and _____ format together in the same piece of music.

    a.   Romantic

    b.   Classical

    c.   Baroque

    d.   Medieval

3. What kind of music, popular in his time, fascinated Gershwin when he was a child?

    _____

4. Name an earlier classical musician whose music was introduced to Gershwin by his music teacher. _____

5. Who wrote the lyrics to George Gershwin's music? _____

6. Which of the following works began the Gershwins' series of successful musicals?

    a.   "When You Want 'Em, You Can't Get 'Em"

    b.   "Swanee"

    c.   *La, La Lucille*

    d.   *Lady, Be Good!*

7. What was Gershwin's first classical piece and one of his most famous?

   a. *Rhapsody in Blue*

   b. *An American in Paris*

   c. Piano Concerto in F

   d. *Of Thee I Sing*

8. *Rhapsody in Blue* fused classical and what other type of music together? _____

9. True or False: Gershwin's folk opera *Porgy and Bess* was about African American life.

10. True or False: Gershwin's life exemplified the "American dream."

Aaron *Copland*

b. 1900 d. 1990

Aaron Copland is often considered the voice of American music. In many of his most popular works, he borrowed melodies from hymns and popular American tunes. What he did with rhythms and harmonies was new to classical music. Aaron Copland was born on November 14, 1900, and grew up in Brooklyn, New York, the youngest of five children. The Brooklyn in which he grew up is very much the same as what is described in the book *A Tree Grows in Brooklyn*. His parents were Russian Jewish immigrants whose original name was Kaplan. For much of his life, Aaron thought that the family name had been Anglicized when the family came through Ellis Island, but he later learned that his father had changed it while they were still in Europe. Upon arriving in America, some of the aunts and uncles continued with the new spelling, while others kept the traditional "Kaplan."

Aaron's parents owned a department store, and the family lived in the three floors above the store. Neither of his parents was particularly musical, but they provided music lessons for several of the older children. His older sister taught Aaron everything she knew in six months and then recommended that he receive lessons from a more qualified teacher. However, Aaron's father didn't want to pay for music lessons anymore. After six years of begging, he finally relented, and Aaron began private piano lessons at the age of 13. By the time he was 15, he knew he wanted to become a composer.

Aaron Copland never went to college. Instead, he started taking the subway into Manhattan to take theory and composition lessons with Rubin Goldmark, a well-known teacher (one of his teachers was **Dvořák**) who had also taught **George Gershwin**. Goldmark was so highly regarded that later, when the Juilliard School of Music opened, Goldmark became the head of the Theory and Composition Department.

From Goldmark, Copland learned a tremendous amount about the structure of classical music. However, Goldmark was a traditional musician, and Copland was interested in learning the newer techniques. One story relates that once Goldmark found Copland "looking at the score of **Ives's** *Concord Sonata* and warned him not to contaminate himself with such things."

Copland finally decided to save up money to travel to Paris and learn more about composition there. In 1921, he arrived at the New School for Americans at Fontainebleau. Copland happened

to hear a class given by Nadia Boulanger. Boulanger left a deep impression on him, and he studied with her privately for three years. This was the beginning of many American would-be composers traveling to Europe to receive training from Boulanger. At that time, Paris was home to many creative souls, including the composers **Igor Stravinsky** (whose music was a great influence on him), **Maurice Ravel**, and **Sergei Prokofiev**, as well as the artist Pablo Picasso, and the writers Ernest Hemingway, Gertrude Stein, and James Joyce. This intellectual atmosphere stimulated Copland's creativity. When his money ran out in 1924, he decided it was time to go home. Boulanger showed her confidence in his abilities by commissioning a piece by him for organ and orchestra. During that year, Copland wrote his Symphony for Organ and Orchestra, which was premiered by the New York Symphony Orchestra.

Copland said, "At the conclusion, there was considerable applause, when Mr. Damrosch (the conductor) pointed to the upper box where I was seated, I rose to bow. As things quieted down, Mr. Damrosch advanced to the footlights and to everyone's surprise, addressed the audience. 'Ladies and Gentlemen,' he began, 'I am sure you will agree that if a gifted young man can write a symphony like this at twenty-three,' and here he paused dramatically, leaving the audience to expect a proclamation of a new musical genius—then continued, 'within five years he will be ready to commit murder.'" Despite this bizarre remark publicly introducing him to New York's music-loving audience, he became tremendously popular.

Next, Serge Koussevitsky, conductor of the Boston Symphony Orchestra, said he felt Copland could "create an authentic musical language." He commissioned Copland to write a score. Still, Copland struggled to make ends meet. He was given the Guggenheim Fellowship and used it to write his Piano Concerto, which was introduced by Koussevitsky with Copland as the piano soloist. His mother said that the proudest moment of her life was watching him perform the Piano Concerto with the Boston Symphony.

Copland's musical career can be divided into four periods. The first was a jazzy phase—between 1925 and 1929. Copland had been greatly influenced by jazz when he was in Paris, as jazz was sweeping Europe then. His second phase began during the Great Depression, when his work became more dissonant and stark. His music was also affected by the popularity of the radio and the phonograph. He said, "It seemed to me that we composers were in danger of working in a vacuum. Moreover, an entirely new public for music had grown up around the radio and the phonograph. It made no sense to ignore them and continue writing as if they did not exist. I felt it was worth the effort to see if I couldn't say what I had to say in the simplest possible terms." His third phase was his most popular, which began around 1936. This was his Americana phase, when he wrote the ballet, *Appalachian Spring*, (which won a Pulitzer Prize for composition); the ballet *Billy the Kid*, and *Fanfare for the Common Man*. *Fanfare* was written at the request of the conductor of the Cincinnati Symphony Orchestra. Later, it was used to open many Democratic National Conventions, and Copland also used it as the main theme in the fourth movement of his Third Symphony.

In the forties, Hollywood began to call him, wanting him to write movie scores. Writing movie music wasn't very highly regarded, but Copland took it very seriously. This was obvious when his score for *The Heiress* (1949) won an Academy Award. He also wrote the score for *The Red Pony*, the film version of a novel by John Steinbeck.

During this period, he also wrote music in the Latin American style. He wasn't sure what audiences would think of it, but it was well received. Copland always kept the audience in mind. He said, "It is not a question of giving an audience what it wants, but of *not* giving it more than you can reasonably expect it to digest. It is difficult to set those limits." Surely, this attitude helped to make his music so enjoyable.

Copland's fourth and final composing phase began in the fifties, when he turned to a style which was popular with classical composers at that time. This style was known as serialism, and although many composers wrote serialist music, it was not especially popular with the public. These pieces weren't well received. By the sixties, Copland felt that he'd lost his creative streak. This was when he began a successful period of conducting—traveling the world and conducting primarily his own works.

As is common with artists, Copland's political views were quite liberal. It was said that he defended the Communist Party USA in 1936. As a result, he was investigated by the FBI in the 1950s and was "blacklisted."[1] In 1953, he was called before Congress during the McCarthy hearings. His piece *Lincoln Portrait* was supposed to be played in 1953 at an inaugural concert for President Eisenhower. However, because of the concern over possible anti-American leanings, it was withdrawn from the concert. Copland maintained his Americanism throughout this time, and it was never proved that he had been a communist.

Despite his great popularity, Copland was a simple man. With a distinctive face—a prominent nose and protruding overbite—he has been called "stunningly ugly" and "endearingly homely." Unlike many composers we have studied, he was very even-tempered and didn't show a lot of emotion. He dressed simply. His good friend **Leonard Bernstein** said, "Can you imagine Aaron wearing a ring, a jeweled cufflink? It's unheard of! Or wearing some kind of leisure suit? Plain, plain, plain! It goes with *Appalachian Spring* and *Our Town*, which we think of as a self-portrait of Aaron. No conspicuous consumption."

A lover of animals, he also enjoyed playing tennis. He never married, though he had many friends. He was close to his siblings and kept in touch with many of his cousins. He wrote and received a lot of letters. Copland was generally a night owl. He explained this by saying, "music is largely the product of the emotions, and I can't get emotional early in the day." Copland's life ended on December 2, 1990, after a battle with Alzheimer's disease. He left America with a rich legacy of beautiful music.

[1]Blacklist: A list of persons who are disapproved of, or who are to be boycotted.

1. Aaron Copland grew up in

   a. Vienna, Austria.

   b. London, England.

   c. Brooklyn, New York.

   d. Atlanta, Georgia.

2. Copland's parents were _____ immigrants.

3. As a child, Copland took music lessons from

   a. his father.

   b. his older sister.

   c. his uncle.

   d. a close family friend.

4. True or False: Copland graduated from the Juilliard School of Music.

5. Copland traveled to _____ to study music with Nadia Boulanger.

6. True or False: As a young composer, Copland was very popular.

7. Copland's most popular phase of music was his _____ phase.

8. Copland wrote all of the following styles of music except

   a. classical.

   b. Latin American.

   c. opera.

   d. jazz.

9. Copland's political views can be described as _____ .

10. Besides music, Copland enjoyed (circle all that apply):

    a. tennis.

    b. baseball.

    c. animals.

    d. hiking.

John *Williams*

b. 1932

Although you may never have heard of **John Williams**, you are probably very familiar with his music! Williams has written the music for many of the most famous movies in the last four decades. These movies include *Jaws*, *E.T.: The Extra-Terrestrial*, *Raiders of the Lost Ark*, *Hook*, all of the *Star Wars* films, the *Home Alone* movies, as well as the first three *Harry Potter* movies—more than a hundred movies altogether!

Because John Williams is still alive at the time of this writing, we have an opportunity to learn more about him and his creative process than other composers we have studied. He has given quite a few interviews throughout his career, and his career has been thoroughly documented.

John Towner Williams was born in the Flushing section of Queens, New York, on February 8, 1932. He is the oldest of four children born to Esther and Johnny Williams. Johnny Williams was a jazz drummer and percussionist with CBS Radio and with ABC's *Hit Parade*. In 1948, the family moved to Los Angeles so that the father could work with film studio orchestras.

His son John began to play the piano at age 7. In addition to the piano, John learned to play the trombone, trumpet, and clarinet. At the age of 15, he decided to become a concert pianist, but while he played for the high school band, he tried his hand at arranging and composing. This must have appealed to him, because after he graduated from North Hollywood High School in 1950, he took courses in piano, composition, and arranging, writing his first serious work at the age of 19.

In 1952, Williams was drafted into the Air Force, where he was able to continue honing his musical skills by conducting and arranging music for service bands. In 1954, after completing his service duties, he studied at the famous Juilliard School of Music in New York City. During this time, he supported himself by playing jazz piano in nightclubs. After only a year, he returned to Los Angeles, where he worked as a pianist in the Twentieth Century-Fox orchestra, under the direction of Alfred Newman. Newman recognized Williams's talent in **orchestration** (writing music for orchestra, or taking music that's been written and adapting it so that all instruments in an orchestra have parts to play) and began having him

orchestrate his scores. He did orchestrating with other Golden Age composers, developing some deep friendships, particularly with **Bernard Herrmann**. This relationship lasted until Herrmann's death in 1975. In the late fifties, Williams began writing music for television. Soon, scores were sent directly to him, and he began to be asked to compose music for television shows, which he did throughout the sixties.

Williams's first major film composition was for the B movie *Daddy-O* in 1958, and his first screen credit came two years later in *Because They're Young*. In 1969, he wrote a film score for a movie called *The Reivers*, which is based on a book written by the well-known author William Faulkner. (Songs used in a film are known as the film's **soundtrack**, while the orchestral music composed for a film is a **film score**.) By the 1970s, John Williams had become a respected composer in Hollywood and was asked to work with the famous director Alfred Hitchcock on his movie *Family Plot* (1976). He wasn't sure he should take the assignment due to some tension between Hitchcock and Williams's good friend Herrmann. However, Herrmann urged him to take the job, pointing out that it would be an excellent experience.

In 1971, the score he had adapted for *Fiddler on the Roof* won him his first Oscar. But this would not be his only one, for just a few years later, something momentous happened. Williams recalls, "I met Steven [Spielberg] at Universal Studios in 1973. I'd been working there for six or seven years doing all manner of television programs, and one of the chief executives at Universal somehow got introduced to this kid off the street who convinced the studio that he was talented and deserved to do something big." The vice president of Universal called Williams, suggesting that he work with Spielberg, an inexperienced director, on his new movie *Sugarland Express*. Williams says, "I agreed to have lunch with him. He looked like he was about 16, but he was then, as he is now, dazzlingly brilliant and wonderfully appealing as a person." They worked together on this first movie and then on a series of "disaster" movies, including *Jaws*, *The Towering Inferno*, and *The Poseidon Adventure*. These were very successful, and the film score to *Jaws* earned him his first Oscar for music that was originally his. His relationship with Spielberg turned out to be another long-lasting friendship. Williams notes, "Here we are thirty-two years later. We're inseparable, and it's been a privilege to be at his side all these years."

Spielberg introduced Williams to the young George Lucas, who was looking for someone to put music to his *Star Wars* idea. As Lucas and Williams discussed the project, they decided to use a full symphonic orchestra. The classic, sweeping themes of heroism and good vs. evil "bring us in the direction of a symphony orchestra rather than a group of synthesizers or computers that might produce the spacey, otherworldly sounds you might expect," Williams explains. And this epic sound—reminiscent of movies of the 1930s scored by **Erich Wolfgang Korngold**, required movies to be fully scored. The original *Star Wars* movie has music through more than two thirds of the film. Williams claims, "Usually scenes will require, because of the style, some kind of orchestral accompaniment. And that's a happy assignment for a composer, because it will mean that you can have a large canvas to work on."

If Williams wasn't famous before *Star Wars*, he certainly was after his third Oscar, which he received in 1977 for the first movie of this series. That same year, he was also nominated for his music for *Close Encounters of the Third Kind*.

Williams is amazingly loyal to his directors and producers. He has scored all of Spielberg's films except *The Color Purple*, as well as George Lucas's major works and several Oliver Stone films. Because of this loyalty, Williams has proved to be a master at scoring sequels—for he has done scores for many movie series. One reason for his success is his technique of assigning musical themes to certain characters and ideas. Williams claims, "It isn't anything new, because it's been done for centuries in operas and also in film, as a way of connecting through a melodic fragment or a full melody in the audience's mind, making a connection between that and a character." Some examples of these themes are the theme for Yoda, and for "The Imperial March"—used for Darth Vader's character. Williams uses these themes to connect one movie to the next, reminding viewers of what they've already seen. However, the reverse chronology of the *Star Wars* films provided Williams with a unique opportunity—because the series, as a whole, is the story of the development of Anakin Skywalker, aka Darth Vader. Says Williams, "I wanted to create a theme for the boy Anakin and within it try, just for fun, . . . to suggest Darth Vader's Imperial March, and begin to put the pieces into something youthful and hopeful and potential, in a positive way." Film music critic Royal Brown points out, "That's quite ingenious. I mean, he's basically giving you a piece of information, just by the music alone, and then, finally, the film catches up with it, the narrative catches up with it."

In 1974, four years before his *Star Wars* success, Williams lost his wife, actress Barbara Ruick. They had been married for 18 years. She died of a cerebral hemorrhage. Together, they had three children, Joseph, Mark, and Jennifer. Williams wrote a violin concerto in memory of his late wife. He has been married since 1980 to Samantha Winslow.

Other non-movie music Williams has written includes seven concerti for flute, tuba (for the one-hundredth anniversary of the Boston Pops), clarinet (for Los Angeles Philharmonic principal clarinetist Michele Zukovsky in 1991), cello (for Yo-Yo Ma in 1994), bassoon (inspired by the poetry of Robert Graves and written for the principal bassoonist of the New York Philharmonic to celebrate the orchestra's one-hundred-and-fiftieth anniversary), and trumpet (for the one-hundredth anniversary of the Cleveland Orchestra). He wrote the symphony *Pops on the March* at the request of **Arthur Fiedler**, (the legendary conductor of the Boston Pops Orchestra); *Liberty Fanfare* for the one-hundredth anniversary of the Statue of Liberty; music for the Special Olympics; themes for four different Olympic Games (1984, 1988, 1996, and 2002 Winter); as well as music to commemorate the five-hundredth anniversary of the Columbus discovery of America; *Happy Birthday Variations* for the birthdays of Seiji Ozawa, Itzhak Perlman, and Yo-Yo Ma; "To Lenny! To Lenny" for **Leonard Bernstein's** seventieth birthday; and so much more!

In addition to all his composing, John Williams followed Arthur Fiedler as the conductor of the Boston Pops Orchestra, serving in this capacity from 1980 to 1993. He is also the artist-in-residence at Tanglewood, the summer home of the Boston Symphony Orchestra— and an outdoor concert facility.

As one of the most prolific composers we've studied, Williams continues to write music, and his music has continued to develop through the years. Where he originally showed the influence of Romantic composers such as **Gustav Mahler**, **Richard Strauss**, and **Richard Wagner**, he now exhibits the more modern influences of **Sergei Prokofiev** and **Dmitry Shostakovich**. Contributing to this development are the challenges of movies such as *Memoirs of a Geisha*, requiring him to become acquainted with Eastern musical instruments and styles and melding them with Western music so that the music is appealing to our ears and appropriate to the film.

Despite technological advances used by up-and-coming composers, who compose in front of a bank of computers while watching a DVD, Williams continues his tried-and-true method of turning back and forth from piano to movie screen. Though his method has not changed, his musical skill continues to mature, and his place in musical history is secure. He has single-handedly earned respect for a new genre of music—film music. In addition, he has exposed millions of people to the plethora of emotions and creative possibilities provided within the vast scope of classical music.

John Williams *Student Review*

1. John Williams's father earned his living as a _____ .

2. True or False: As a child, Williams lived on both the east and west coasts of the United States.

3. Williams continued to develop his musical skills while serving in the

   a. Army.

   b. Air Force.

   c. Marines.

   d. None of the above.

4. What is orchestration? _____

5. Orchestral music composed for a film is called a _____ _____.

6. Williams has received Oscars for his music in (circle all that are correct):

   a. *The Sound of Music.*

   b. *Fiddler on the Roof.*

   c. *Star Wars.*

   d. *Willie Wonka and the Chocolate Factory.*

7. George Lucas and John Williams decided to create an epic sound for the *Star Wars* movie by using _____ .

8. One character trait of John Williams is his

   a. loyalty.

   b. shyness.

   c. playfulness.

   d. honesty.

9. One technique that Williams uses is to assign _____ _____ to certain _____ ____ _____.

10. True or False: Besides writing music for movies, John Williams has also conducted the Boston Pops Orchestra.

Appendix

Composer Info-Card

Directions:

- Copy the Info-Card onto sturdy paper or front and back on card stock. (If paper, then cut it out and paste the front and back onto a 5" x 7" index card.)
- Cut the illustration of the composer out of the appendix section of the book and place it in the appropriate place on the front of the card. (Artistic students may prefer to color in or draw their own picture.)
- Fill in the name and the musical period on the front as well.
- The back of the card is fairly straightforward. Answer the questions, fill in the birth and death dates, and color in the country of origin on the map. Choose the Composer Info-Card with the correct map on the back for each composer. (For example, almost all of the composers we study were born in Europe, so you will predominantly use the Europe back. But Tchaikovsky was born in Russia and a number of the Contemporary period composers were born in the USA.)
- The trickiest part for some of the cards will be the question regarding the composer's faith. You may need to discuss this with the student or help him or her to decide if there are any clues available in the lesson.

Composer Info-Card Game and Review

- A simple but effective manner of reinforcing the chronology of composers is to mix up the cards on the table, picture side up. Ask the student to stack them in the order of the composers' birth dates. Students can then easily self-check by turning the cards over to check the dates to see if they were right.
- A quick review game is for the parent or one student to hold up the card, picture side facing outward to a student. The student states the name and then lists either the names of the composer's works or three facts.
- Cards should be brought out and reviewed often and can be
  - ~ stored in a 5" x 7" index box.
  - ~ wrapped in a rubber band.
  - ~ placed in envelopes.
  - ~ inserted into a Folderbook. (See Folderbook Directions.)

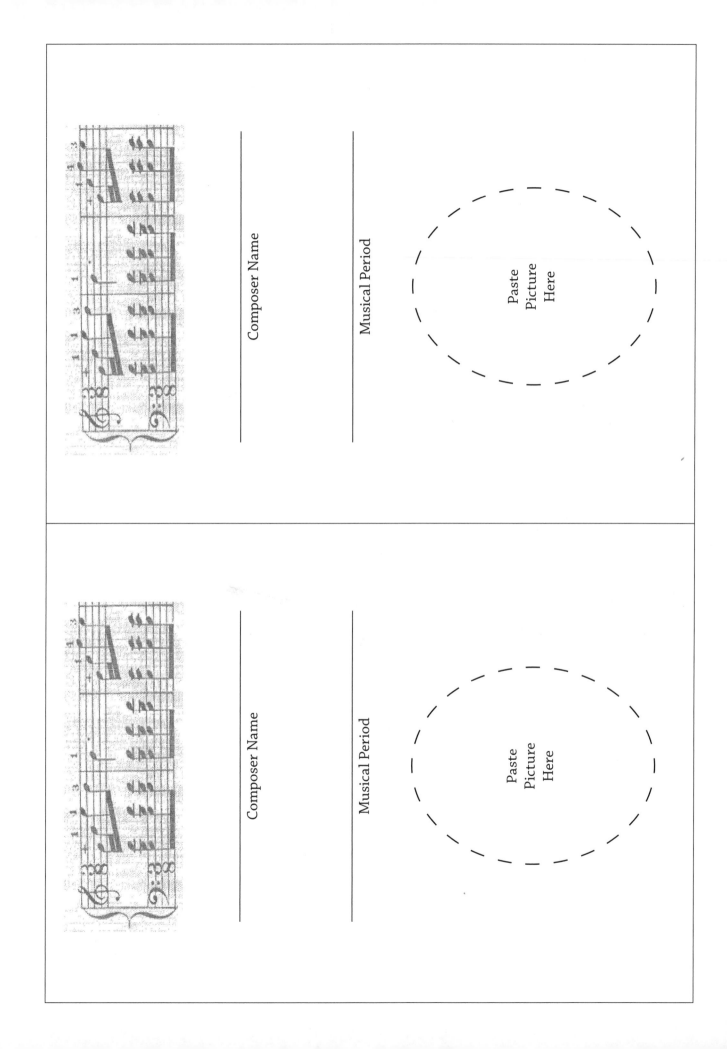

Composer's Name: _____

Lived from _____ to _____

In what country was he born? _____

List 3 facts you learned about him:

1. _____

2. _____

3. _____

Name at least two of his compositions:

1. _____

2. _____

What evidence do we have that he was or was not a Christian?
List as much as you can find.

_____

_____

_____

Composer's Name: _____

Lived from _____ to _____

In what country was he born? _____

List 3 facts you learned about him:

1. _____

2. _____

3. _____

Name at least two of his compositions:

1. _____

2. _____

What evidence do we have that he was or was not a Christian?
List as much as you can find.

_____

_____

_____

Composer's Name: _____

Lived from _____ to _____

In what country was he born? _____

List 3 facts you learned about him:

1. _____

_____

2. _____

_____

3. _____

Name at least two of his compositions:

1. _____

2. _____

What evidence do we have that he was or was not a Christian?
List as much as you can find.

_____

_____

_____

_____

Composer's Name: _____

Lived from _____ to _____

In what country was he born? _____

List 3 facts you learned about him:

1. _____

_____

2. _____

_____

3. _____

Name at least two of his compositions:

1. _____

2. _____

What evidence do we have that he was or was not a Christian?
List as much as you can find.

_____

_____

_____

_____

Composer's Name: _____

Lived from _____ to _____

In what country was he born? _____

List 3 facts you learned about him:

1. _____
   _____

2. _____
   _____

3. _____
   _____

Name at least two of his compositions:

1. _____

2. _____

What evidence do we have that he was or was not a Christian?
List as much as you can find.

_____
_____
_____
_____

Composer's Name: _____

Lived from _____ to _____

In what country was he born? _____

List 3 facts you learned about him:

1. _____
   _____

2. _____
   _____

3. _____
   _____

Name at least two of his compositions:

1. _____

2. _____

What evidence do we have that he was or was not a Christian?
List as much as you can find.

_____
_____
_____
_____

Bach

Beethoven

Brahms

Bruckner

Chopin

Copland

Debussy

Dvořák

Elgar

Fauré

Foster

Gershwin

Handel

Haydn

Ives

Joplin

Liszt

Mendelssohn

Mozart

Schubert

Schumann

Strauss

Tchaikovsky

Verdi

Vivaldi

Williams

Listening Suggestions

The Websites listed below were all active at the time of writing this Appendix. Unfortunately, there is no guarantee that they will still be active when this book is read. In that case, a search on a good Internet browser such as Google should locate other relevant sites.

Ancient Music to Music in the Middle Ages

Gregorian Chant:

Google some Gregorian chants and listen to them, or borrow a CD from the library. Listen to enough that you get a feel for their sound.

Or try these:

"Salve Regina"

http://www.youtube.com/watch?v=d5p_U8J0iRQ&feature=related

"Dies Irae"

http://www.youtube.com/watch?v=-fMHms5Cvsw

- How many musical lines (also called "voices") do you hear? (Do you hear "harmony" or only "melody"?)
- Is the tune catchy? (These are sung prayers—do they convey feelings?)
- Could you turn off the music and sing the melody? Why or why not?

Music in the Renaissance

Madrigals—secular songs for several voices—were very popular during this time. Listen to some and answer the following questions:

Piffaro (name of the ensemble)

http://www.youtube.com/watch?v=_tTRxffTC5Y&feature=related

"Sumer Is Icumen In"

http://www.youtube.com/watch?v=o4uzKTLmETQ&feature=related

- How is this music different from the chants you listened to?
- How many musical lines do you hear?
- When you stop the recording, can you sing back the melody?
- Are there instruments playing, too? If so—what kind of instruments do you think they are?

Antonio Vivaldi

Listen to Vivaldi's *Four Seasons:* "Spring I"

http://youtube.com/watch?v=St9wYu_WeAM

In his *Four Seasons*, Vivaldi wrote a poem to go with each season. Here is a translation of the poem he wrote to go with "Spring":

Joyful Spring has arrived,

The birds welcome it with their happy songs,

And the brooks in the gentle breezes

Flow with a sweet murmur.

The sky is covered with a black mantle,

Thunder and lightning announce a storm.

When they are silent, the birds

Take up again their harmonious songs.

And in the flower-rich meadow,

To the gentle murmur of leaves and plants

The goatherd sleeps his faithful dog at his side.

To the merry sounds of a rustic bagpipe

Nymphs and shepherds dance in their beloved spot

when Spring appears in its brilliance.

Listen to the music all the way through, first just relaxing and enjoying what you hear.
Listen again for the various elements (birds, brook, storm, dog, etc.) in his poem.
- Can you identify them?
- How do you think Vivaldi made it sound that way?
- What instrument is featured as a solo instrument?

Much music of the Baroque uses the harpsichord to support the orchestra. Here you can see the harpsichord (it is the one that has keys like a piano).
- Can you hear it also?
- How is the sound similar to the sound of a piano?
- How is the sound different from the sound of a piano?

"Gloria in Excelsis Deo" from the Gloria in D
http://www.youtube.com/watch?v=pR-eTkk8T50
Listen to the instrumental introduction.
- Do you hear how similar the introduction is to what the choir sings when they start singing?
- Note the use of silence—this recording is careful to preserve those moments of silence with absolute stillness. Listen to the way silence is used. We don't always have to have a lot of noise to be effective!

George Frideric Handel

Messiah is what we most often think of when we think of Handel. There are any number of recordings of it to be found. If you just want a taste of it, the "Hallelujah Chorus" is a must.

Here are some links:

http://youtube.com/watch?v=Up3TIPoVh-M&feature=related

http://youtube.com/watch?v=Abcgpn2UTV8&feature=related

- Does the music portray the majesty of the text?
- Can you hear the different voices as they have the melody/ important parts?
- Can you hear how the orchestra supports the singers?
- Can you hear the trumpets when they support the singers?
- When the trumpets have their own melody, there is a lot of music happening—can you hear it all?

Water Music, written for King George I, is an hour-long, joyous, majestic orchestral score that was widely performed during Handel's day.

Music for the Royal Fireworks was composed to celebrate the end of the War of the Austrian Succession and the signing of the Treaty of Aix-la-Chapelle. Watch and listen to ten minutes of it here: www.youtube.com/watch?v=I38Kw-oG0kE

- Do you hear how the music is overall joyful and buoyant, but there are quieter moments? Listen for the different sections of the orchestra to be featured: strings (violins, violas, cellos, and basses), woodwinds (flutes, clarinets, oboes, bassoons), brasses (trumpets, horns, and trombones) as well as the timpani.
- Does each section have its own individual sound?

Johann Sebastian Bach

There's a wonderful amount of music to listen to while studying Bach. But there are too many for you to do an in-depth job of listening over just one week. We suggest you listen to the following once, then choose three other pieces to get familiar with during the rest of the week.

Toccata and Fugue in D Minor

Here's one recording of it: http://www.youtube.com/watch?v=Zd_oIFy1mxM

- What does this make you think of?
- Where have you heard it before?
- What instrument is it played on?

As you listen this week, see if you can get so you can hum the parts beyond the first familiar lines.

Listen and watch!

- As you watch the hands change from one keyboard (manual) to the next, can you hear how the sound of the organ changes?

- At about 4:30, you will see the second person pushing in some of the knobs on the sides of the organ. Can you hear how the sound changes once more?
- At about 5:45, you will see what makes the organ such a different instrument. What does the camera focus on at this point?

The Well-Tempered Clavier
Book One—Prelude and Fugue in C Major
http://tinyurl.com/5zjbgd
Another recording—unusual to watch: http://www.youtube.com/watch?v=LSdxJXX_NQU
- Have you heard this before?
- What instrument is it played on?
- It may be interesting to compare both of the recordings. The music was written for the second instrument (harpsichord), but it is most frequently played on the first instrument (piano).

"Air on the G String" (originally part of Bach's Orchestral Suite no. 3 in D Major)
This particular version is played on original instruments.
http://www.youtube.com/watch?v=WZXM2eq46_s
- Can you hear some of the different instruments?
- Can you name them?
- Is one instrument a solo instrument?
- What instrument is playing the melody?

Mass in B Minor
Here is some of his choral music. The Mass is very famous. For now, listen to the "Kyrie Eleison I."
http://youtube.com/watch?v=dZvkSSVp3H8&feature=related
- You don't have to listen to the whole thing—just the vocal part at the beginning, before the instruments come in. Do you hear the "tension" in it? The way it kind of makes your stomach hurt—especially at the end of the word "Kyrie"—the "ay" part—if it stopped before the notes changed at the end of the word, you'd feel like it wasn't done—like if the notes didn't move, you'd kind of go crazy—the sound that creates that "not finished" feeling is called an "unresolved chord." When it moves and you feel that the musical sound or line is complete—that's called the "resolution." The way Bach stretches those unresolved chords is what creates the tension.
- Again, listen to the instruments—can you name some of them?

Brandenburg Concertos
Listen to any of them, really. They're so beautiful. Here's a link to Melissa's favorite:
http://www.youtube.com/watch?v=49IOKnhX0Sk
- What instruments do you see/hear?
- Can you identify them by sight? By sound?
- You can see the harpsichord in the video—can you hear it? Do you hear how it helps keep everyone together as they play?

- What's the main "theme," or tune, of the music? (Hint: You hear it right at the beginning.) See how Bach gives you a theme, strays from it a bit and gives you something else to listen to, then brings you back to it—you feel like you're home when you hear it again. How many times do you hear it in this particular concerto?

If you want to hear more, check out:
- More Brandenburg Concertos, especially no. 2—these are some of Melissa's favorites
- *Goldberg Variations*
- *Magnificat*
- Unaccompanied Cello Suites—more of Melissa's favorites

(Franz) Joseph Haydn

Symphony no. 94 (*Surprise Symphony*)—Second Movement.
http://www.classicsforkids.com/music/music_view.asp?id=26
- Listen for "surprises." Do you hear anything that would make people stay awake and pay attention?
- What happens at about 2:05? We have a theme that is similar to the beginning, but how is it different?
- What instruments are added to the strings to help create the "surprise"?

The Creation—Introduction.
http://youtube.com/watch?v=Q5RHDwdaanQ
- No. 1— Introduction: Remember that this is the work where Haydn says that "God speaks." And this is the very beginning—the Bible says, "In the beginning, God..."
- What did Haydn do with the music to make listeners think of God? When you listen, close your eyes—how does it make you feel?
- How did Haydn depict the "void" at the beginning of time?
- Did you hear when God began "creating"? What happened? (What instruments were added? How did the mood change?)

No. 14—"The Heavens Are Telling"
Same as above link—follows the Introduction.
- This is a choral piece from Haydn's *Creation*. It is quite famous, and it follows several numbers that depict God creating light, water, etc. It is worth knowing the main line of this work—the melody at the beginning.
- Listen for the whole chorus/orchestra and then moments when only the soloists are singing (three of them— they are "angels.")

Symphony no. 45 in F (*Farewell Symphony*)—Finale. Presto.

A Young Scholar's Guide to Composers

Do you remember reading about the *Farewell Symphony*? This is the Finale in which orchestra members leave. Can you hear the different instruments stop playing? How does it end? Wouldn't it be fun to SEE this music performed? This YouTube link gives you a little taste.

http://youtube.com/watch?v=PP89Av0fdS4

- As the orchestra instruments are done, they turn out their stand lights—in the original performance, they blew out their candles. Do you hear how the music gets softer as more instruments quit playing?

Wolfgang Amadeus Mozart

Mozart wrote A LOT of music. And much of it is famous or recognizable. I (Melissa) love Mozart, so it's hard to choose. His operas are quite famous, and his choral music, and his piano sonatas...you see why this has been difficult. I've given a lot of listening suggestions. Please read that word again— suggestions. They are not required listening. If you're not interested in listening to everything, stick with the selections with asterisks.

Someone's going to ask about the K numbers. I'll beat you to it. The K numbers came about in 1862, when a man named Ludwig von Köchel (pronounced Kerchel) decided to organize and number Mozart's compositions. The numbering system is intended to be chronological, though as historians have learned more about Mozart, they've found that it isn't quite. At any rate, because of Mr. Köchel, each composition has a K number, and that's often how his works are distinguished from one another.

We'll start with opera:
Marriage of Figaro
"Sull Aria"
http://www.youtube.com/watch?v=BLtqZewjwgA&mode=related&search=

- Here you are listening in on a conversation between the two ladies— listen to hear the differences and similarities between the two voices.
- Do you hear how the oboe occasionally takes up the melody, giving the voices a small break?

*"Voi che sapete"
http://www.youtube.com/watch?v=KwrgrSoAVdc

- Listen to the beginning 43 seconds of this clip: Notice that the accompaniment is by harpsichord and not orchestra—and the accompaniment is minimal. This is called "recitative."
- "Voi Che Sapete" begins after 43 seconds and you hear the entrance of the orchestra and the "aria," or solo singing.
- (In opera, most of the action happens quickly in the recitative sections, things come to a standstill during the arias so that the soloists may flex their voices and the composer can use all of the resources of the orchestra as well as the singers.)

Now some piano...
*Sonata no. 16—K. 545.

Appendix: Listening Suggestions

http://www.youtube.com/watch?v=8NNvsYhuErk

- Listen as the melody gets passed between the right hand and the left hand. Can you hear how the top part and the bottom part imitate each other?
- Listen for crescendos (music getting louder) and diminuendos (music getting softer) in this piece. Before the "pianoforte" was invented, it was difficult to make things gradually louder or softer. Mozart took advantage of this new instrument's ability.

More opera...
The Magic Flute
"The Queen of the Night Aria"—This is VERY famous.
PREVIEW THIS, PLEASE! Costuming will be questionable in some homes, and it's a bit like showing only the scene in *Snow White* where the queen poisons Snow White. So—if you don't want your students watching it, this is still the best I've found. You might want to have them sit where they can't see it but can still listen to it.
Here's the scoop: The deranged Queen commands her daughter Pamina to slay her father, Sarastro. Mandy Watsham as the Queen. Pamela Hay as Pamina.

The aria itself starts at about 2:08—you can fast-forward until then. Up to that point, it's all German dialogue.
http://www.youtube.com/watch?v=DvuKxL4LOqc&mode=related&search=

- Listen for the unusual effects that the soloist is able to perform. The words are nearly lost to some of these vocal demands. Do you think the aria is effective in portraying the deranged queen?
- Opera is a marriage of singing, story, orchestra, drama, and costuming. How do all of these elements combine to bring the story to life?

Here's a symphony...
Symphony no. 41 (Jupiter Symphony)
Give the notes on this clip a read—pretty interesting if you can hold out until the end!
http://www.youtube.com/watch?v=Fcly8-RGhgw

- Were you able to find a "theme" to the work? (There may be more than one that you caught throughout the entire piece.)
- This uses a larger orchestra—are you able to tell that several people on each instrument are playing the same thing? (Watch their bows as they go up and down together.) This give a fuller sound to the orchestra.

"Lacrimosa" from Requiem
http://www.youtube.com/watch?v=gqPz5B-TA1w

- Listen to the differences in dynamics and moods as the piece progresses. Do you hear the extremely soft portions? Do you hear the contrasting loud sections?
- Does the orchestra support the choir or is it independent of what the choir is singing?

Serenade no. 13 for strings in G Major (*Eine Kleine Nachtmusik*)
This is played on period instruments:

http://youtube.com/watch?v=wKhH2hRa-WQ
- Once again, do you hear how the instruments can begin softly and make a huge crescendo? And then do the opposite?
- The violins often have the melody, but can you hear the occasions (where the theme returns) where ALL of the instruments play the same thing?

Ludwig van Beethoven

Symphony no. 5 in C Minor—Movement I. Allegro con Brio.
http://youtube.com/watch?v=zhcR1ZS2hVo
- This clip is movements one and two. The conductor in this clip is Karajan, one of the most renowned conductors of the 20th century. He is known for often conducting with his eyes closed.
- The theme of this piece is quite famous— how many notes make up this theme? Can you believe that so few notes can be so well known?
- Listen for the theme to bounce between the sections of the orchestra. Can you hear it in the strings, the woodwinds, the brass? Can you hear when all of the sections play it together?

Symphony No. 9 in D Minor "Choral"—Movement IV. Finale: Allegro assai.
http://youtube.com/watch?v=PtU8dm08XCE&feature=related
- Hang in—you will recognize it!
- Do you hear the faster parts? The slower parts? See how the music seems to be broken into sections.
- We finally hear a hint of the theme that is so famous at about 2:15. Did you catch it? The theme we all know so well begins around 2:40. Beethoven takes that theme and plays with it for a long time and it appears in all of the sections of the orchestra before the choir sings even their first note.
- Can you tell that something dramatic is about to occur as you listen to the orchestra at about 6:16? The harmonies Beethoven chooses are stunning to any audience!

Bagataelle for Piano in A Minor: "Fur Elise"
http://youtube.com/watch?v=TWP6UoyQ--s
- The opening material is very familiar. Did you recognize it?
- Something different happens at 1:08—do you hear that the theme is different here?
- The original theme returns at 1:30—did you catch it?
- And something new happens at 2:05—did you hear this totally different theme?
- Again, at 2:39, the original theme returns.
- This form (where the theme keeps returning) is called a "Rondo."

Piano Sonata no. 14 in C-sharp Minor (*Moonlight*)—Movement I. Adagio sostenuto.
http://www.youtube.com/watch?v=O6txOvK-mAk

- Do you recognize this piece? How do you think it came up with the nickname "Moonlight Sonata"?
- Again, do you hear how the pianist is able to bring out the melody and make the accompaniment softer?
- How many different thematic ideas do you hear throughout this piece?
- Does it stay in one mood or does it change moods as it progresses?

Franz Schubert
Symphony no. 8 in B Minor (*Unfinished*)
http://www.youtube.com/watch?v=DItLZ5UsgyU&feature=related
- How would you describe the beginning of this symphony? It starts out with a solo melody played by the string basses—very unusual.
- The main theme follows this opening—how is it different?
- How many different themes can you count?

Piano Quintet in A (*The Trout*)— Movement IV.
http://www.youtube.com/watch?v=Hx8_mv7CzTg&feature=related
- Listen for the theme as it passes between all of the instruments. Do you hear how the theme gets changed throughout the piece?
- Some variations are quiet, some bombastic— how many different words can you use to describe the many variations?

"Ave Maria"
http://www.youtube.com/watch?v=bPvAQxZsgpQ
- Have you heard this before?
- Is the orchestra an equal partner or is it only accompaniment?
- Is the choir an equal partner or is it accompaniment?

Song: "Heidenröslein"
http://www.youtube.com/watch?v=zbLp8LABNnk&feature=related
- Do you hear sections that come back and repeat the melody?
- Is the piano an equal partner or simply accompaniment?
- Do you hear different moods or does it maintain one mood throughout?

Fantasie in C Major (*Wanderer*)
http://www.youtube.com/watch?v=4WmABGMV3tw&feature=related
- Do you hear the sudden and frequent changes of dynamic?
- Do you hear the calm sections and the stormy sections?
- Why do you think this is called a "Fantasy"?

Felix Mendelssohn

Violin Concerto in E, op. 64

http://youtube.com/watch?v=CCLxso5XDN4&mode=related&search=

- Once again, the solo instrument begins instead of the orchestra. Does this beginning set the mood for this fiery and big movement?
- Does the orchestra keep up the fire when it has its solo section?
- Are there changing moods or styles in this piece?

A Midsummer Night's Dream: "Wedding March"

http://www.youtube.com/watch?v=EfsTXzAgp6c

- This was originally written for orchestra. Does the organ imitate the sounds of an orchestra successfully?
- Is this piece familiar to you?

A Midsummer Night's Dream: "Overture"

http://www.youtube.com/watch?v=oUoB55XKEL4

- This piece opens a very long series of pieces that are a "dream." Does it sound like any dream you have had?
- In what ways does the composer make this dream come alive? What do you imagine when you first hear this music?
- Listen to all of the instruments as they pass the thematic material around. Can you name the different instruments as they play?

Symphony no. 3 (*Scottish*)—Movement II. Vivace non troppo.

http://youtube.com/watch?v=HKcVPOo4le4

- Listen to the full orchestra. Then listen to the solos as they are played.
- Do they imitate what the whole orchestra did?
- Do they have their own themes?
- Can you name any of the solo instruments?

Songs Without Words, Book 1, op. 19, no. 1 in E

http://youtube.com/watch?v=k4yf-V2LQE0&feature=related

Listen for the melody. Can you hear it clearly?

- The difficult part about playing this piece is keeping the accompaniment softer than the melody. How would you describe the accompaniment?
- Does it flow?
- Is it made out of chunky chords?

"Lift Thine Eyes" from *Elijah*

http://youtube.com/watch?v=wtiD9_OlTIM&feature=related

Frédéric (Fryderyk) Chopin
Waltz in D-flat, op. 64, no. 1 (*Minute Waltz*)
http://youtube.com/watch?v=7q82qUpRfGI
- Do you hear the faster notes at the beginning and then the slower section in the middle?
- Do you think this is a waltz that you could dance to?

Piano Sonata, op. 35, no. 2 (*Funeral March*)
http://youtube.com/watch?v=Q5UrVdvk1Ao
- Does this sound like a funeral march to you? Why or why not?
- Does this use the higher or lower registers (sounds) of the piano?

Piano Étude, op. 10, no. 12 (*Revolutionary*)
http://youtube.com/watch?v=3zikmAirQqQ
- Do you hear a contrast between this piece and the *Funeral March*?
- Why do you think it is called the *Revolutionary Étude*?

Fantasie Impromptu, op. 66
http://youtube.com/watch?v=w0m6uOdW-LI&mode=related&search=
- Do you hear more of the higher or lower notes in this piece?
- The right hand has some very fast notes. Does the left hand do the same thing?

Robert Schumann
Fantasy in C, op. 17
http://youtube.com/watch?v=oe0hRv_ZHOA
- Does this sound similar in style to the Chopin piano works or is it different in some way? How is it similar or different?
- Does it keep the intensity of sound from beginning to end or are there moments of calm?

Album for the Young, op. 68:
No. 2 "Soldier's March"
No. 8 "The Wild Rider"
http://youtube.com/watch?v=PpTP2WeZJLg
No. 10 "The Happy Farmer"
- This was a series of pieces written for young pianists.
- Is it similar in any way to the Fantasy?

Franz Liszt
Hungarian Rhapsody, no. 2. Allegretto in G.

http://youtube.com/watch?v=ru84UVcPHDo&feature=related
- Does the opening use more of the lower or higher sounds of the piano?
- Does the tempo stay the same or does it change a lot?

Piano Sonata in B Minor

http://youtube.com/watch?v=QHe0kUUvaU4
- The opening is very soft. Do you hear how the composer uses silence?
- Does the piece seem to flow or does it seem to stop and start?

Les Preludes

http://youtube.com/watch?v=6BZgte0ObLw&feature=related
- How would you describe the mood at the opening of the piece?
- When does the mood begin to change?
- Can you recognize some of the instruments as they are played?

Giuseppe Verdi

Rigoletto: "La donna è mobile"

http://youtube.com/watch?v=8A3zetSuYRg
- Does the orchestra give a hint of the melody in the introduction?
- Can you recognize the instrument that joins in a duet with the tenor?

La Traviata: "Libiamo ne' lieti calici"

http://youtube.com/watch?v=NcKdnkGBSgA
- Watch the text as the music is sung. Does the music reflect the text?
- Do you hear how the whole piece builds from orchestra to solos, to duets, and finally to the full chorus?

Requiem: "*Dies Irae*"

http://youtube.com/watch?v=pd0KdGxIUbg
- *Dies Irae* means "Days of Wrath." Does the music reflect the title? How?
- You can hear several instruments playing small solo lines at about 1:50. Can you name some of them?

Anton Bruckner

Symphony no. 7—First Movement. Allegro.

http://youtube.com/watch?v=NhawE1zfu5M
- What family of instruments opens this work?
- This movement opens in a soft and haunting way, but a distinct melody emerges. Can you pick it out?

"Ave Maria"

http://youtube.com/watch?v=3imMJrs-IxI&feature=related

- This was written for seven parts—a three-part women's choir and a four-part men's choir. How many of these parts can you hear?
- Does this remind you of the Gregorian chants you've heard? Why or why not?

Stephen Foster

"Oh! Susanna"

http://youtube.com/watch?v=yCnQsfWQHog

- Does this sound like some of the operatic solos you have heard before? Why or why not?
- Is this tune familiar?

"Camptown Races"

www.youtube.com/watch?v=PFZTz0JnNew&feature=related

- What instruments are featured here?
- What makes these tunes "American"?

The New Christy Minstrels version:

www.youtube.com/watch?v=peZseIp3QGI&feature=related

"Old Folks at Home"

http://www.youtube.com/watch?v=IOqh-dNeQ-o&feature=related

- Does this sound similar in any way to some of the operatic arias you have heard earlier?
- What kinds of emotions are portrayed in this song?

Johannes Brahms

Piano Quartet in G Minor

http://youtube.com/watch?v=V0ca3yUElVc

- Can you name the four instruments in the quartet?
- Is any instrument more important or prominent that any of the others or are they equal partners?

Hungarian Dance no. 5 in F-sharp

http://youtube.com/watch?v=HglV1pZDf7I&feature=related

- Do you think it is easy to coordinate two pianists at the same piano?
- Are they together when the tempo changes?
- Can you hear how it gets faster/slower/faster/...? How many times does the speed (tempo) change?

Violin Concerto in D Major

http://youtube.com/watch?v=UkIULqYxiPU

- The orchestral opening is beautiful—what instrument is featured? (It is not the violin.)
- Does the violin theme sound similar to the orchestral opening theme or not?

"How Lovely Is Thy Dwelling Place"

http://youtube.com/watch?v=mTW1-ncCrbc&feature=related

Pyotr Ilyich Tchaikovsky

1812 Overture

http://youtube.com/watch?v=k-vQKZFF-9s&mode=related&search=

- This piece begins softly, but that doesn't last long. What percussion instruments are featured within the first minute (and then throughout)?
- Around 5:00, can you hear all of the additional "noise" that Tchaikovsky adds to this piece? By 5:20, he has added cannons to the carillon (bells). This is one of the loudest pieces ever written when played with all of the extra instruments!

The Nutcracker: "March," "Dance of the Sugar Plum Fairy," or any others

http://youtube.com/watch?v=EHQ7gPuZ3Qw

- Here the music and the choreography go together. Does the music seem to match the actions of the performers on the stage?
- Which is more important: the music or the staging?
- Do you think the music could exist without the staging?
- Do you think the staging could exist without the music?

Antonín Dvořák

Symphony no. 9 in E Minor (*From the New World*) op. 95—Movement 4. Allegro con fuoco.

http://youtube.com/watch?v=Vlci-kCEaKE

- What instruments state the theme toward the beginning? (Hint: They are loud!)
- What instrument is doing the solo work at about 2:00?
- Is this music exciting or calming?

Humoresque, op. 101, no. 7 in G-flat Major

http://youtube.com/watch?v=ScSCILXXLnM

- What instrument has the solo at the beginning?
- Which instrument takes over the melody at about 0:55?
- Do you hear the two instruments in a duet after each one has a solo?

String Quartet no. 12 in F (*American*)—Movement 4. Vivace ma non troppo.
http://youtube.com/watch?v=B6QjtpCTRvw
- Name the instruments in the quartet. (Two instruments are the same, so there are only three instruments to name.)
- Which instrument seems to be featured? (the highest one)

Gabriel Urbain Fauré
Élégie (cello and orchestra), op.24
http://youtube.com/watch?v=okSW0QNquv8&feature=related (performance begins around 1:55)
- An "Élégie" would generally refer to a funeral piece. Does it sound like something that would be used at a funeral?
- Is the whole piece soft and slow?
- Can you hear how the orchestra and cello duet back and forth around 5:20?

Cantique de Jean Racine (choral & beautiful!!!), op. 11
http://youtube.com/watch?v=tADRPwVHxZA&feature=related
- What instrument is featured with the orchestra at the beginning?
- What kind of mood would you say this piece evokes?

Sir Edward Elgar
Pomp & Circumstance March no. 1
www.youtube.com/watch?v=gxqFdcZz974
- This is an old black-and-white recording of Elgar himself conducting!
- This is used at graduation ceremonies frequently. Why do you think it would be good for those occasions?
- Does this sound more like a march or a waltz?

Enigma Variations
www.youtube.com/watch?v=sUgoBb8m1eE
- Can you hear how the piece crescendos and then draws to a quick, very soft end?
- Which instruments really make the biggest crescendo?

Claude Debussy
Clair de Lune
www.youtube.com/watch?v=bINSmhssRRs&feature=related
- How is this similar to other piano music we have heard? How is it different?
- Is this piece familiar to you?

Le Petit Negre

http://www.youtube.com/watch?v=Ss03VfDcVTM&feature=related

- You should listen to this piece again after you hear some of the music of Scott Joplin!

Richard Strauss

Till Eulenspiegel

www.youtube.com/watch?v=2mbatJgtNk0

- Have you ever heard this piece before?
- Where do you think you've heard it?
- Look up the reference to this piece in Wikipedia and see what that encyclopedia says about it.

Scott Joplin

"The Entertainer"

www.youtube.com/watch?v=tqR-DQYcmP0

- Is this tune familiar to you? Where have you heard it before?
- What would be the most distinctive characteristic of this piece (melody, harmony, or rhythm)?

Any of the ragtime piano works—there are many!

Charles Ives

Variations on "America"

www.youtube.com/watch?v=R_N9PF2JwIc

- Things to listen for:
- The introduction. Can you tell that "America" will follow?
- The theme follows the introduction ("My Country 'Tis of Thee"). Does it sound just like a hymn?
- The five variations come after that. Listen for the theme ("My Country 'Tis of Thee…")
- Does the third variation (3:53) sound a bit like a waltz?
- What does the fourth variation remind you of? (4:50)
- At 5:40, where is the interest? (Ives wrote: "The organist may hold on to the bench with the left hand at this point.")

The Unanswered Question

www.youtube.com/watch?v=5JBfjPO7B8o

- Does the music in any way suggest a "question" to you?
- Describe the mood of this piece.
- How is this orchestral piece different from those that you have heard earlier in the course?

George Gershwin

Rhapsody in Blue

www.youtube.com/watch?v=3efPg1UKKgA&feature=related

- What instrument starts this piece? (It is one of the most famous solos for this instrument!)
- What is the real solo instrument for this piece? (It is really a concerto for this instrument.)

Porgy and Bess: "Summertime"

www.youtube.com/watch?v=dRvVBKLxCgU

- This is a truly "American" opera. What makes this piece so American?
- How does this sound like the arias from the Verdi operas and how does it sound different?

"Someone to Watch Over Me"

www.youtube.com/watch?v=KvoiNvcYI-M&feature=related

- This is Katharine McPhee on *American Idol* (song itself starts at 1:02). If the link is broken, you might try doing a search for it.
- Does this sound like it was written a long time ago or only a short time ago?
- Do the words match the music?

www.youtube.com/watch?v=rTrlX_M7_LA

- Here is another version of this song, this time by Joni James, an American singer of traditional pop music.

Three Preludes for the Piano, (short and familiar)

http://youtube.com/watch?v=JSDUW8PhK7A&feature=related

- Listen to all three preludes (there is a LOT of applause between each one). How are they similar? How are they different? Does the second prelude remind you of some of the Gershwin songs that you have heard?

Aaron Copland

Fanfare for the Common Man

http://youtube.com/watch?v=Xzf0rvQa4Mc

- What section of the orchestra begins this fanfare (quite unusual)?
- The actual fanfare is played by what instruments?
- Where have you heard this piece before?

Appalachian Spring—You MUST listen to this! It is everywhere, and now you will know the name of the piece when you hear it again.

www.youtube.com/watch?v=96Zc9enoGCg

- Does this remind you of spring? How would you describe the piece as it progresses?
- What instruments stand out to your ears? Some are more prominent than others.

John Williams

"Olympic Fanfare" includes interview with Williams interspersed:
www.youtube.com/watch?v=BiCGgt4SKb8&feature=related
- John Williams describes his music well. Does he describe his music adequately?
- Would you add anything to his comments?

Here Williams conducts a medley of movie themes:
http://www.youtube.com/watch?v=sE_vbrj0MqU
- The very beginning of this clip is not from *Star Wars*. Do you know what movie that opening theme is from?
- How would you describe this movie music? A good composer of movie music makes the scene on the screen come alive just as a ballet composer makes the dancers come alive!

Reproducible Timeline

Timeline Directions

There is a Comparative Timeline page for every fifty-year period, beginning with Vivaldi, the first composer in our study who has been given his own lesson. Use a different color for each musical period: Baroque – red, Classical – blue, Romantic – green, Contemporary – orange. We have provided the birth and death dates for the composers and a shaded line connecting these two dates. The student's assignment is to use the appropriate color to highlight or draw over this shaded line for each composer. This is a simple method that enables students to see at a glance which composers composed in which period, visually reinforcing what they are learning in the lessons.

We also want students to recognize the relationships between the composers. In this study students will learn that some composers influenced other composers, and some composers were friends. We have assigned a different color for each of those relationships. Friendship will be marked with gold; influence will be marked with purple. If one composer influenced another, draw a vertical line, in purple, from the "influencer" to the one who was influenced. Put an arrow at the end of the line, so the direction of the influence is clear. If the composers were friends, draw a vertical line in gold from one friend to the other. There may be relationships that are difficult to draw because the related composers may not have "lifelines" on the same page. In this case, the student can hand-write the missing composer's name on the timeline page and draw the vertical line to the hand-written name. For further clarification, see the Exhaustive Timeline Reference Key at www.BrightIdeasPress.com, discussed further under "Timeline Answer Key" below.

At the bottom of each timeline page, there is a "Significant Events" line. On it, you'll see that one or two significant events have already been labeled. This is a quick and painless technique useful for seeing where each composer fits into world events. You might like your older students to find a few additional events to add to this line. The significance of these timeline pages is that these composers did not live in isolation but were, indeed, influenced by the people and events around them. This is an effortless visual way to present this information.

Timeline Answer Key

The Exhaustive Timeline Reference Key found at www.BrightIdeasPress.com is a thorough answer key for these timeline activities. The charts in this Reference Key are provided in full color and can be downloaded and printed out. The charts show ALL relationships, both explicit and implied, from within the lessons. DO NOT expect your student to find all the relationships on these charts. However, the relationships your student does find SHOULD be on them. You can use these charts to check and make sure the relationships your student found are correct.

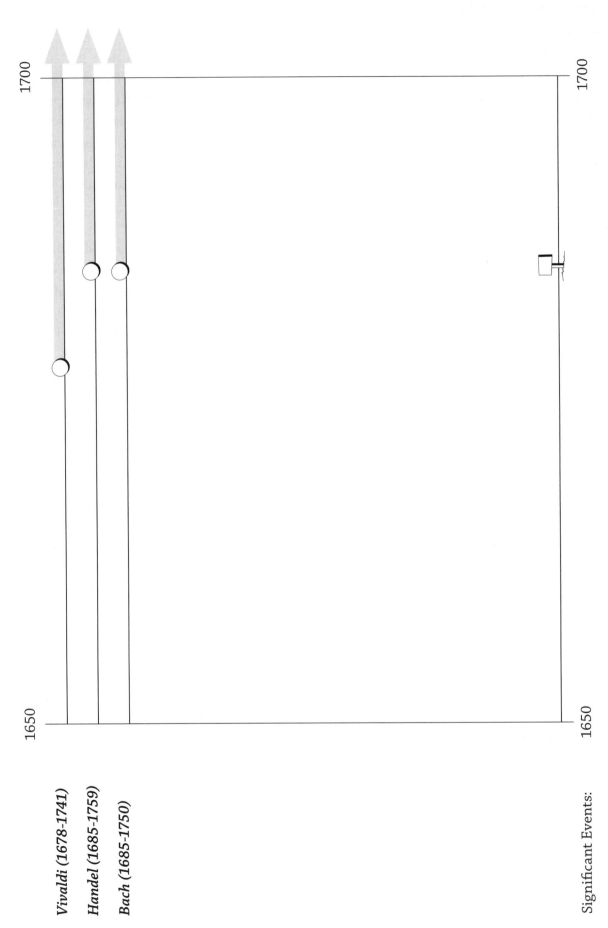

1700

1650

Vivaldi (1678-1741)

Handel (1685-1759)

Bach (1685-1750)

1700

1650

Significant Events:

1665 - Great Plague of London

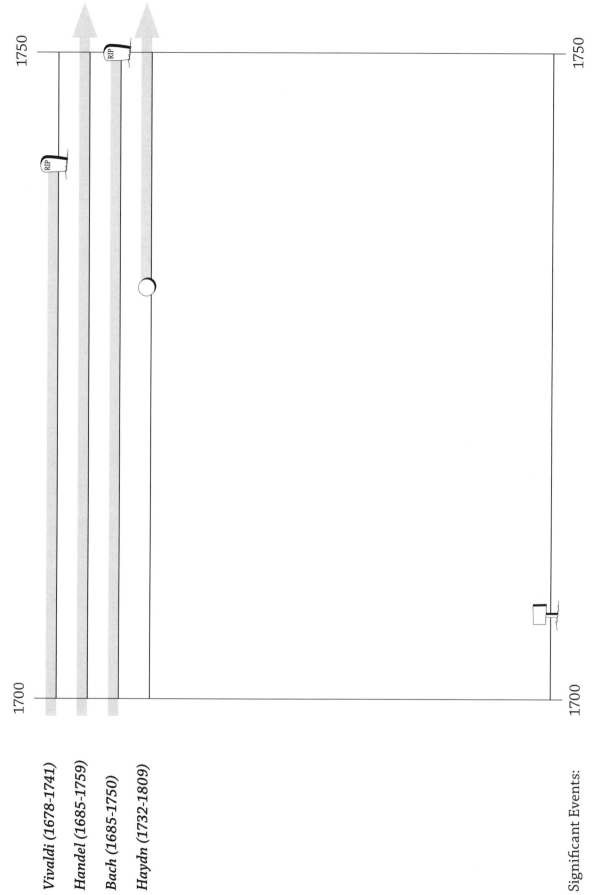

1750

Vivaldi (1678-1741)

Handel (1685-1759)

Bach (1685-1750)

Haydn (1732-1809)

1700

Significant Events:

1707 - Mughal Empire ends

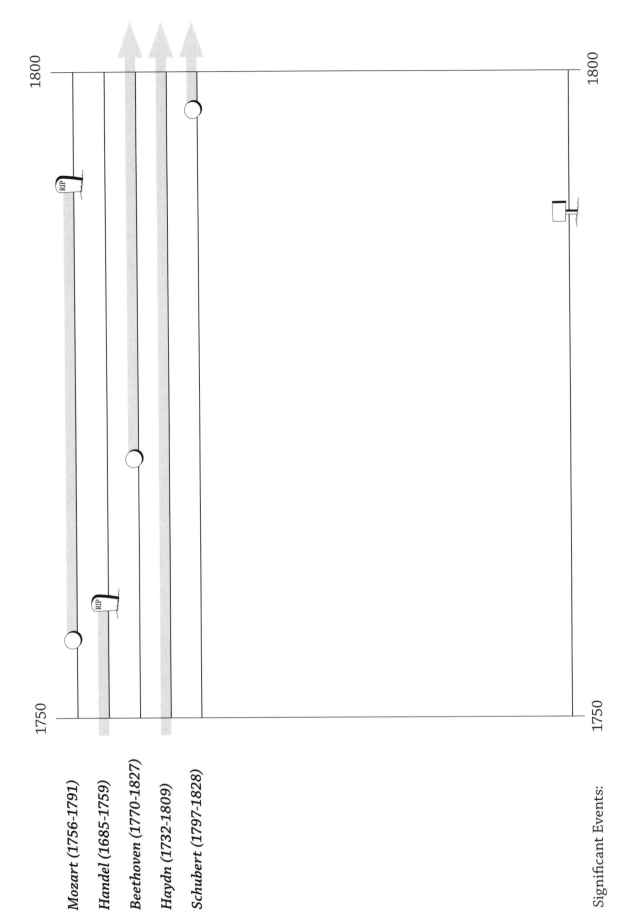

Mozart (1756-1791)

Handel (1685-1759)

Beethoven (1770-1827)

Haydn (1732-1809)

Schubert (1797-1828)

Significant Events:

1789 - French Revolution

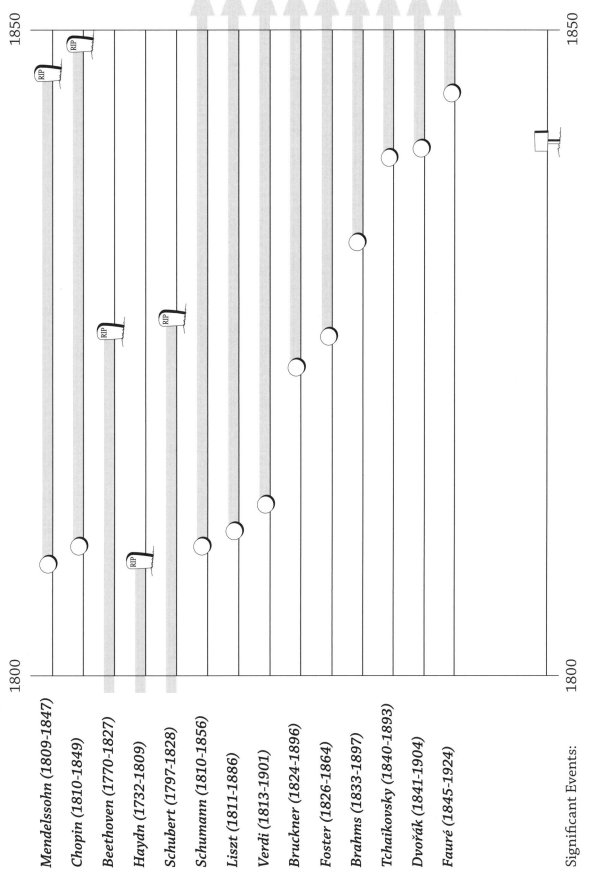

Mendelssohn (1809-1847)

Chopin (1810-1849)

Beethoven (1770-1827)

Haydn (1732-1809)

Schubert (1797-1828)

Schumann (1810-1856)

Liszt (1811-1886)

Verdi (1813-1901)

Bruckner (1824-1896)

Foster (1826-1864)

Brahms (1833-1897)

Tchaikovsky (1840-1893)

Dvořák (1841-1904)

Fauré (1845-1924)

1800

1850

1800

1850

Significant Events:

David Livingstone goes to Africa - 1841

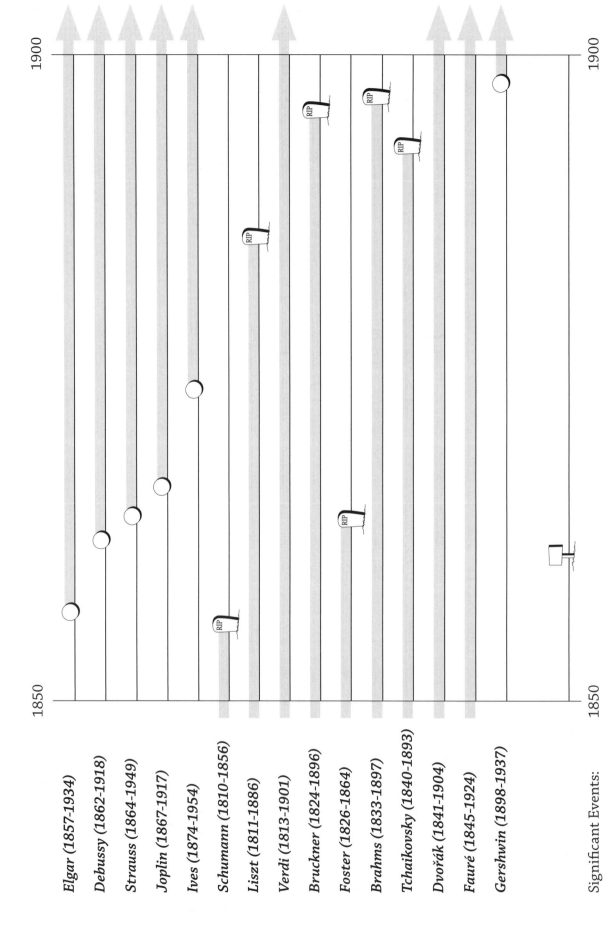

1900

Elgar (1857-1934)

Debussy (1862-1918)

Strauss (1864-1949)

Joplin (1867-1917)

Ives (1874-1954)

Schumann (1810-1856)

Liszt (1811-1886)

Verdi (1813-1901)

Bruckner (1824-1896)

Foster (1826-1864)

Brahms (1833-1897)

Tchaikovsky (1840-1893)

Dvořák (1841-1904)

Fauré (1845-1924)

Gershwin (1898-1937)

1850

1850

1900

Significant Events:

1861 – American Civil War

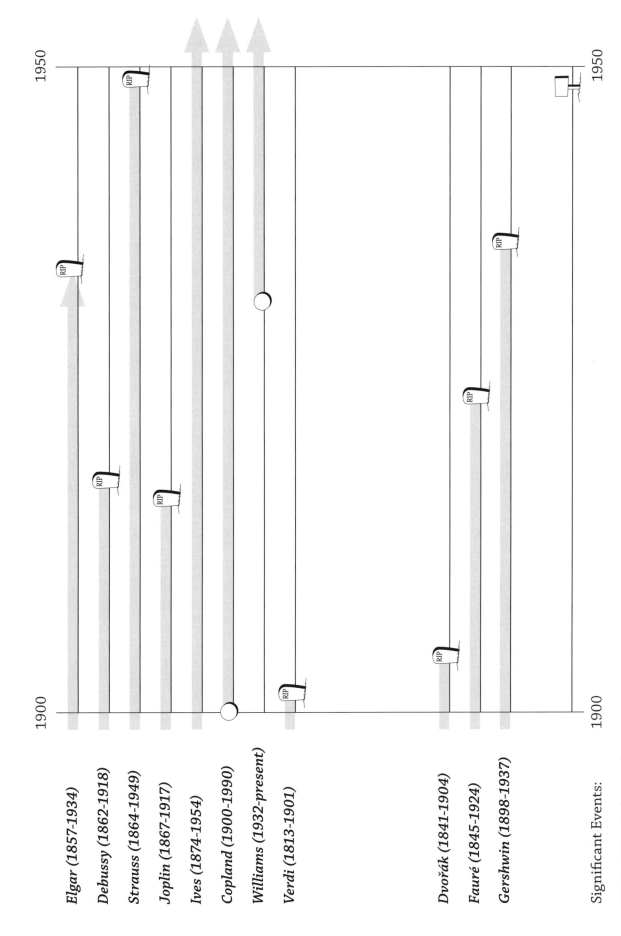

Elgar (1857-1934)

Debussy (1862-1918)

Strauss (1864-1949)

Joplin (1867-1917)

Ives (1874-1954)

Copland (1900-1990)

Williams (1932-present)

Verdi (1813-1901)

Dvořák (1841-1904)

Fauré (1845-1924)

Gershwin (1898-1937)

1900

1950

Significant Events:

1949 - Mao Zedong takes power

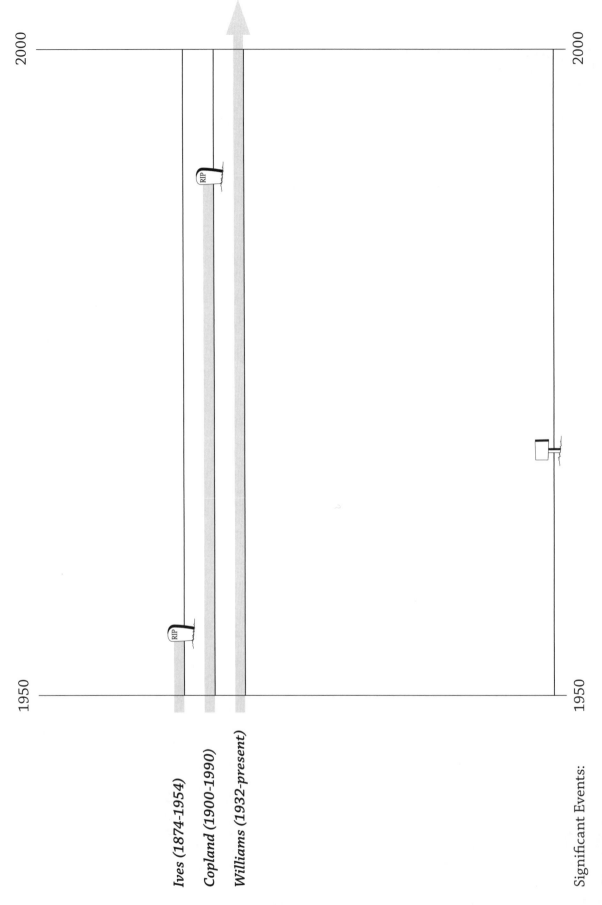

Ives (1874-1954)

Copland (1900-1990)

Williams (1932-present)

1950

2000

2000

Significant Events:

1950

1969 – First man on the moon

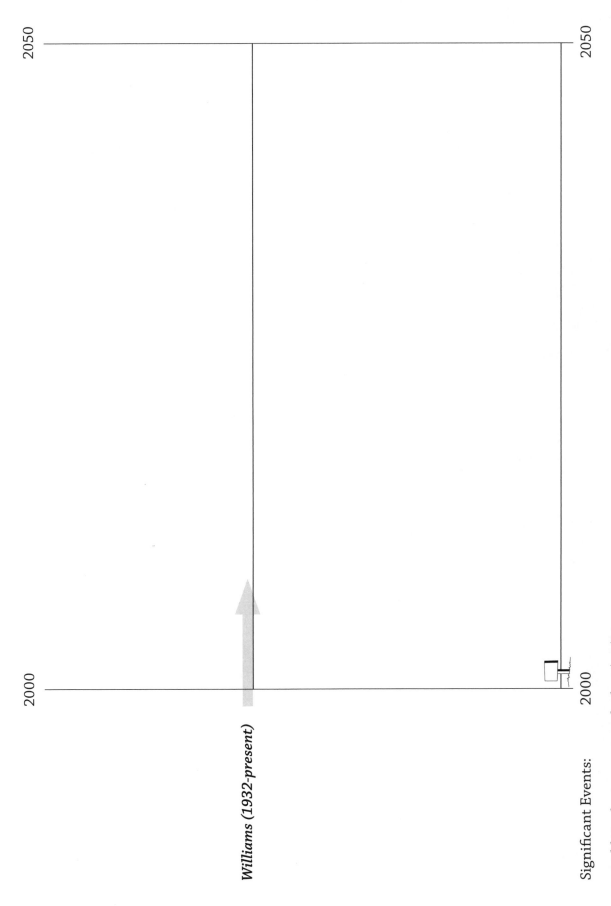

2000   2050

Williams (1932-present)

2000   2050

Significant Events:

World Trade Center Attacked - 9/11/2001

European Composers - Baroque & Classical Periods

Draw a line from the composer's portrait to the country in which he was born. Use the same color-coding system for musical periods on the map as you used on the timelines.

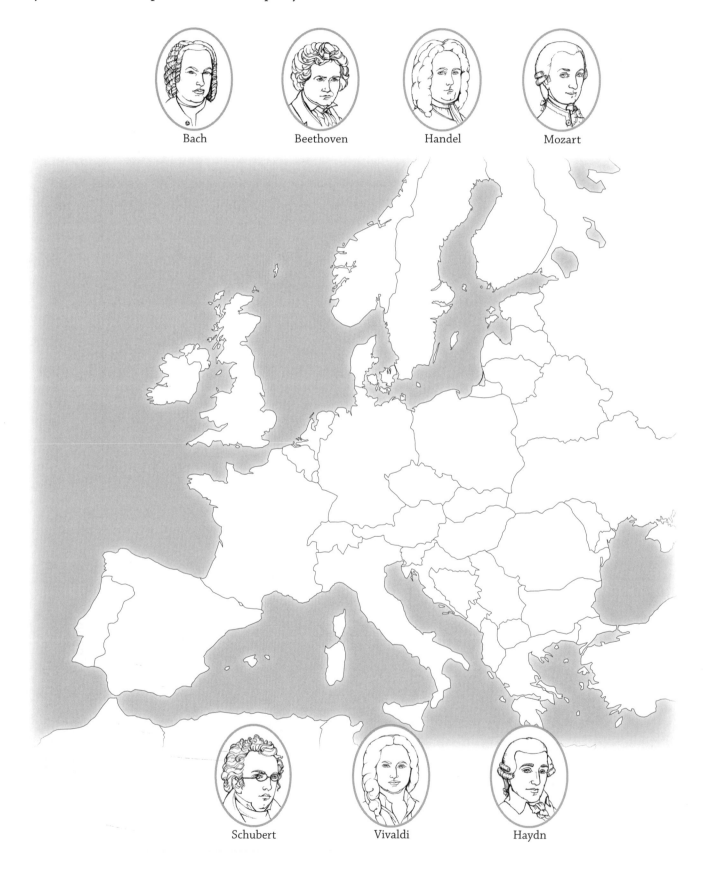

Bach

Beethoven

Handel

Mozart

Schubert

Vivaldi

Haydn

European Composers - Romantic Period

Draw a line from the composer's portrait to the country in which he was born. Use the same color-coding system for musical periods on the map as you used on the timelines.

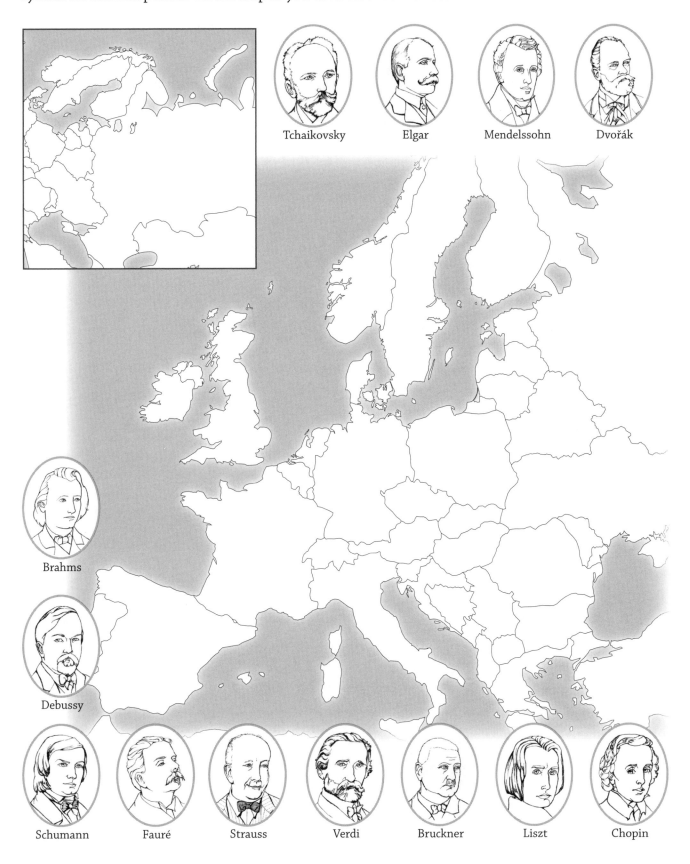

Tchaikovsky

Elgar

Mendelssohn

Dvořák

Brahms

Debussy

Schumann

Fauré

Strauss

Verdi

Bruckner

Liszt

Chopin

American Composers - Contemporary Period

Draw a line from the composer's portrait to the state in which he was born. Use the same color-coding system for musical periods on the map as you used on the timelines.

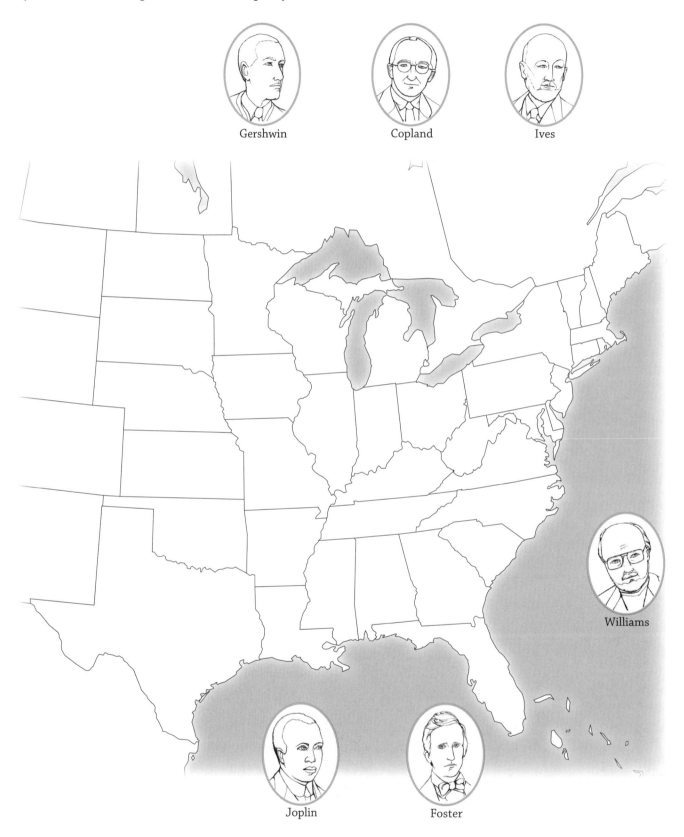

Games

The following games will help your children grow in familiarity with the composers. You can make the games yourself, but we recommend that you include your student because the process will be a good review.

Several of the games require creating a deck of cards. This deck is easily made by copying the composers' pictures (use the reproducible composer illustrations in this Appendix), cutting them out, and pasting them to index cards or card stock. If your children are artistic, they may want to produce a design for the back of the cards. The cards will last longer if you laminate them or cover them in clear packing tape.

Composer Memory
What You Need to Play
- Players – This game can be played alone or with 2-4 players.
- Playing Cards – Make two copies of each composer's picture. Paste the pictures on index cards or card stock.

Playing the Game
- Arrange the cards face down on a flat surface in rows in a rectangular pattern.
- The group chooses a player to start the play. The turns proceed in a clockwise order.
- The first player selects a card and turns it face up so that all players can see. He then chooses a second card and turns it face up.
- If the cards do not match, they are turned back over and that player's turn is over.
- If the cards do match, the player removes them and keeps that pair of cards.
- The player continues to turn over pairs of cards until he turns over two cards that do not match.
- The game is over when all of the pairs of cards are matched.
- The winner is the player with the most cards.

Advanced Game
Make this game more challenging for older students by creating a deck of cards where students will match the picture of the composer to his musical period, one of his compositions, or his birthplace.

Go Fish for Composers
What You Need to Play
- Players – This game can be played by 2-6 players.
- Playing Cards – Make three copies of each composer's picture. Paste each picture on an index card or card stock.

Playing the Game
- Deal five cards to each player. The remaining cards are placed face down in the middle to form a "fishing pool."

- The player to the left of the dealer begins play.
- A turn consists of asking a specific player for a specific composer card. ("Ben, do you have Bach?") She must have at least one of those cards in her hand in order to ask for it. If the person asked has any cards with that composer in his hand, he must give them all to the person asking. She may continue asking specific players for specific cards as long as she continues to be successful.
- If the person does not have any cards of the composer named, he says, "Go Fish." The asker then chooses a card from the fishing pool. If the card picked is the one asked for, she gets another turn. If not, she keeps the card and it is the next player's turn.
- As soon as a player collects a "book" of three of the same composer, she lays them down in front of her.
- The game proceeds until either someone has no cards left or the fishing pool is empty.
- The winner is the player with the most books.

Composer Bingo

What You Need to Play
- Players – Any number.
- Bingo Card – Use the template at the end of this section to create a Bingo card for each player. Each space on the card will need a different composer's name in it. Each player's card should have the composers arranged in a different pattern. Note: There will be more composers than spaces on the card.
- Markers – Pennies, beans, cereal, mini-marshmallows or some other type of marker for the card.
- Easy Version: Index cards or slips of paper with a different composer's name on each one.
- Advanced Version: Index cards or slips of paper that have one fact about one of the composers. You may want to make new fact cards each time you play or create a set to reuse each time.

Playing the Game

Easy version
- Put the slips of paper in a basket or bag and mix them up.
- Draw one out and read the name written on it.
- If the players have that composer on their board, they cover that space with a marker.
- Set aside the slips of paper that have been read until the next game.
- The first player to get five in a row in any direction wins.

Advanced Version
- Put the fact cards in a basket or bag and mix them up.
- Draw one out and read the fact written on it.
- If the players can identify the composer, and they have that name on their card, they cover that space with a marker.
- Set aside the fact cards that have been read until the next game.
- The first player to get five in a row in any direction wins.

Composer Jeopardy!

What You Need to Play

- Players – Any number but probably works best with 4 or less. Could also be played with 2 or 3 teams.
- Question-and-Answer Cards – Use the information from the lessons or the composer cards that you filled out. Create five questions for the composers from each musical period that could be the answer to "Who is (fill in the name of one of the composers)?" Put the answer on one side of a card and "Who is _____?" on the other side of the card. For example:
  - ~ At the end of his manuscripts, he always wrote the initials, S.D.G., or *Soli Deo Gloria*—"To God Alone the Glory." The answer is "Who is Bach?"
  - ~ He was totally deaf by the age of 48, but continued to compose. The answer is "Who is Beethoven?"
- A *Jeopardy!* Game Board – You can use the graphics at the end of this section or create your own. It should have six rows and five columns. Set the board up so each musical period is displayed across the top row. Then place your Q & A cards (answer side up) in the appropriate columns. Then cover each card with a card that has a dollar amount on it so that the answers remain hidden until they are chosen.
- Buzzers – Provide buzzers or some other device so that players can "buzz in" if they think they know the answer. A wooden spoon on a pot will work nicely.

Playing the Game

- Decide who will start the game.
- That player chooses a time period and dollar amount.
- The host of the game reads the question in that box.
- Any of the players may "buzz in" if they know the answer.
- If they answer correctly, they receive the money card that covered the question and may choose the next category and dollar amount.
- If they answer incorrectly, any other player may "buzz in." The other players are not required to "buzz in" and guess.
- If none of the players answer correctly, whichever player originally chose the question may choose again.
- Play continues until all of the questions have been answered.
- The player with the most money wins.

Composer Info-Card Timeline Game

What You Need to Play
- Players – One, although this could be adapted to work as a team game.

Playing the Game
- Place all the Composer Info-Cards on the table with the Picture/Name side facing up.
- Scatter/shuffle the cards about.
- Now place the cards in proper chronological sequence.
- Self-check by turning the cards over and looking at the dates.
- Advanced Version: Set a timer and beat your own time or race against another player.

Note: We designed the Composer Info-Card with this game in mind. Hence, there are no dates on the front of the card; only on the back.

Composer Bingo Game Form

Composer *Jeopardy!* Game Forms

Baroque	Classical	Early Romantic	Late Romantic	Contemporary
$100	$100	$100	$100	$100
$200	$200	$200	$200	$200
$300	$300	$300	$300	$300
$400	$400	$400	$400	$400
$500	$500	$500	$500	$500

$100	$100	$100	$100	$100
$200	$200	$200	$200	$200
$300	$300	$300	$300	$300
$400	$400	$400	$400	$400
$500	$500	$500	$500	$500

A Young Scholar's Guide to Composers

Who is
Vivaldi?

Who is
Handel?

Who is
Bach?

Who is
Haydn?

Who is
Mozart?

Who is
Beethoven?

Who is
Schubert?

Who is
Mendelssohn?

Who is
Chopin?

Who is
Schumann?

Who is
Liszt?

Who is
Verdi?

Who is
Brahms?

Who is
Foster?

Who is
Tchaikovsky?

Who is
Dvořák?

Who is
Fauré?

Who is
Elgar?

Who is
Bruckner?

Who is
Debussy?

Who is
Strauss?

Who is
Ives?

Who is
Gershwin?

Who is
Copland?

Who is
Joplin?

Who is
Williams?

Vivaldi tests out his concertos at an all-girls' orphanage.

Messiah composer Handel works on a masterpiece.

Bach, an amazing organist, playing an amazing organ.

Haydn's orchestra says, "Farewell!"

The Mozart family enjoys a special dinner with King Louis XV.

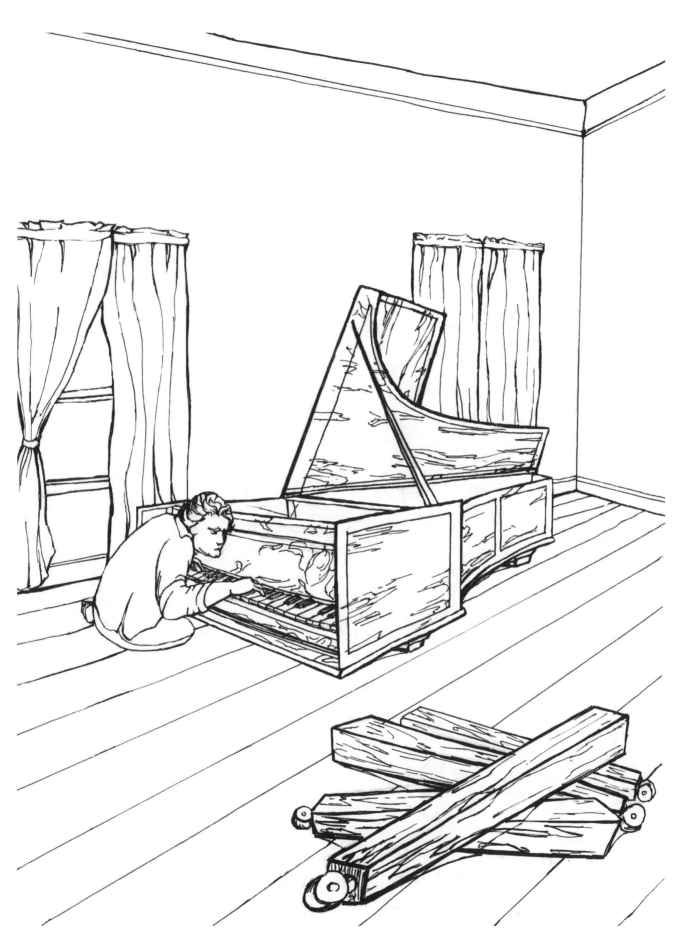

Beethoven "hears" his notes through the piano's vibrations on the floor!

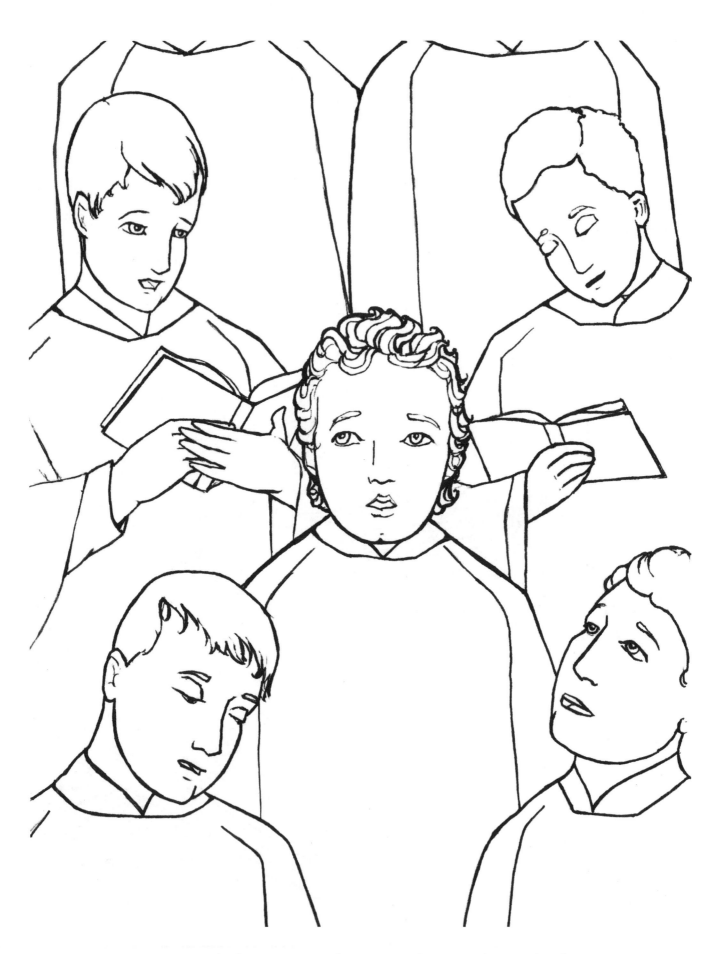

Young Schubert sings in the Imperial Court Choir School.

Siblings Felix and Fanny Mendelssohn enjoy playing music together.

Chopin plays beautiful music for friends Liszt and Mendelssohn.

Poet-musician Schumann gets creative.

Proud performer Liszt prepares to take a bow.

Verdi outside the stunning La Fenice Theater in Venice.

The Bruckner Organ in the St. Florian Monastery.

Forty-niners belt out Foster's "Oh! Susanna."

One of Brahms's many visits to the Schumann family.

Clara dances to the music of Tchaikovsky's *Nutcracker*.

A faithful Dvořák heads for St. Mary's Church.

Fauré grades his students' unique compositions.

Elgar creates emotional compositions during World War I.

Debussy appreciated color in both paintings and music.

Not everyone approved of Strauss's new opera!

Lively sheet music composed by Joplin.

Even baseball could inspire Ives.

Gershwin gets his inspiration from everyday sounds.

A relieved Copland leaves the McCarthy hearing.

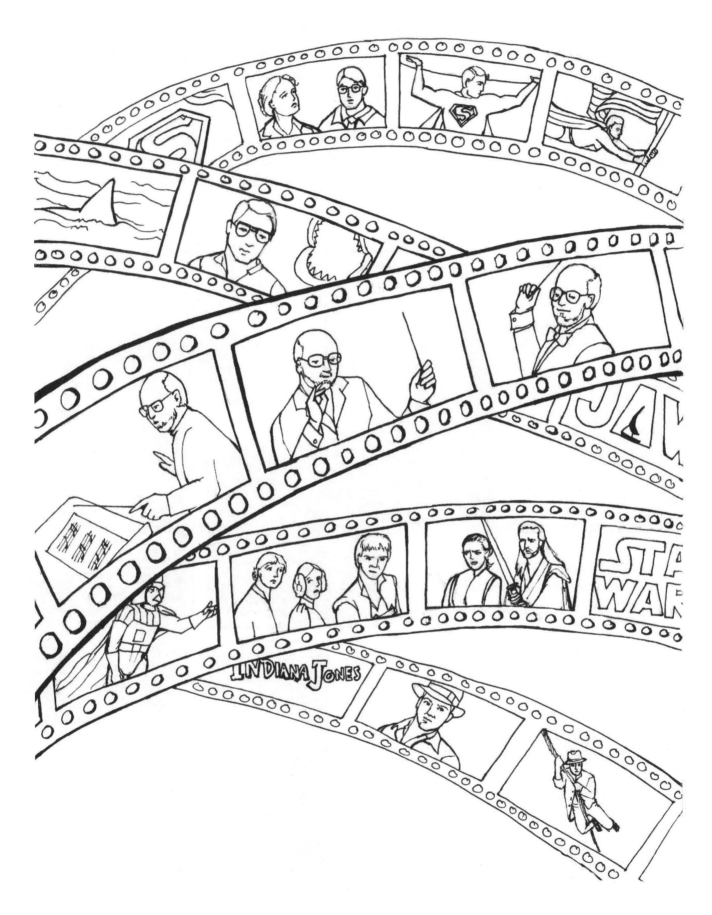

John Williams is the composer of many famous movie scores.

Folderbook Directions

Folderbooks are a simple and interesting way to show what one has learned. Think of them as a place to store tidbits of information, pictures, drawings, maps, etc. By helping your students to learn to organize and display what they have studied, you are training them to sift through ideas, choose what is important, and present it in a logical manner. This kind of learning will be useful for the rest of their lives!

If you are familiar with Lap Books, think of folderbooks as the simple, quicker version. Instead of multiple layers, a folderbook consists of just one file folder. Instead of elaborate, clever folds and time-consuming layouts, a folderbook can be assembled rapidly. Although Lap Books are a wonderful learning tool, sometimes all we have time for is simple!

Other ideas for your composer folderbook:

- Paste envelopes inside and put cards with information or smaller books inside the envelopes.
- Include pictures, maps, or timelines as appropriate.
- Make small books or flip books and paste them inside.
- Decorate lists and glue them on.
- Let imagination and creativity be your guide.
- Decorate the cover in an appropriate fashion. Coloring pages make easy covers.

Composers Resource List

General Music History

Classical Music, Phil G. Goulding. ISBN# 978-0449910429. 656 pages.

Spiritual Lives of the Great Composers, Patrick Kavanaugh. ISBN# 978-0310208068. 256 pages.

The Essential Canon of Classical Music, David Dubal. ISBN# 978-0865476646. 800 pages.

The Lives of the Great Composers, Harold C. Schonberg. ISBN# 978-0349109725. 761 pages.

The Lives and Times of the Great Composers, Michael Steen. ISBN# 978-0195222180. 992 pages.

700 Years of Classical Treasures: The Complete History of Classical Music...the Composers, Their Instruments, and Works. Reader's Digest, ISBN# 978-0762107155. 104 pages, Grades 9-adult. Comes with 8 CDs.

Music Is, Lloyd Moss. ISBN# 978-0399233364. 32 pages, PK-2.

The Usborne Story of Music, David Cuzik. ISBN# 978-0794514037. 32 pages, Grades 1-8.

Classical Composers for Dummies, ISBN# 978-0764550096. 384 pages, Grades 7-adult.

Ah, Music! Aliki. ISBN # 978-0064462365. 48 pages, Grades 1-4.

Music, (DK Eyewitness Books). ISBN# 978-0756607098. 72 pages, Grades 3-adult.

Story of the Orchestra: Listen While You Learn About the Instruments, the Music and the Composers Who Wrote the Music! Robert Levine. ISBN#978-1579121488. 96 pages, Grades 1-8.

General Music Information on orchestras, instruments, and genres like opera

Classical Cats: Children's Introduction to the Orchestra, David Chesky. Chesky Records, 1997, ISBN# 978-0965878708.

The Story of the Incredible Orchestra: An Introduction to Musical Instruments and the Symphony Orchestra, Bruce Koscielniak. ISBN# 978-0618311125. 40 pages, Grades K-6.

Story of the Orchestra: Listen While You Learn About the Instruments, the Music and the Composers Who Wrote the Music! Robert Levine. ISBN#978-1579121488. 96 pages, Grades 1-8.

Brovo! Brava! A Night at the Opera: Behind the Scenes with Composers, Cast, and Crew, Anne Siberell. ISBN# 978-0195139662. 64 pages, Grades 3-8.

Ticket to the Opera: Discovering and Exploring 100 Famous Works, History, Lore, and Singers, (with Recommended Recordings), Phil G. Goulding. ISBN# 978-0449005668. 720 pages, Grades 7-adult.

Meet the Orchestra, Ann Hayes. ISBN# 978-0152002220. 32 pages, Grades PK-3.

The Orchestra: An Introduction to the World of Classical Music, Alan Blackwood. ISBN# 978-1562947088. 96 pages, Grades 4-8.

André Previn's Guide to the Orchestra. ISBN# 978-0399128653. 192 pages, Grades 7-adult.

700 Years of Classical Treasures: The Complete History of Classical Music...the Composers, Their Instruments, and Works. Reader's Digest, ISBN# 978-0762107155. 104 pages, Grades 9-adult. Comes with 8 CDs.

Ah, Music! Aliki. ISBN # 978-0064462365. 48 pages, Grades 1-4.

Young Person's Guide to the Orchestra, book and CD set. ISBN# 978-0152013042. Book – 64 pages, Grades 3-6.

Baroque
Vivaldi

I, Vivaldi, Janice Shefelman. ISBN# 978-0802853189. 32 pages, Grades K-4.

Introducing Vivaldi, (Great Composers Series), Ronald Vernon. ISBN# 978-0382396342. 32 pages, Grades 2-6.

Antonio Vivaldi and the Baroque Tradition, Donna Getanger and David Felsenfeld. ISBN# 978-1931798204. 144 pages, Grades 4-adult.

Vivaldi, Voice of the Baroque, H.C. Robins Landon. ISBN# 978-0226468426. 208 pages, Grades 9-adult.

Handel

George Frideric Handel, Composer of Messiah, Charles Ludwig. ISBN# 978-0880620482. 185 pages, Grades 7-adult.

Handel at the Court of Kings, (Great Musicians Series), Opal Wheeler. ISBN# 978-1933573038. 166 pages, Grades 4-8.

Handel, Who Knew What He Liked, M.T. Anderson. ISBN# 978-0763625627. 48 pages, Grades K-6.

Hallelujah Handel, Douglas Cowling. ISBN# 978-0439058506. 48 pages, Grades 1-4.

George Handel (Getting to Know the World's Greatest Composers), Mike Venezia. ISBN# 978-0516445397. 32 pages, Grades K-4.

Handel (Famous Children Series), Ann Rachlin. ISBN# 978-0812049923. 24 pages, Grades K-3.

Bach

Sebastian, A Book About Bach, Jeanette Winter. ISBN# 015200629X. 40 pages, Grades PK-3.

Bach (Famous Children Series), Ann Rachlin. ISBN# 978-0812049916. 24 pages, Grades K-3.

Sebastian Bach, The Boy from Thuringia, (Great Musicains Series), Opal Wheeler & Sybil Deucher. ISBN# 978-0974650517. 127 pages, Grades 4-8.

Introducing Bach (Great Composers Series), Roland Vernon. ISBN# 978-1841384689. 32 pages, Grades 2-6.

Johann Sebastian Bach (Getting to Know the World's Greatest Composers Series), Mike Venezia. 32 pages, Grades K-4.

Classical
Haydn

Haydn (Famous Children Series), Ann Rachlin. ISBN# 978-0812049886. 24 pages, Grades K-3.

Joseph Haydn, the Merry Little Peasant, Opal Wheeler & Sybil Deucher. Zeezok Publishing. 120 pages, Grades 4-8.

The Farewell Symphony, Anna Harwell Celenza. Charlesbridge Publishing, 2005, ISBN# 978-1570914072. 32 Pages, Grades PK-6.

Haydn (Composer's World Series), Wendy Thompson. ISBN# 978-0670841714. 48 pages, Grades 4-8.

Mozart

Mozart, the Wonder Boy, Opal Wheeler & Sybil Deucher. ISBN# 978-0974650531. 127 pages, Grades 4-8.

Mozart Tonight, Julie Downing. ISBN# 978-0689718083. Grades K-4.

Mozart (Famous Children Series), Ann Rachlin. ISBN# 978-0812049893. 24 pages, Grades K-3.

Wolfgang Amadeus Mozart (Getting to Know the World's Greatest Composers), Mike Venezia. ISBN# 978-0516445410. 32 pages, Grades K-4.

Introducing Mozart (Great Composers Series), Roland Vernon. ISBN# 978-0382391583. 32 pages, Grades 2-6.

Wolfgang Amadeus Mozart (Composer's World Series), Wendy Thompson. ISBN# 978-0670836796. 48 pages, Grades 4-8.

Beethoven

Ludwig Van Beethoven (Getting to Know the World's Greatest Composers), Mike Venezia. ISBN# 978-0516200699. 32 pages, Grades K-4.

Beethoven (Famous Children Series), Ann Rachlin. ISBN# 978-0812019964. 24 pages, Grades K-3.

Introducing Beethoven (Great Composers Series), Roland Vernon. ISBN# 978-1841384672. 32 pages, Grades 2-6.

Ludwig Beethoven and the Chiming Tower Bells, Opal Wheeler. ISBN#0-9746505-6-0. 144 pages, Grades 4-8.

Ludwig Van Beethoven (Composer's World Series), Wendy Thompson. ISBN# 978-0670836789. 48 pages, Grades 4-8.

Schubert

Franz Peter Schubert (The Primary Source Library of Famous Composers), Eric Michael Summerer, ISBN # 978-1404227682. 32 pages, Ages 9-12.

Franz Schubert (Composer's World Series), Wendy Thompson. ISBN# 978-0670841721. 48 pages, Grades 4-8.

Franz Schubert and His Merry Friends, Opal Wheeler & Sybil Deucher. 127 pages, Grades 4-8.

Early Romantic

Mendelssohn

    The Life and Times of Felix Mendelssohn, Susan Zannos. ISBN# 978-1584152101. 48 pages, Grades 4-8.

    Mendelssohn and His World, R. Larry Todd. ISBN# 978-0691027159. 428 pages. Grades 8-adult.

Chopin

    Chopin (Famous Children Series), Ann Rachlin. ISBN# 978-0516084916. 24 pages, Grades K-3.

    Frédéric Chopin (Getting to Know the World's Greatest Composers), Mike Venezia. ISBN# 978-0516265346. 32 pages, Grades K-4.

    Introducing Chopin (Great Composers Series), Roland Vernon. ISBN# 978-1841384719. 32 pages, Grades 2-6.

    Frédéric Chopin, Son of Poland, Early Years, Opal Wheeler. Zeezok Publishing. 160 pages, Grades 4-8.

    Frédéric Chopin, Son of Poland, Later Years, Opal Wheeler. Zeezok Publishing. 166 pages, Grades 4-8.

Schumann

    Robert Schumann and Mascot Ziff, Opal Wheeler. Zeezok Publishing, 1975. 978-1-933573-06-9. 167 pages, Grades 4-8.

    Schumann (Famous Children Series), Ann Rachlin. ISBN# 978-0812015447. 24 pages, Grades K-3.

Liszt

    Liszt (Master Musicians Series), Derek Watson. ISBN# 978-019864999. 424 pages, Grades 8-adult.

    Reflections on Liszt, Alan Walker. ISBN# 978-0801443633. 304 pages, Grades 8-adult.

    The Life and Times of Franz Liszt (Masters of Music), Jim Whiting. ISBN # 978-1584152804. 48 pages, Ages 9-12.

Verdi

    Introducing Verdi, (Great Composers Series), Roland Vernon. ISBN# 978-1841384733. 32 pages, Grades 2-6.

    The Life and Times of Giuseppe Verdi: The World's Greatest Composers (Masters of Music), Jim Whiting. ISBN# 978-1584152811. 48 pages, Ages 9-12.

    Verdi (The World of Composers), Greta Cencetti. ISBN# 978-1588454737. 40 pages, Ages 9-12.

    Verdi With a Vengeance: The Energetic Guide to the Life and Complete Works of the King of Opera, William Berger. ISBN# 978-0375705182. 512 pages, Grades 9-adult.

Brahms

Brahms (Famous Children Series), Ann Rachlin. ISBN# 978-0812015423. 24 pages, Grades K-3.

The Young Brahms, Opal Wheeler & Sybil Deucher. Zeezok Publishing. 127 pages, Grades 4-8.

Johannes Brahms (Getting to Know the World's Greatest Composers), Mike Venezia. 32 pages, Grades K-4.

The Life and Times of Johannes Brahms (Masters of Music Series), ISBN# 978-1584152149. 48 pages, Grades 4-8.

Late Romantic
Foster

The Life and Times of Stephen Foster (Masters of Music Series), Susan Zannos. ISBN# 978-1584152132. 48 pages, Grades 4-8.

With My Banjo on My Knee: The Minstrel Songs of Stephen Foster, Daniel Partner. ISBN# 978-1574242294. 64 pages, Grades 6-adult.

He Heard America Sing: The Story of Stephen Foster, Clair Lee Purdy. Grades 7-adult.

Tchaikovsky

Pyotr Ilyich Tchaikovsky (Composer's World Series), Wendy Thompson. ISBN# 978-0756775339. 48 pages, Grades 4-8.

Tchaikovsky (Famous Children Series), Ann Rachlin. ISBN# 978-0812015454. 24 pages, Grades K-3.

Peter Tchaikovsky (Getting to Know the World's Greatest Composers), Mike Venezia. ISBN# 978-0516445373. 32 pages, Grades K-4.

Dvořák

Dvořák in America: In Search of the New World. Joseph Horowitz. ISBN# 978-0812626810. 160 pages, Grades 6-12.

Fauré

www.classiccat.net/faure_g/biography.htm

http://tinyurl.com/aqpw78

http://tinyurl.com/ajck3c

Elgar

www.elgar.org/2welcome.htm

The Rochester Philharmonic Orchestra has a section of nice lesson plans, including one on Elgar, in PDF format here: http://tinyurl.com/djj8mr

Bruckner

This site is in German but has nice pictures of his home and more: http://tinyurl.com/bh3g9k

www.geocities.com/Vienna/4291/florian.htm

www.geocities.com/Vienna/4291/youth.htm

Debussy

Claude Debussy (Composer's World Series), Wendy Thompson. ISBN# 978-0670844821. 48 pages, Grades 4-8.

Strauss

This site, dedicated to ". . . our grandfather Richard Strauss," contains lots of pictures and interesting tidbits: http://tinyurl.com/ckpjfh

You'll find pictures of Strauss here: http://w3.rz-berlin.mpg.de/cmp/strauss_r_pic.html

Contemporary

Ives

What Charlie Heard: The Story of the American Composer Charles Ives, Mordicai Gerstein. ISBN# 978-1591122784. Grades 3-6.

Gershwin

George Gershwin (Getting to Know the World's Greatest Composers), Mike Venezia. ISBN# 978-0516445366. 32 pages, Grades K-4.

Gershwin's Rhapsody in Blue, Anna Harwell Celenza and Joann E. Kitchel. ISBN# 978-1570915567. 32 pages, Grades 1-5.

Introducing Gershwin (Great Composers Series), Roland Vernon. ISBN# 978-1841384702. 32 pages, Grades 2-6.

The Life and Times of George Gershwin (Masters of Music), Jim Whiting. ISBN# 978-1584152798. 48 pages, Grades 4-6.

Copland

Aaron Copland (Getting to Know the World's Greatest Composers), Mike Venezia. ISBN# 978-0516445380. 32 pages, Grades K-4.

Joplin

Raggin': A Story About Scott Joplin, Barbara Mitchell. ISBN# 978-0876145890. 56 pages, Grades 4-8.

The Life and Times of Scott Joplin (Masters of Music), John Bankston. ISBN# 978-1584152705. 48 pages, Grades 4-8.

Williams

www.johnwilliams.org

http://tinyurl.com/8tphw9

http://tinyurl.com/cu7rdj

CDs

Peter and the Wolf, Sergei Prokofiev. Can be found in many versions as a CD or book and CD set.

Carnival of the Animals, Camille Saint-Saëns. Can be found in many versions as a CD or book and CD set.

Beethoven's Wig: Sing-Along Symphonies (CD). Several volumes of funny lyrics set to great classical music.

Classical Kids CD Series – produced by NAXOS – Each CD is a combination of music, history and story-telling, designed to introduce children to the composers and their music. Titles include:

> *Beethoven Lives Upstairs*
>
> *Hallelujah Handel*
>
> *Vivaldi's Ring of Mystery*
>
> *Mozart's Magic Fantasy*
>
> *Mozart's Magnificent Voyage*
>
> *Mr. Bach Comes to Call*
>
> *Tchaikovsky Discovers America*

DVDs

Classical Kids Series on DVD:

> *Mr. Bach Comes to Call*
>
> *Beethoven Lives Upstairs*

Coloring Books

Musical Instruments Coloring Book, Ellen J. McHenry. Dover Publications, 1995, ISBN#0-486-28785-8. 48 pages.

Great Composers Coloring Book, John Green & Paul Negri. Dover Publications, 2007, ISBN# 978-0486462141. 32 pages.

Composers (Fandex Family Field Guides), David Bouchier. Workman Publishing Company, 1999. ISBN# 978-0761112068.

More Coloring Books – Bellerophon has a large selection of coloring books on the composers and other musical classics like *Peter and the Wolf* and *Sleeping Beauty*. www.bellerophonbooks.com

Games

Composers Card Game – Available at unclesgames.com and other sources.

Multimedia History of Music and Great Composers – CD-ROM game by Voyetra.

Useful Websites

www.classicalarchives.com

The Classical Archives is the largest classical music site on the web: 40,042 full-length classical music files by 2,091 composers. Free users are welcome and may access 5 unprotected files per day after logging-in. Subscribe for $25/year to have full access to 1,000 files/month for 12 months.

www.lessontutor.com/musicgenhome.html

Awesome site filled with worksheets, lesson plans, bios, links, and more!

www.classicsforkids.com/links

A fun site filled with games, links, wonderful activity sheets, and much more for kids

www.dsokids.com/2001/rooms/musicroom.asp

The Dallas Symphony Orchestra has a kids' site with loads of music examples: see and hear the families of instruments and more.

www.creatingmusic.com

Creative music site where children can compose as well as play with musical performance, music games, and music puzzles.

w3.rz-berlin.mpg.de/cmp/classmus.html

For upper-level students—classical music history, biographical information about composers (with portraits and short sound examples), explanations of the various musical forms, and a dictionary of musical terminologies.

www.eclassical.com

MP3 files here have no restrictions. Copy to your MP3 player or burn your own CDs.

www.gutenberg.net

Thousands of e-books for the use of anyone anywhere at no cost and with almost no restrictions whatsoever.

www.gutenberg.org/catalog/world/readfile?fk_files=90760&pageno=1

The World's Great Men of Music by Harriette Brower, circa 1922. (Simple biographies in short chapters—great for read-alouds.)

www.baroquemusic.org

Lovely portrait gallery of famous Baroque composers as well as their biographies plus two hours of Baroque music.

Ancient Music to Music in the Middle Ages

Years: __Creation__ to __circa 1350__

People have been making music since __accept different answers—the beginning of time/ Adam and Eve, Creation . . .__

Genesis 4:21 tells us that Jubal was the "__father of all who play the harp and flute.__"

From __paintings and writings__ found in ancient Mesopotamia, China, and Egypt, we know that there were musical instruments in those civilizations.

We don't know what ancient music sounded like because __it was not written down.__

The beginning of the growth of Western classical music started with __church music of the Middle Ages.__

The first written music didn't appear until __A.D. 1000__.

This music was called __plainchant or Gregorian chant.__

Characteristics of chants:
1. __sung in unison__
2. __no instruments__
3. __non-metrical rhythm__—you can't __tap__ your foot
4. __smooth progression__—notes move by __step__
5. words sung in __Latin__
6. Tunes are __modal__—they do not follow the major or minor scales used today.

Gregorian chant was used during the Christian church service, which became known as __Mass.__

Mass is divided into two parts:

__Ordinary__—the prayers that don't change

__Proper__—the prayers that do change according to the church calendar

The parts of the Ordinary that are sung:
1. Kyrie: a plea for __mercy.__

2. Gloria: proclaims God's __glory.__

3. Credo: the __Nicene Creed.__

4. Sanctus: proclaims God's __holiness.__

5. Agnus Dei: proclaims the power of Christ's __redemption.__

Music in the Renaissance

During the Renaissance, the __royal courts__ became supporters of the arts.

Court songs: __love poetry__ set to music.

Court songs were written by troubadours in southern France, __trouvères__ in northern France, __minnesingers__ in Germany.

Court songs were sung by bards, __minstrels, jongleurs.__

Because __musical notation__ and literacy were limited, we don't know how this music was performed.

Polyphony—music with __more than one__ voice, or musical line, at a time.

Organum—a type of polyphony in which a composer adds another line sung at the __same time.__

Between A.D. 900 and A.D. 1300, several musical changes took place:

At first, harmony moved along with melody a certain __distance__ from it.

Then, harmony became more __independent__.

Next, more __notes__ were added. Several notes were sung at the same time as one chant note.

Later, composers began to add two lines of __harmony.__

Finally, __rhythm__ became more structured.

Notable composers from this period:

Guillaume de Machaut, who was French and wrote the first ballades

Guillaume Dufay, also French, who brought many styles together and helped establish the form of the Mass

Thomas Tallis, considered the "Father of English Cathedral Music"

Giovanni Palestrina, considered the greatest representative of sixteenth century counterpoint

Orlando de Lassus, the most published composer of the age

William Byrd, an English Catholic living in Protestant England who built a bridge between the older musical sounds and the new sounds

Giovanni Gabrieli, an Italian who used instruments with choral music

Carlo Gesualdo, an Italian who wrote madrigals

John Dowland, the finest lute player in England, who is often considered the greatest English songwriter ever

Claudio Monteverdi, who linked Renaissance music to the Baroque and added instrumental parts to the madrigal

Vincenzo Galilei, the father of the scientist Galileo Galilei, who challenged composers to make music sound like the words it expressed

Gregorio Allegri, who wrote *Miserere*, a piece for nine voices, which was so beautiful it was allowed to be performed only at the Sistine Chapel during Holy Week

Ballad: • __secular song__
   • sung in __courtly language__
   • accompanied by __musical instruments__

Madrigal: Song
   • written for several __voices__ to sing at the same time
   • always __secular__ (not about God)
   • usually about __love__
   • generally sung at a __quick tempo__
   • popular among the __aristocracy__ of the time

Counterpoint: describes the combination of simultaneously sounding musical lines according to a system of __rules__

The Baroque Period

During the Baroque period, music was characterized by the phrase, "<u>never one note when five will do</u>."

Musicians were employed by <u>wealthy households.</u>

Two composers we are introduced to in the Baroque period:
- Georg Philipp <u>Telemann</u>
- Johann <u>Pachelbel</u> [besides Johann Sebastian Bach]

Musical Forms
Opera
Like a play, it has <u>scenery</u>, <u>actors</u>, <u>costumes</u>.

Unlike a play, it is <u>sung</u>, not spoken, and is accompanied by an <u>orchestra</u>.

Oratorio
Like an opera, it is <u>sung</u>.
Unlike an opera, it uses <u>biblical stories</u> and is not <u>staged</u>.
People liked oratorios because they were similar to operas but could be performed in <u>church</u>.

Cantata
Like oratorios but short enough to take up the same time as a <u>church service</u>

Suite
Made of different dance movements, including:
1. <u>allemande</u>   5. <u>gigue</u>
2. <u>bourrée</u>   6. <u>minuet</u>
3. <u>courante</u>   7. <u>sarabande</u>
4. <u>gavotte</u>   8. <u>waltz</u>

Dance music tends to have:
- steady <u>rhythm</u>
- <u>repetition</u>

Concerto
- written for an instrumental <u>soloist</u>
- accompanied by an <u>orchestra</u>
- has three movements: <u>fast</u>   <u>slow</u>   <u>fast</u>

Baroque Instruments
Most common:
- <u>organ</u>
- <u>harpsichord</u>
- <u>recorder</u>
- <u>trumpet</u>
- <u>violin</u>

Baroque orchestras were larger/<u>smaller</u> than orchestras we have today.

Antonio Vivaldi

1. Why is Vivaldi called the "Red Priest"?
   [Because he had bright-red hair and he entered the priesthood.]

2. With which place was Vivaldi connected for most of his life?
   a. church
   b. [orphanage]
   c. vineyard
   d. hospital

3. What is a benefactor?
   [A benefactor is someone who pays a composer to write and play music.]

4. How many movements does a concerto have?
   a. one
   b. two
   c. [three]
   d. four

5. Which famous composer was influenced by Vivaldi's concertos?
   [Bach or Johann Sebastian Bach]

6. True or False: Vivaldi remained a devout priest all his life. [False]

7. Vivaldi is best known for his development of the
   a. opera.
   b. fugue.
   c. [concerto.]
   d. clarinet.

8. True or False: Vivaldi's works were almost lost, but they were eventually recovered in the early twentieth century. [True]

9. During which musical era did Vivaldi compose?
   a. Dark Ages
   b. [Baroque]
   c. Renaissance
   d. Classical

10. Vivaldi's most famous concertos belong to a set of four entitled _The Four Seasons._

A Young Scholar's Guide to Composers

George Frideric Handel

1. Handel shares a birth year (1685) and some similarities with another famous composer named
    a. Beethoven.
    b. Vivaldi.
    c. Mozart.
    d. [Bach.]

2. True or False: Handel stayed in Germany throughout his career. [False]

3. A Kapellmeister is the director of music for a monarch, nobleman, or church.

4. True or False: During the performance of an opera in Handel's time, people would play cards and talk. [True]

5. In 1714, when Queen Anne of England died, the Elector of Hanover became King George I. What was his relationship to Handel?
    a. father
    b. son
    c. [employer]
    d. conductor

6. Which anthem did Handel write that has been sung at British coronations ever since?
    a. "God Save the Queen"
    b. Messiah
    c. [Zadok the Priest]
    d. Water Music

7. What are the differences between an oratorio and an opera?

Opera	Oratorio
Secular—not specifically religious	Sacred—of, or relating to, religion
Scenery	No scenery
Actors	No actors
Costumes	No costumes

8. What form of music is Handel's famous work Messiah? [oratorio]

9. At what part of Messiah do people usually stand? ["Hallelujah Chorus"]

10. True or False: Handel wanted to change lives with his music, not just entertain his listeners. [True]

Johann Sebastian Bach

1. True or False: Bach shared the same attitude toward music (viewing it as a means to glorify God) as the Protestant reformer Martin Luther. [True]

2. The Wartburg Castle still sits high on a hilltop overlooking the city of Eisenach, where Bach was raised.

3. True or False: Bach was from a famous family of wheelwrights. [False]

4. The orphaned Bach went to live
    a. in the local monastery.
    b. in boarding school.
    c. [with his brother.]
    d. with his uncle.

5. Bach once walked 200 miles to hear a famous _____ named Dietrich Buxtehude.
    a. pianist
    b. [organist]
    c. opera singer
    d. violinist

6. True or False: Bach became known as one of the greatest organists in Germany. [True]

7. While Bach was in prison, he made good use of his time by _____. [examples of correct answers: writing music, or composing, or writing "organ chorale preludes"]

8. Bach wrote at the bottom of all of his works the initials S.D.G. (Soli Deo Gloria). What does that phrase mean? [To God Alone the Glory]

9. Name one of Bach's compositions or books: _____. [Compositions mentioned in the lesson were: the St. John Passion, Mass in B Minor, and Goldberg Variations. Books mentioned were: Little Organ Book and The Well-Tempered Clavier.]

10. Which statements are true of Bach?
    a. [He composed nearly 1,000 works.]
    b. He was a master composer in the Romantic era.
    c. [He wrote The Well-Tempered Clavier.]
    d. [He fathered 20 children.]
    e. He was most famous for his operas.
    f. [He left a legacy of faith.]

The Classical Period

The Classical period took place between the years 1750 and 1820.

Name two major political events that were happening in the world during this time:
1. The American Revolution
2. The French Revolution

What was different about concerts during this period? They were public concerts.

What was different about the audiences attending these concerts? Common people, not just the nobility, began attending.

Composers began writing in homophony, instead of counterpoint.

Homophony occurs in a work that contains one melody.

This melody is supported by harmony, which accompanies the melody in chords.

New forms:
1. sonata   2. minuet   3. rondo   4. theme and variations

Sonata form contains three sections.

Section #	Name	Music Contains	Format
1	exposition	theme	A
2	development	different theme	B
3	recapitulation	similar theme	A'

The minuet is the one dance form that carried over from the Baroque period.

The rondo takes a tune and repeats it.

Some possible structures for a rondo: ABACA OR ABACABA

The theme and variations form introduces a theme and repeats it with different variations.

A symphony is made up of four movements.

These movements are actually other forms.

Movement	Tempo (fast or slow)	Form
first	fast or moderate	sonata
second	slow	any—sonata or rondo or variation
third	moderate	minuet
fourth	fast	sonata or rondo

(Franz) Joseph Haydn

1. Where was Haydn born?
   a. Hungary
   b. Germany
   c. France
   d. [Austria]

2. True or False: Composing did not come easily to Haydn. [True]

3. Circle all of the following characteristics that describe Haydn and his personality:
   a. [sense of humor]
   b. stingy
   c. angry
   d. [generous]
   e. [easygoing]
   f. impatient
   g. [respected]

4. Haydn was one of the last musicians to work in a noble household.

5. Was Haydn a Christian? [yes]

6. Define a Kapellmeister: [the head court musician]

7. What part of Haydn's personality shows most strongly through his music?
   a. [his cheerfulness]
   b. his temper
   c. his generosity
   d. his love

8. Haydn is known as the "Father of the Symphony."

9. *The Creation* is one of Haydn's well-known works. The words for it were taken from the writings of John Milton and from the Bible.

10. Haydn was a dear friend of another famous composer, Mozart, who called him "Papa Haydn."

Wolfgang Amadeus Mozart

1. Mozart's father began teaching his son keyboard and composition when he was just <u>4</u> years old.

2. As a child prodigy, young Mozart performed all over Europe, even for Marie Antoinette, the future <u>queen</u> of France.

3. Mozart had the amazing ability to memorize music after hearing it played just <u>once</u>.

4. Mozart relaxed by (circle all that apply):.
   a. [writing music.]
   b. [solving math problems.]
   c. gardening.
   d. [playing pool.]

5. Were Mozart and his wife Christians? [yes]

6. Which of the composers that we've studied was Mozart's mentor?
   a. [Haydn]
   b. Bach
   c. Handel
   d. Vivaldi

7. True or False: Mozart was a famous court musician. [False]

8. Once, when a beggar asked Mozart for money, he
   a. gave him cash.
   b. bought him lunch.
   c. [wrote him music to sell.]
   d. gave him a free concert ticket.

9. True or False: Mozart died young. [True]

10. Which of the following of Mozart's compositions is a testimony to his faith?
    a. [Requiem]
    b. Piano Concerto no. 24
    c. Symphony no. 40
    d. *The Marriage of Figaro*

Ludwig van Beethoven

1. Beethoven was born only 14 years after which of these composers?
   a. Bach
   b. Haydn
   c. Handel
   d. [Mozart]

2. Which of the composers that we've studied so far were born in Germany? (Circle all that apply.)
   a. Haydn
   b. [Bach]
   c. [Handel]
   d. [Beethoven]
   e. Mozart

3. Beethoven studied under the famous composer Joseph <u>Haydn</u>.

4. When his mother died, Beethoven became the head of the house and took on the support of his <u>brothers</u>.

5. Beethoven became well known as a gifted player of the then-new instrument, the <u>pianoforte</u>.

6. Beethoven wrote many famous pieces, including (circle all that apply):
   a. [the *Pastoral Symphony*.]
   b. [the Fifth Symphony.]
   c. the *Farewell Symphony*.
   d. [*Moonlight Sonata*.]
   e. ["Ode to Joy."]

7. How would you describe Beethoven's personality? [Answers will vary.]

8. What was one of the biggest inspirations for Beethoven's music?
   a. God
   b. people in general
   c. his father
   d. [nature]

9. By the time he was 48, Beethoven was totally <u>deaf</u>.

10. True or False: Beethoven had an outwardly visible, obvious relationship with Jesus Christ. [False]

The Romantic Period

The Romantic period took place between the years 1820 and 1910.

Romantics:

- Were fascinated by the unknown
- Relied on emotion and imagination
- Were interested in what happened long ago or far away
- Emphasized the way they felt, not necessarily what was true
- Were particularly interested in nature and man's struggle with nature

In Romantic Music:

- Melodies began to flow.
- Harmony became rich.
- Chromaticism, in which composers use extra notes outside the major and minor scales, was used.
- Pieces became longer.
- Contrast within the music was greater.

New Forms of Music:

- Lieder — art songs or poems set to music. (The composer tries to give the listeners a feeling of the emotion in the poem.)
- Étude—French word for "study"—develops a certain technique on an instrument
- Ballade—a ballad
- Fantasia—like a fantasy — very imaginative
- Nocturne—commonly used by Chopin for many of his beautiful songlike pieces

Romantic Dance Forms:

- mazurka
- polonaise
- waltz

Program Music:
Tone Poem/Symphonic Poem

- Type of orchestral composition
- Followed an actual story or expressed a certain concept

Program Symphony:

- Similar to a tone poem
- More than one movement
- Often, the themes of a symphonic poem will appear in more than one movement.

During the Romantic era, the Industrial Revolution was occurring and there were improvements also in musical instruments. Some new instruments even came into use during this period, such as the following:
contrabassoon, bass clarinet, piccolo, English horn, cymbals, gongs, bells, triangles

Two women who composed during this time:
Fanny Mendelssohn Hensel
Clara Wieck Schumann

Franz Schubert

1. Franz Schubert was born in 1797 in the musical city of Vienna.

2. Franz would often come home and join with his father and two brothers in a string quartet in order to try out new compositions.

3. The gatherings that Schubert's friends would have that included dancing, poetry reading, and Franz improvising on the piano were called
   a. Franz parties.
   b. Schubert days.
   c. [Schubertiads.]
   d. Franziads.

4. Schubert, along with Beethoven, is considered to be the "bridge" between the Classical period and the Romantic period.

5. One of Schubert's most famous symphonies is his Eighth Symphony, which has only two movements. It is also called the Unfinished Symphony.

6. Schubert was most in awe of the composer Beethoven and asked to be buried next to him.

7. True or False: People were amazed at Schubert's ability to compose so quickly and perfectly. [True]

8. Schubert was always poor. Which group did he rely on to support him?
   a. the government
   b. the church
   c. [his friends]
   d. his family

9. Schubert is most famous for his 600 songs for voice, also known as
   a. symphonies.
   b. operas.
   c. librettos.
   d. [lieder.]

10. True or False: His lifestyle showed his strong commitment to Christ. [False]

A Young Scholar's Guide to Composers

Felix Mendelssohn

1. True or False: Mendelssohn's family was well-to-do and educated. [True]

2. Felix Mendelssohn, along with his family, converted from Judaism to
   a. Buddhism.
   b. Hinduism.
   c. [Christianity.]
   d. Agnosticism.

3. In addition to music, Mendelssohn was talented in (circle all that apply):
   a. [painting.]
   b. engineering.
   c. [memorization.]
   d. [languages.]
   e. [writing.]

4. Mendelssohn became a very good friend of Goethe, a <u>poet</u> and <u>philosopher.</u>

5. One of Mendelssohn's greatest works was the overture to Shakespeare's
   a. [A Midsummer Night's Dream.]
   b. Romeo and Juliet.
   c. King Lear.
   d. Hamlet.

6. One of Mendelssohn's achievements was the founding and directing of the Leipzig <u>Conservatory.</u>

7. His Fifth Symphony (the Reformation Symphony) ends with a setting of Luther's "A Mighty Fortress Is Our God," a hymn that is still sung today.

8. Mendelssohn died young, after composing important works in every form except <u>opera.</u>

9. Do we have evidence that Mendelssohn loved the Lord? <u>Yes</u>

10. True or False: Mendelssohn often rearranged words of Scripture to make the words fit better into his music. [False]

Frédéric Chopin

1. Chopin was born in <u>Poland</u> but lived his entire adult life in <u>France.</u>

2. True or False: Before age 6, Chopin could play on the piano every melody he had ever heard and had even begun to improvise. [True]

3. Which of the characteristics below describe Chopin? (Circle all that apply.)
   a. ["Polish Prodigy"]   e. [fun-loving]
   b. shy   f. sloppy
   c. [mannerly]   g. silly
   d. unintelligent   h. [snobbish]

4. From what disease did both Chopin and his beloved sister die?
   a. muscular dystrophy
   b. AIDS
   c. [tuberculosis]
   d. hepatitis B

5. True or False: Chopin preferred playing in large concert halls as opposed to small, intimate salons. [False]

6. Match the following musical terms with their description:
   a. étude =   French for "studies"
   b. tempo rubato =   "stolen time"
   c. nocturnes =   "music of the night"

7. Chopin knew many writers, artists, musicians, and other famous people. Which of the following had he met? Circle all that apply.
   [Charles Dickens]   Michelangelo
   [Victor Hugo]   Mark Twain
   Jane Austen   Georgia O'Keeffe
   Queen Elizabeth   [Franz Liszt]
   [Eugene Delacroix]   [George Sand]

8. What country was Chopin referring to when he said, "Their orchestra resembles their roast beef and their turtle soup; it's strong, it's famous . . . but that is all"? <u>England</u>

9. Chopin, along with some other composers, is considered a "bridge" between the <u>Romantic</u> period and the <u>Classical</u> period.

10. Chopin requested that Mozart's Requiem be played at his funeral, which was attended by thousands.

Robert Schumann

1. Schumann's works (along with Chopin's and Mendelssohn's) mark the beginning of the Romantic period of music.

2. When Schumann's father died, Schumann's mother wanted him to study
   a. medical science.
   b. music.
   c. art.
   d. [law.]

3. What happened to Schumann that forced him to give up his dream of being a concert pianist? [His finger became crippled.]

4. Because of his love for literature, Schumann, along with being an excellent composer, was also an excellent
   a. novelist.
   b. English teacher.
   c. librarian.
   d. [editor.]

5. Schumann and another composer we've studied, named Chopin, were born in the same year.

6. True or False: Schumann married his piano teacher's daughter and they had eight children. [True]

7. In 1853, Schumann became a mentor to and a great friend of the composer Johannes Brahms.

8. True or False: Schumann died at home of tuberculosis. [False]

9. Who provided most of the income for the Schumann family? Clara Schumann

10. Clara Schumann was considered the best female pianist of the nineteenth century.

Franz Liszt

1. Franz Liszt was born in rural
   a. Germany.
   b. England.
   c. America.
   d. [Hungary.]

2. Franz's father died when Franz was
   a. 9.
   b. 4.
   c. [16.]
   d. 18.

3. True or False: Franz could perform his complete recitals from memory. [True]

4. Because he wanted to be the sole performer in concerts, Liszt "invented" the recital.

5. Circle all the following characteristics that describe Franz Liszt:
   a. humble
   b. [kind]
   c. discouraging
   d. moral
   e. [vain]
   f. [generous]
   g. slow to learn

6. Which composer that we've studied was an admirer of Liszt and possibly even a little jealous of him? Chopin

7. True or False: Liszt was probably the originator of charity concerts, or benefits. [True]

8. Liszt was called the "Grand Old Man" of European music.

9. True or False: Liszt had weak performance skills. [False]

10. Liszt introduced the symphonic or tone poem.

Anton Bruckner

1. True or False: Anton Bruckner was born to an aristocratic family in Vienna. [False]

2. Anton wrote to his mother "Only the thought that all God does is for the best keeps me going." What difficulty that he experienced might he have been referring to? [His father's illness and eventual death; typhoid fever]

3. Why did Bruckner feel out of place in Vienna? [He was a country boy in a sophisticated city, he dressed poorly, had poor manners, was socially awkward]

4. Some of Bruckner's character qualities were (circle all that apply):
   a. [his devotion to God.]
   b. [his outgoing personality.]
   c. his idleness.
   d. [his willingness to keep working on his music despite little success or recognition.]

5. True or False: Bruckner preferred Wagner's music to that of Brahms. [True]

6. Anton Bruckner was in his sixties before his reputation and fame began to grow.

7. One of the composers who appreciated Bruckner's work was Mahler.

8. Circle the names of the composers who influenced Bruckner.
   a. [Wagner]
   b. Mozart
   c. Paul McCartney
   d. [Beethoven]

9. Toward the end of his life, Bruckner received financial support from [the Habsburg emperor Franz Josef].

10. Bruckner will always be remembered
    a. for his operas.
    b. [as a religious composer.]
    c. for his innovative use of new instruments.
    d. as a lyricist.

Giuseppe Verdi

1. Verdi was born in which European country? [Italy.]

2. Like Richard Wagner, Verdi was known for his
   a. symphonies.
   b. jazz music.
   c. [operas.]
   d. All of the above.

3. True or False: Verdi came from a wealthy, educated family. [False]

4. Verdi's first instrument was a
   a. flute.
   b. [spinet.]
   c. organ.
   d. clarinet.

5. What relationships did Antonio Barezzi have with Verdi?
   a. [mentor]
   b. employer
   c. uncle
   d. [father-in-law]
   e. priest

6. True or False: Verdi was not very respectful toward the church. [True]

7. True or False: Verdi's first opera, Oberto, was written during a happy time in his life. [True]

8. What personal tragedies did Verdi live through? [death of his first wife and his two young children]

9. Besides music, Verdi was involved in
   a. [politics.]
   b. science.
   c. art.
   d. the church.

10. Which of the following operas were composed by Verdi? (Circle all that apply.)
    a. [Aida]
    b. [Rigoletto]
    c. The Pirates of Penzance
    d. [Otello]
    e. [Nabucco]
    f. [Macbeth]

Johannes Brahms

1. How would you describe Brahms's childhood? [difficult, poor]

2. Two of Brahms's favorite composers were <u>Bach</u> and <u>Beethoven</u>.

3. What did Brahms do with his compositions that he didn't think were good enough to publish? [He burned them.]

4. <u>Robert Schumann</u> helped to launch Brahms's career by writing about him in a musical journal.

5. Brahms gave music lessons to the family of
   a. Queen Victoria.
   b. [Prince Leopold III.]
   c. Henry VIII.
   d. All of the above.

6. True or False: Brahms was a part of the progressive "New German School." [False]

7. Brahms's personality could best be described as
   a. shy.
   b. outgoing, the life of the party.
   c. self-centered.
   d. [difficult yet lovable.]

8. Brahms is remembered best for composing <u>symphonies</u>.

9. How was Brahms's German Requiem different from a traditional Requiem Mass? [Instead of using a standardized Latin text, Brahms derived his text from Martin Luther's German Bible. A traditional Requiem Mass begins with prayers for the dead; Brahms began his with "Blessed are they that mourn: for they shall be comforted."]

10. True or False: It is difficult to know exactly what Brahms believed about God. [True]

Stephen Foster

1. Stephen Foster grew up in
   a. Vienna, Austria.
   b. Cincinnati, Ohio.
   c. Atlanta, Georgia.
   d. [Pittsburgh, Pennsylvania.]

2. True or False: As a child, Foster received much encouragement from his family to become a musician. [False]

3. In his family, Stephen was closest to <u>his brother Morrison, or Mit</u>.

4. Foster's music was influenced by (circle all that apply):
   a. Beethoven.
   b. [minstrel performers.]
   c. jazz.
   d. ["Ethiopian" music.]

5. Foster's first musical success was the song <u>"Oh! Susanna"</u>.

6. The song "Oh! Susanna" was the "theme song" for the <u>forty-niners</u> on their way to the California Gold Rush.

7. True or False: Foster never married. [False]

8. Which of Stephen Foster's songs is the state song of Florida? ["Old Folks at Home" or "Way Down Upon the Swanee River"]

9. True or False: In spite of publishing many popular songs, Foster did not make much money from his musical career. [True]

10. True or False: Stephen Foster leaves a legacy as a great American composer and a strong spiritual leader. [False]

Pyotr Ilyich Tchaikovsky

1. In which country was Tchaikovsky born? [Russia]

2. True or False: Tchaikovsky's family was very musical. [False]

3. True or False: It was decided that Tchaikovsky, at the age of 10, would begin training for a career as an architect. [False]

4. True or False: Throughout his life, Tchaikovsky suffered from many torments and fears. [True]

5. Tchaikovsky was a friend and an associate of two brothers in the music field, Anton and Nikolai [Rubinstein.]

6. There is a sad story behind *Marche slave*. He composed it for a benefit concert to give aid (or help or money) to the kingdom of Serbia.

7. What is a patron? [One who provides money for another to live on so that the person can follow his art, or a wealthy or influential supporter of an artist or writer.]

8. Did Tchaikovsky ever meet his patron, the widow Nadezhda von Meck? [No]

9. Tchaikovsky wrote the music for a ballet that we often hear at Christmastime. What is the name of this ballet? [*The Nutcracker*]

10. Tchaikovsky's Sixth, and final, Symphony, which was written to describe life and death, was called the
    a. [*Pathétique.*]
    b. *Marche slave.*
    c. *1812 Overture.*
    d. Piano Concerto no. 1 in B-flat Minor.

Antonín Dvořák

1. Besides the violin, what else did Dvořák become interested in at an early age? [Trains]

2. Which composer's works did Dvořák study the most?
    a. Bach
    b. Tchaikovsky
    c. [Beethoven]
    d. Chopin

3. Which composer was Dvořák's lifelong mentor and friend?
    a. [Brahms]
    b. Joplin
    c. Haydn
    d. Mozart

4. True or False: Dvořák's first concert consisting entirely of his own works went so well that it became the springboard for his career. [True]

5. Dvořák wouldn't move to Vienna because he was a
    a. homebody.
    b. [nationalist].
    c. patriot.
    d. paraplegic.

6. Dvořák told a reporter for the *New York Herald* that black music (which he was personally fascinated with) would play a role in future American music.

7. This prediction was correct, because just around the corner were the beginnings of jazz music.

8. Dvořák was born and died in Prague.

9. Besides being influenced by black culture, Dvořák was also influenced by
    a. European culture.
    b. South American culture.
    c. [Native American culture.]
    d. Eskimo culture.

10. True or False: Dvořák was a Christian. [True]

Appendix: Lesson Answer Keys

Gabriel Urbain Fauré

1. True or False: Fauré was a noisy, ill-behaved child who loved to make music. [False]

2. Fauré was sent to boarding school because
   a. [he had talent.]
   b. he was a great student.
   c. he drove his parents crazy.
   d. he was orphaned.

3. Where was Fauré's boarding school located?
   a. Prague
   b. Germany
   c. Austria
   d. [Paris]

4. Saint-Saëns took special note of him because he excelled at which instrument? [piano]

5. Was Fauré a "model" church organist? [No]

6. Fauré served his country in which war? [Franco-Prussian]

7. Fauré is considered the master of what type of song? The [French art song.]

8. A Requiem Mass is a specific type of service performed in some churches immediately preceding what event? [burial]

9. Which two composers/teachers had a strong impact on Fauré? [Chopin and Saint-Saëns]

10. Fauré lost his hearing in later life, similar to [Beethoven,] another composer we have studied.

Sir Edward Elgar

1. Elgar was born near this large cathedral city, which was one of the famous "Three Choir" cities.
   a. [Worcester]
   b. London
   c. Athens
   d. Dover

2. Elgar's appearance as a composer ended a 200-year "drought" of music in which country? [England]

3. True or False: Elgar was from a rich upper-class family. [False]

4. True or False: Elgar was formally trained in music and composing. [False]

5. Elgar married one of his piano students, Caroline Roberts, whose family opposed the union because of Elgar's [Roman Catholic] religion and his [lower middle-class] social status.

6. What is an enigma, and how did Elgar use it in his music? [An enigma is a puzzle or something that contains a hidden meaning. One of Elgar's compositions included an enigma; one in which the main theme was known only to Elgar, his wife, and his publisher.]

7. Which piece of music did Elgar consider "the best of me," despite its poor debut?
   a. *Enigma Variations*
   b. Violin Sonata
   c. [*The Dream of Gerontius*]
   d. *Falstaff*

8. During which war did Elgar compose *Pomp and Circumstance*? [World War I]

9. Elgar's *Pomp and Circumstance* is commonly played at what type of American event? [graduations]

10. How were Elgar's last four masterpieces described? [moving, melancholy]

Claude Debussy

1. At age 10, Debussy was accepted into the prestigious <u>Paris</u> Conservatoire.

2. True or False: Debussy was a model pupil, conforming to his professors' ideals of music. [False]

3. When Debussy returned to Paris after studying in Rome, much was happening. Which of the following events were going on when Debussy returned?
   a. [There were rumors of war.]
   b. [Mass transit appeared.]
   c. [The Eiffel Tower opened.]
   d. The rural economy and banks were doing well.
   e. [Construction began on the Panama Canal.]

4. Which American writer/poet did Debussy admire? (He even started an opera based on one of his/her works.)
   a. [Edgar Allan Poe]
   b. Emily Dickinson
   c. William Wordsworth
   d. Henry David Thoreau

5. What is Debussy's most famous composition?
   a. *Pelléas et Mélisande*
   b. *The Sea*
   c. [*Prelude to the Afternoon of a Faun*]
   d. *Children's Corner*

6. Debussy's music is called by some "<u>impressionistic</u>," after the famous French painters of the time.

7. True or False: Debussy died during World War I. [True]

8. Debussy's daughter, who was 12 years old when he died, had an unusual nickname. What was it? ["Chouchou"]

9. On which twentieth-century composers did Debussy have a strong influence? [any of the following: Béla Bartók, Igor Stravinsky, Steve Reich, Philip Glass, Thelonious Monk, and Duke Ellington]

10. True or False: We can tell by his lifestyle that Debussy was a believer. [False]

Richard Strauss

1. During which period did Richard Strauss compose music?
   a. Classical
   b. Modern
   c. Romantic
   d. [Both b and c.]

2. Some thought Richard, touring Europe as a child prodigy at a young age, could be the next <u>Mozart</u>.

3. Richard's style became more modern because of his friendship with the composer
   a. [Alexander Ritter.]
   b. Robert Schumann.
   c. Hans von Bülow.
   d. Johannes Brahms.

4. In a short essay, describe a symphonic poem. How does it compare to a symphony?

5. (Circle all that apply.) Strauss's works were
   a. [loved.]   d. few.
   b. [hated.]   e. old-fashioned.
   c. forgotten.   f. [attention getting.]

6. Strauss became well known for his outrageous and scandalous operas.

7. True or False: Strauss was the Music Director for the Nazis. [True]

8. For which of the following works of literature did Strauss write music?
   a. *Don Quixote*
   b. *Don Juan*
   c. *Macbeth*
   d. [All of the above.]

9. Unlike the other musicians we've studied, Strauss was a good <u>businessman</u>, known for driving a hard bargain.

10. True or False: Strauss made headline news with his controversial opera *Salome*. [True]

The Contemporary Period

The Contemporary period took place between the years 1910 and the present.

Three important events happened during this era:

Who	What	Why It's Important
1. Darwin	Wrote *On the Origin of Species*	People thought maybe God was not the creator.
2. Freud	Studied people's behavior	People thought maybe they couldn't control their behavior.
3. Einstein	Theory of Relativity	People thought maybe nothing was absolutely true.

During the twentieth century, composers made up new scales.

They tried writing music without melody.

Serialism

- Invented by Arnold Schoenberg
- Each note is assigned a numerical value
- Music is based on mathematical formulas

John Cage wrote a piece called 4'33". He did not use traditional instruments.

Much of the music in the twentieth century is still written in the Romantic style.

Although man may come up with new theories, God's Word is true and unchanging.

Scott Joplin

1. (Circle all that apply.) Scott Joplin lived in which of the following towns during his lifetime?
   a. [Texarkana]
   b. New Orleans
   c. [New York City]
   d. Pittsburgh

2. By age 7, Joplin was taking piano lessons from a German immigrant.

3. For what style of music is Scott Joplin famous? [ragtime]

4. Ragtime music can be described as: syncopated piano music.

5. True or False: Ragtime is the style of music that led to today's rock music. [False]

6. Joplin's most famous rag is called "Maple Leaf Rag."

7. (Circle all that are true.) Scott Joplin wrote
   a. [waltzes.]
   b. [opera.]
   c. [a ballet.]
   d. a requiem.
   e. [marches.]

8. One of the reasons that Joplin's work was not respected as art during his lifetime was probably because [music critics were prejudiced against him because he was an African American].

9. *Treemonisha*, Joplin's second opera, was performed for the first time in what year? 1970

10. True or False: Joplin was awarded a Pulitzer Prize in 1976 for his contributions to American music. [True]

288

A Young Scholar's Guide to Composers

Charles Ives

1. In what part of the United States did Ives live?
   a. Northwest (Oregon, North Dakota)
   b. South (Georgia, Alabama)
   c. Southwest (New Mexico, Texas)
   d. [Northeast (Connecticut, New York)]

2. Charles Ives received much of his musical education from his father, who was the town band director.

3. Charles's music lessons with his father could be described as unconventional or experimental.

4. Besides music, as a young man Ives enjoyed (circle all that apply):
   a. soccer.
   b. [football.]
   c. lacrosse.
   d. [baseball.]

5. What kind of industry did Charles work in as his career? [insurance]

6. True or False: Ives lived in conflict with his wife, who wanted him to write a different kind of music. [False]

7. What health problem did Ives have? [heart attacks]

8. True or False: Ives's music was popular in his day. [False]

9. What was a common technique of Ives?
   a. borrowing melodies from other composers
   b. borrowing themes from other composers
   c. incorporating his father's experiments
   d. [All of the above.]

10. What kind of prize did Ives receive for his Third Symphony?
   a. the Nobel Prize
   b. third place
   c. [the Pulitzer Prize]
   d. a new car

George Gershwin

1. George Gershwin's parents were Jewish immigrants from what country? [Russia]

2. Gershwin brought popular sounds and classical format together in the same piece of music.
   a. Romantic
   b. [Classical]
   c. Baroque
   d. Medieval

3. What kind of music, popular in his time, fascinated Gershwin when he was a child? [ragtime]

4. Name an earlier classical musician whose music was introduced to Gershwin by his music teacher. [any of the following: Chopin/Debussy/Ravel/Liszt]

5. Who wrote the lyrics to George Gershwin's music? [his brother Ira]

6. Which of the following works began the Gershwins' series of successful musicals?
   a. "When You Want 'Em, You Can't Get 'Em"
   b. "Swanee"
   c. La, La Lucille
   d. [Lady, Be Good!]

7. What was Gershwin's first classical piece and one of his most famous?
   a. [Rhapsody in Blue]
   b. An American in Paris
   c. Piano Concerto in F
   d. Of Thee I Sing

8. Rhapsody in Blue fused classical and what other type of music together? [jazz]

9. True or False: Gershwin's folk opera Porgy and Bess was about African American life. [True]

10. True or False: Gershwin's life exemplified the "American dream." [True]

John Williams

1. John Williams's father earned his living as a <u>drummer or musician</u>.

2. True or False: As a child, Williams lived on both the east and west coasts of the United States. [True]

3. Williams continued to develop his musical skills while serving in the
   a. Army.
   b. [Air Force.]
   c. Marines.
   d. None of the above.

4. What is orchestration? [writing music for an orchestra or adapting music so that it can be played by an orchestra]

5. Orchestral music composed for a film is called a <u>film score</u>.

6. Williams has received Oscars for his music in (circle all that are correct):
   a. *The Sound of Music.*
   b. [*Fiddler on the Roof.*]
   c. [*Star Wars.*]
   d. *Willie Wonka and the Chocolate Factory.*

7. George Lucas and John Williams decided to create an epic sound for the *Star Wars* movie by using a <u>full symphonic orchestra</u>.

8. One character trait of John Williams is his
   a. [loyalty.]
   b. shyness.
   c. playfulness.
   d. honesty.

9. One technique that Williams uses is to assign <u>musical themes</u> to certain <u>characters or ideas</u>.

10. True or False: Besides writing music for movies, John Williams has also conducted the Boston Pops Orchestra. [True]

Aaron Copland

1. Aaron Copland grew up in
   a. Vienna, Austria.
   b. London, England.
   c. [Brooklyn, New York.]
   d. Atlanta, Georgia.

2. Copland's parents were <u>Russian Jewish</u> immigrants.

3. As a child, Copland took music lessons from
   a. his father.
   b. [his older sister.]
   c. his uncle.
   d. a close family friend.

4. True or False: Copland graduated from the Juilliard School of Music. [False]

5. Copland traveled to <u>Paris</u> to study music with Nadia Boulanger.

6. True or False: As a young composer, Copland was very popular. [True]

7. Copland's most popular phase of music was his <u>Americana, or third</u> phase.

8. Copland wrote all of the following styles of music except
   a. classical.
   b. Latin American.
   c. [opera.]
   d. jazz.

9. Copland's political views can be described as <u>liberal</u>.

10. Besides music, Copland enjoyed (circle all that apply):
    a. [tennis.]
    b. baseball.
    c. [animals.]
    d. hiking.

Glossary

absolute music
Music that stands alone, needing no words to describe it.

absolute pitch
The ability to recognize or sing a given isolated note; also called perfect pitch.

Agnus Dei
A part of the Mass that is traditionally sung. It proclaims the power of Christ's redemption: "Lamb of God who takes away the sin of the world."

aristocracy
Upper-class or wealthy people.

ballades
Secular songs that were sung in the courtly language (not Latin) and were accompanied by instruments. Originally popular in the 1300s, they became popular again during the Romantic period.

bards
Singers who performed the works of troubadours in the courts. Also known as minstrels or in French, *jongleurs*.

Baroque period
A historic period characterized by ornamental art, architecture, and music.

basso continuo
See *continuo*.

Benedicamus
A part of the Mass that is traditionally sung. It is a closing blessing: "Let us bless the Lord."

benefactor
Someone who gives money to a composer so he can play music or pays a composer to write music for them.

Bohemian
A person with artistic or literary interests who disregards conventional standards of behavior.

bourgeois
Of, relating to, or typical of the middle class.

cantata
A short oratorio, written to fit within a church service.

cantor
Choir leader.

catechism
A brief summary of the basic principles of Christianity in question-and-answer format.

chant
See *plainchant*.

chromaticism
The use of notes that are not within the major or minor scales.

Classical period
A historical period that falls circa 1750–1820. During this period, people challenged the established religions and monarchies. This period is characterized by the rise of the common man so the art and music reflected that change. Musically, this era dropped the ornamentation of the Baroque era and presented melodies in a cleaner fashion. Composers continued to follow an established pattern of rules.

clavichord
An early stringed instrument similar to a piano.

concerto
A musical work that is written for an instrumental soloist, usually accompanied by an orchestra. The work typically has three movements. The first is a fast one, the second is a slow one, and the third is another fast one. A concerto can be remembered as fast-slow-fast.

concerto grosso
Translated as "grand concerto." Instead of featuring a solo instrument, this work uses a small group of instruments, perhaps two violins or some other combination, playing together as the featured instruments. The featured instruments are accompanied by a larger group of instruments (similar to a small orchestra) called a continuo.

Contemporary period
A historical period that began in the early twentieth century. In response to such thinkers as Darwin, Einstein, and Freud, people began to question all they previously believed to be true. In music, composers did away with rules, and much of the music didn't sound harmonious. Consequently, much of the music from this period still follows a developing Romantic style.

continuo
Short for "basso continuo," which means "continuous bass." Used in a concerto grosso, the continuo was a group of instruments usually made up of a keyboard instrument (harpsichord or organ) along with a lower instrument (cello or bassoon). Its purpose was to provide the harmony for the featured instruments.

coronation
The act (or occasion) of crowning (typically, a monarch).

counterpoint
A term describing music that features two or more melodies working together at the same time within a piece.

Credo
A statement of the Nicene Creed: "I believe…"

dissonant
Harsh and inharmonious sound.

étude
The French word for "study." An étude is a piece that is written to develop a certain technique on an instrument.

fantasia
Like a fantasy; a composition free in form and inspiration; very imaginative.

film score
The orchestral music that is written for a film.

fugue
A musical work, usually written for the organ, in which the melody starts, and then another line comes in, sometimes the same melody, played higher, or a different melody altogether. A fugue may have two, three, or four musical lines playing simultaneously and somehow it all sounds beautiful together.

Gloria
A part of the Mass that is traditionally sung. It proclaims God's glory: "Glory to God on high…"

Gregorian chant
See *plainchant*.

harmonium
A keyboard instrument similar to an organ, using reeds instead of pipes. Air is pushed through the reeds by pumping a pedal.

harmony
Another note that is played at the same time as the main note, the melody. It is usually pleasing to the ear.

harpsichord
Any of a family of European keyboard instruments; all these instruments generate sound by plucking a string rather than striking one, as in a piano or clavichord, thus there is little chance for a true crescendo or diminuendo.

homophony
A musical term describing music that features a melody with some accompaniment.

humanist
Someone who does not believe in God but thinks that people hold the greatest power.

Javanese gamelan
An Indonesian orchestra comprised of bells, gongs, and percussion instruments.

jongleurs
French word for singers who performed the works of troubadours in the courts. Also known as bards or minstrels.

Kapellmeister
Musical director for a monarch, nobleman, or church.

Kyrie
A part of the Mass that is traditionally sung. A plea for mercy: "Lord, have mercy; Christ have mercy. . ." It is sung in Greek instead of Latin.

lieder
German for "songs." In particular, songs written in the nineteenth century. Usually poetry from the literary tradition set to ornamental accompaniment.

lute
A plucked, stringed instrument with a neck and a deep, round back. It was popular during the Renaissance era.

madrigals
Songs that were written during the Renaissance for several voices to sing at the same time. They were always secular and usually about love. They were generally sung at a quick tempo and were popular among the aristocracy.

Mass
Certain prayers said in the early church (and in some churches still today) that are standardized and said in a certain order.

Mass Ordinary
Standard prayers in the Mass that do not change from day to day.

Mass Proper
Prayers of the Mass that change according to the holiday or part of the church calendar.

microtones
Notes that fall between the notes that are on the piano.

Middle Ages
A historical time period also known as the Medieval period. It is considered to begin in approximately the fifth century and last until the fourteenth century. Characterized by castles, knights, and feudalism; the music we are aware of during this time period was mostly chants that were sung in churches.

minnesingers
The troubadours of Germany.

minstrels
Singers who performed the works of troubadours in the courts. Also known as bards or, in French, jongleurs.

minuet
A dance form that became popular during the Baroque period.

modal
Pattern of tones that does not follow the major or minor scales used today.

monarchy
A form of government in which a monarch (king or queen) is the head of state.

musical line
A melodic statement that runs through a composition; can be vocal or instrumental.

nocturne
A word commonly used by Chopin for many of his beautiful songlike pieces.

opera
A dramatic composition in which all dialogue is sung, accompanied by an orchestra. In an opera, individual performers sing whole songs, called arias, or many performers join together and sing choruses.

oratorio
A musical work similar to an opera, but about biblical stories and unstaged: no scenery, actors, or costumes.

orchestration
Writing music for orchestra, or taking music that's been written and adapting it so all instruments in an orchestra have parts to play.

organ
A keyboard instrument that makes noise by pushing air through pipes. It is capable of making a variety of musical sounds.

organ chorale preludes
Relatively short organ pieces used to introduce the hymn to be sung by the congregation.

organum
Plainchant to which a composer or singer has added another line, sung at the same time, with the same words.

Passion
An oratorio based on a Gospel narrative of the suffering of Jesus Christ.

philharmonic
A society or group that is designed to sponsor a symphony orchestra. Or, an orchestra that is sponsored by such a group.

pianoforte
A keyboard instrument played by depressing keys, causing hammers to strike tuned strings to produce sounds. By striking the key harder, the hammer will strike the string harder, and thus it was possible to create a crescendo or diminuendo or to make true fortes (louds) and pianos (softs); hence, the name "pianoforte." An early version of today's piano.

pizzicato
A musical technique in which the string player plucks the string with his finger instead of using the bow.

plainchant
Early written music; sung in church during the Middle Ages. Also called "chant." Characteristics include: sung in unison; sung without instruments; sung without a rhythm; sung with a smooth progression; sung in Latin, not English (except for the Kyrie, which is sung in Greek); and all modal. Also known as Gregorian chant.

player piano
A piano that is mechanically operated.

polyphony
Music in which one hears more than one musical line.

polyrhythm
Two different rhythms played at the same time.

polytonality
Music played in two different keys at the same time.

program music
Popular during the Romantic era, it is music that describes specific nonmusical things without using words and is often about nature or feelings or people.

program symphony
Very similar to a tone poem, except that there is more than one movement, as in a symphony.

ragtime
Syncopated piano music.

recital
A musical presentation that highlights solo performances.

Renaissance
A historical time period lasting from the end of the Middle Ages, approximately the fourteenth century through early seventeenth century. This was a period of revival that marked great change in music, bringing it from a simple, ancient sound to the classical sounds we are familiar with today.

Requiem
Mass for a deceased person and/or a musical composition for such a Mass.

rhythm
A pattern of regular beats.

Romantic period
A historical period spanning the early 1800s to the early 1900s. During this era, artists and thinkers challenged the established rules and looked toward emotion and imagination. Artists wanted their art to reflect nature. Melodies began to flow more and harmonies became rich. Composers used new note combinations that had not been used before.

rondo
A musical form that developed during the Classical period. The rondo form takes a tune and repeats it—a lot, with some extra stuffing in between its appearances so that the listener doesn't get bored. It is light and especially easy to listen to. A rondo could be structured like this: ABACA or ABACABA (notice that A keeps recurring).

royalties
Money paid to an artist for each copy of his work sold in a year.

Sanctus
A part of the Mass that is traditionally sung. It proclaims the holiness of God: "Holy, holy, holy..."

score
A musical composition written down.

serialism
Musical technique in which each note is assigned a numerical value and, instead of following a melody, the music is based on mathematical formulas.

solo concerto
See *concerto*.

sonata
Musical work, written for a solo instrument, that consists of several (usually three) movements or sections—exposition, development, recapitulation.

song plugger
A piano player employed by music stores in the early twentieth century to promote new music.

soundtrack
Songs used in a film.

spinet
A small piano.

suite
A group of musical works or songs that were written to go together.

symphonic poem
See *tone poem*.

symphony
A musical form that arose during the Classical period. It is a longer work written for orchestra and typically consists of four movements, or shorter pieces.

syncopated
Stress on a normally unstressed beat.

tempo rubato
Literally, "stolen time." Musical term for slightly speeding up or slowing down the tempo of a piece at the discretion of the soloist or the conductor. Especially common in piano music.

theme and variations
A musical form that became popular during the Classical period. It introduces a main theme and then repeats it with variations.

tonal
A form of musical writing in which the music relates to a particular "home" tone. Almost all of the Western music since the Renaissance has been tonal.

tone painting
Work in which a composer tries to describe something with music, such as running water or tweeting birds.

tone poem
Also known as a symphonic poem. A piece of orchestral music in one movement in which some extra-musical program provides a narrative or illustrative element. This program could come from a poem, a novel, a painting, or some other source.

tremolo

Musical technique in which a string player moves the bow back and forth rapidly on the strings.

troubadours

Poets during the Renaissance who wrote love songs that were performed by bards or jongleurs in the courts.

trouvère

A troubadour of northern France.

unison

Sung together, with everyone singing the same notes; without harmony.

zither

A stringed instrument with thirty to forty strings, no neck, and a shallow sounding board. It is primarily used in folk music.

A Young Scholar's Guide to Composers

Certificate of Completion

awarded to

_____

for completion of
"A Young Scholar's Guide to Composers"

_____   _____
Signed   *Date*

A Young Scholar's Guide to
Composers

ALSO AVAILABLE FROM BRIGHT IDEAS PRESS...

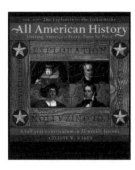
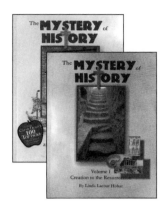

All American History by Celeste W. Rakes
Containing hundreds of images and dozens of maps, *All American History* is a complete year's curriculum for students in grades 5 – 8 when combined with the Student Activity Book and Teacher's Guide (yet adaptable for younger and older students).

There are 32 weekly lessons, and each lesson contains three sections examining the atmosphere in which the event occurred, the event itself, and the impact this event had on the future of America.

- Vols. I & II Student Reader
- Vols. I & II Student Activity Book
- Vols. I & II Teacher's Guide

The Mystery of History Volumes I, II, & III by Linda Hobar
This award-winning series provides a historically accurate, Bible-centered approach to learning world history. The completely chronological lessons shed new light on who walked the earth when, as well as on where important Bible figures fit into secular history. Grades 4 – 8, yet easily adaptable.

- Volume I: Creation to the Resurrection
- Volume II: The Early Church & the Middle Ages
- Volume III: Renaissance, Reformation, Growth of Nations Student Reader
- Volume III: Renaissance, Reformation, Growth of Nations Companion Guide (Book or CD version)

Christian Kids Explore Biology
by Stephanie Redmond
One of Cathy Duffy's 100 Top Picks! Elementary biology that is both classical and hands-on. Conversational style and organized layout make teaching a pleasure.

Christian Kids Explore Earth & Space
by Stephanie Redmond
Another exciting book in this award-winning series! Author Redmond is back with more great lessons, activities, and ideas.

Christian Kids Explore Chemistry
by Robert W. Ridlon, Jr., and Elizabeth J. Ridlon
Authors Robert and Elizabeth Ridlon team up for 30 lessons, unit wrap-ups, and even coloring pages all about the fascinating world of chemistry.

Christian Kids Explore Physics
by Robert W. Ridlon, Jr., and Elizabeth J. Ridlon
Both college professors and creation scientists, the Ridlons offer their depth of knowledge about science and Scripture.

Illuminations: Totally planned and scheduled English, Geography, Bible, and more for *The Mystery of History* series—we've done the work for you!

For Ordering Information, Call 1.877.492.8081
or visit www.brightideaspress.com